The Toga and Roman Identity

Also published by Bloomsbury

Roman Military Clothing (1): 100 BC–AD 200, Graham Sumner
Roman Military Clothing (2): AD 200–400, Graham Sumner
Roman Military Clothing (3): AD 400–640, Graham Sumner
Reconstructing the Slave, Kelly L. Wrenhaven
Expurgating the Classics, edited by Stephen Harrison
and Christopher Stray

The Toga and Roman Identity

Ursula Rothe

BLOOMSBURY ACADEMIC
LONDON • NEW YORK • OXFORD • NEW DELHI • SYDNEY

BLOOMSBURY ACADEMIC
Bloomsbury Publishing Plc
50 Bedford Square, London, WC1B 3DP, UK
1385 Broadway, New York, NY 10018, USA
29 Earlsfort Terrace, Dublin 2, Ireland

BLOOMSBURY, BLOOMSBURY ACADEMIC and the Diana
logo are trademarks of Bloomsbury Publishing Plc

First published in Great Britain 2020
Paperback edition first published 2021

Copyright © Ursula Rothe, 2020

Ursula Rothe has asserted her right under the Copyright,
Designs and Patents Act, 1988, to be identified as Author of this work.

For legal purposes the Acknowledgements on p. viii constitute
an extension of this copyright page.

Cover design: Terry Woodley
Cover image © Lararium, House of the Vettii, Pompeii.
PRISMA ARCHIVO/Alamy Stock Photo

All rights reserved. No part of this publication may be reproduced or
transmitted in any form or by any means, electronic or mechanical,
including photocopying, recording, or any information storage or retrieval
system, without prior permission in writing from the publishers.

Bloomsbury Publishing Plc does not have any control over, or responsibility for,
any third-party websites referred to or in this book. All internet addresses given
in this book were correct at the time of going to press. The author and publisher
regret any inconvenience caused if addresses have changed or sites have
ceased to exist, but can accept no responsibility for any such changes.

A catalogue record for this book is available from the British Library.

Library of Congress Control Number 2019949553

ISBN: HB: 978-1-4725-7154-0
PB: 978-1-3501-9441-0
ePDF: 978-1-4725-7156-4
eBook: 978-1-4725-7155-7

Typeset by RefineCatch Limited, Bungay, Suffolk

To find out more about our authors and books visit
www.bloomsbury.com and sign up for our newsletters.

Contents

List of Figures	vi
Acknowledgements	viii
List of Abbreviations	x
1 Introduction	1
2 The Toga: A Brief History	17
3 The Toga and the Roman Man	37
4 The Toga and Social Status	71
5 The Toga and Politics	101
6 The Toga in the Provinces	123
7 The Toga in Late Antiquity	147
Epilogue	159
Glossary	163
Notes	165
Bibliography	209
Index	235

Figures

1.1	Relief panel on the western side of the Ara Pacis showing Aeneas sacrificing	10
1.2	Detail of a mosaic from Hadrumetum showing Vergil and Muses	11
2.1	Detail of a wall painting in the Tomb of the Augurs, Tarquinia	18
2.2	Cloak 2 from Grave 89, Verucchio (top) and reconstruction (bottom)	19
2.3	How the toga was draped	27
2.4	Reverse of a silver *denarius* of C. Minucius Augurinus from Rome	29
2.5	'Arringatore' statue from Lake Trasimeno	29
2.6	Grave portrait of a Roman couple from the Via Statilia, Rome	30
2.7	Statue of the 'Togatus Barberini' from Rome	31
2.8	'Brothers' sarcophagus'	32
2.9	Detail of the forum frieze, Arch of Constantine, Rome	33
2.10	Statue of the 'young magistrate' from Rome	34
3.1	Statue of a mother and daughter from Rome	39
3.2	*Lararium* painting in the House of the Vettii, Pompeii	47
3.3	Fresco from the House of Julia Felix, Pompeii	53
3.4	Relief from Çukurbağ (Nicomedia) showing part of an *adventus* scene	61
4.1	Detail of the south frieze of the Ara Pacis	75
4.2	*Transvectio equitum* scene on the base of a column of Antoninus Pius	80
4.3	Funerary relief of a family, Rome	90
4.4	Funerary relief of a potter and his wife	98
5.1	Reverse of a bronze *sestertius* of Nero from Rome	115
5.2	Reverse of a gold *aureus* of Trajan from Rome	117
5.3	Reverse of a bronze *sestertius* of Hadrian from Rome	119
6.1	Grave stele for M. Valerius Celerinus from Cologne	129
6.2	Grave stele for Apana and family from Prado de Arriba, Lugo	131
6.3	Igel Pillar in the village of Igel near Trier	134
6.4	Scenes from the south face of the Igel Pillar	135
6.5	Grave stele for Quartus, Licovia and family from Celje	137

6.6	Detail of the base of a sarcophagus from Palmyra showing a sacrificial scene	144
7.1	Consular diptych of Magnus(?)	152
7.2	Detail of the south-east face of the pedestal of Theodosius' obelisk, Istanbul	155
7.3	Detail of a miniature showing Nicephorus III	158
E.1	Statue of Napoleon Bonaparte by Jérôme Maglioli in the Place-du-Maréchal-Foch, Ajaccio, Corsica	160
E.2	Musée de la Romanité, Nîmes	161

Acknowledgements

This book is the end result of a conversation I had with a senior colleague several years ago in which we shared our frustration about the lack of a comprehensive cultural study of the toga that we could use in our work on Roman dress and social history. After a while, the colleague looked at me and said, 'well, you're just going to have to write one, aren't you?' And so I did. As such, from its inception, this book was the result not only of my own desire to place antiquity's most iconic garment into the limelight of scholarly discussion, but also of substantial input from colleagues and friends to whom I am extremely grateful.

A large part of the research took place during a three-month stint as Hugh Last Fellow at the British School at Rome in 2018, and I am truly thankful to the BSR for giving me the opportunity to disappear into the blissful oblivion of uninterrupted research in such a beautiful and productive environment. I am especially grateful to the BSR staff – in particular Val Scott, Stefania Peterlini and Christine Martin – for helping me find materials and access collections. I am also indebted to Lara Pucci, Janet Wade, Krešimir Vuković and all my fellow-fellows at the BSR for allowing me to bounce my ideas off them, and for showing such enthusiasm for my work that toga-spotting in the streets and museums of Rome became a regular hobby of the cohort; many of the ideas presented in this book only took shape through those interactions, and I can only hope that I was able to contribute as much to their work as they did to mine. Whilst in Rome I also benefitted from working in the libraries of the DAI, the AAR, the Bibliotheca Hertziana and the Koninklijk Nederlands Instituut: my sincere thanks to those institutions and their invariably helpful staff.

Apart from my time in Rome, my work writing up the manuscript was greatly helped by several extended periods of self-imposed exile abroad, and I am grateful to Petros Diveris and Rachel Robertson for the use of their residences in Astypalea and Paris for this purpose. It would be disingenuous of me not to also thank the cats of the Ballo in Astypalea for keeping me sane through those long, isolated days and nights on the island. (Cannello, Vivienne, Klikli – you know who you are.)

Finally, and most importantly, I would like to express my heartfelt gratitude to those various colleagues who read and commented on parts of this book or provided expert advice: Costas Panayotakis, Mary Harlow and Ortolf Harl, Claire Holleran for a very useful conversation about buying togas, Jen Baird, Ted Kaizer and Lucinda Dirven for their help with the section on Palmyra, Jonathan Edmondson for his advice on the Quartus inscription, and Glenys Davies, Mark Humphries and James Thorne for reading and providing copious and extremely helpful comments on drafts of chapters. I am also grateful for the questions and comments provided by the audiences of papers in which I presented sections of this material, especially Elena Theodorakopoulos, Hannah Cornwell and those at the University of Birmingham who, in a truly enjoyable and fruitful post-paper discussion, helped me to expand my ideas about the toga and status. I am thankful also to the anonymous reviewers at Bloomsbury, through whose diligence and insight many significant improvements have been made to the manuscript. Any errors remaining in it are, of course, my own.

Abbreviations

All abbreviations have been taken from the *Oxford Classical Dictionary*, except the following:

LSA *Last Statues of Antiquity* database: http://laststatues.classics.ox.ac.uk/

LUPA *Ubi Erat Lupa* database: http://lupa.at/

MuM Münzen und Medaillen AG auction house, Basel, Switzerland

RGDA Augustus, *Res Gestae Divi Augusti*

RPC *Roman Provincial Coinage*, Volumes I–X (London/Paris: British Museum Press/Bibliothèque Nationale 1992–)

1

Introduction

In 390 BCE, after defeating the Romans at the Battle of the Allia, a band of Gallic forces moved south and sacked the city of Rome.[1] This event went on to play a significant role in the Romans' sense of their own history, and centuries later the so-called *metus Gallicus* remained a central paradigm of military ideology and foreign policy.[2] But it is one later historical account of it that is particularly illuminating for the subject of this book:

> At Rome the appropriate arrangements for defending the *arx* were complete, and the old men returned to their homes to await the arrival of their enemies with hearts that were steeled to die. Those of them that had held curule magistracies put on their stately robes (*augustissima vestis*), so that they might face death dressed in the symbols of their ancient rank and office ... and, thus clothed, they sat down on ivory chairs in the middle of their houses.... [The Gauls] found the houses of the plebeians locked, but the halls of the nobles open; and they hesitated almost more to enter the open houses than those that were shut, so close to religious awe were they when they saw, seated in the vestibules, beings who, apart from the fact that their ornaments and clothing (*ornatus habitusque*) seemed more splendid (*augustior*) than could adorn human beings, appeared also, in the majesty of their countenance and the gravity of their expression, almost like gods.
>
> Livy 5.41[3]

The *augustissima vestis* to which Livy refers is, of course, the toga, and the passage neatly encompasses all of the main themes in what is to follow. We are invited to admire, with the ransacking Gauls, the perfect image of the Roman elite man: stern, dignified and steeped in public duty. These attributes cannot be separated from the peculiar garment in which such a man was ideally clothed for most of Rome's history, and the further details given by Livy make it clear that the men awaiting death by the Gallic sword took care to each dress in the garment to which they were entitled. Readers would have known this meant the ornate *toga picta* for those who had celebrated a triumph, and the purple-bordered *toga praetexta* – together with ivory chairs the insignia of high office – for the others. For the toga acted as both a vital tool for the expression of Roman status distinctions, and as a canvas for the constant status anxieties of an unusually fluid society. Along with gender and status, the passage also alludes to the role of politics in the mindset of the ideal toga-clad Roman man: the decision to make provisions for the defence of the Capitol and to return home to face certain death is a collective one. Finally, written as it was in the Augustan period, a time of consolidation of Roman ideas of imperial destiny, the passage deliberately contrasts the image of the stately Roman in his characteristic dress with that of the marauding barbarians who recognize his superiority. The toga was Roman and distinctive, but it was also the dress of an empire.

The purpose of this book is to explore the toga as a garment and symbol from its origins in Rome's earliest history to its decreasing use and transformation in late antiquity; in particular, it focuses on its multifarious and constantly evolving meaning in Roman society, rather than merely on its form. It also serves to correct the recent scholarly tendency to see the toga as an elite garment of Italy that served only a symbolic role for most of Roman history by showing the role it played in the lives of provincial populations and the non-elite. The toga is like a prism that allows us to turn the light stream of Roman identity into a whole spectrum of different sub-identities, and the approach taken in this book is largely thematic in nature, drawing out the various strands and explaining how these served to make the toga the quintessential symbol of Romanness: its role in the formation and enforcement of (elite) Roman masculinity (Chapter 3), its use in the marking out and negotiation of status divisions (Chapter 4), its function in the political sphere (Chapter 5), and the myriad ways in which it was embedded in the development of provincial societies (Chapter 6). It is true that Roman culture does not easily allow for this kind of compartmentalization, and many cross-connections will be drawn as the discussion progresses; but it is only through a thematic perspective that it is possible to do justice to the many dimensions of the toga as a cultural instrument and symbol. The book begins with a preliminary discussion (Chapter 2) of the origins of the toga in Rome's earliest history and of basic details such as its production and main draping styles. It only returns to a chronological focus in Chapter 7, which traces its evolution in late antiquity.

In terms of geographical scope, the first chapters look at Rome and Italy together, whilst the provinces are treated separately in Chapter 6. This could be viewed as an arbitrary, even retrogressive division, not least given the importance of the provinces in shaping Roman culture, the long history of Rome's conquest of Italy and the enduring cultural diversity of the Italian peninsula that has been the focus of much recent work.[4] However, at least to the Roman elite, Italy had come to be seen as an extension of Rome by the time of the late Republic and early Empire, the period to which most of our evidence dates and, as such, the main chronological focus of this book. Roman villa culture, both in reality and in the Roman imagination, wedded the capital to the Italian countryside in a way that simply does not apply to other provinces. And whilst as late as the middle of the first century BCE Cicero could state that town-born people like him possessed two *patriae* – their hometown and Rome (*Leg.* 1.5–6), he meant that one was by birth and the other by citizenship; only a century later Pliny quite naturally spoke of Italy as synonymous with Rome when he described it as the motherland of all other countries and races (*HN* 3.39).[5]

Why the toga?

The Romans were intensely preoccupied with personal appearance, and especially with dress.[6] It is perhaps unsurprising, given the centuries of scholarship focusing on the great deeds, profound political struggles and courageous military feats of Roman statesmen, that the pettiness and viciousness with which those same statesmen often conducted themselves in relation to each other's appearance is often overlooked. Take the following account by Polybius – a Greek living in Rome but surely reflecting the view held by his elite Roman friends – of King Prusias II of Bithynia meeting Roman delegates in the second century BCE:

> This Prusias was a man by no means worthy of the royal dignity, as may easily be understood from the following facts.... [W]hen some Roman legates had come to his court, he went to meet them with his head shorn, and wearing a white hat and a toga and shoes, exactly the costume worn at Rome by slaves recently manumitted or 'liberti' as the Romans call them. 'In me,' he said, 'you see your libertus who wishes to endear himself and imitate everything Roman'; a phrase as humiliating as one can conceive.
>
> 30.18, trans. Paton 1927

Prusias' catastrophic clothing choices, whilst well-meant, earned him nothing but derision from his elite male Roman audience, and it is characteristic of Roman attitudes that it is this ostensibly trivial aspect of an important state event that made it into the history books.[7] But it is within the Roman elite itself that we often find the snidest of sartorial commentary. When Cicero heard of Caesar's victory over Pompey in the first triumviral war he is reported as saying he was surprised that Pompey could be defeated by someone who couldn't even tie his tunic properly (Dio Cass. 43.43.5); and on Cicero himself Pliny is said to have commented that he wore his toga extra long to cover his varicose veins (Quint., *Inst.* 11.3.143). And if the ancient authors are to be trusted, such interactions could go beyond the barbed tongue: earlier on in the Dio passage cited above it is reported that Sulla was so annoyed by Caesar's loose tunic that he nearly physically attacked him (43.43.4) and Macrobius would have us believe that the famous late Republican orator Hortensius once took a colleague to court for upsetting his toga in a narrow alleyway (*Sat.* 3.13.4–5). The imperial biographies would be incomplete – and less entertaining – without the accounts of the dress behaviour of individual emperors that are given in minute and dubious detail; and Suetonius himself wrote an entire book on dress – *De genera vestium* – which is sadly now lost, although we have fragments of it in other works.[8] Satirists like Martial and Juvenal give us perhaps the most comprehensive, if comically exaggerated, insight into this mindset, and their works are replete with crushing remarks on the clothing of people around them.

But to see this fixation with appearance within the Roman male elite as merely a trivial diversion of a self-important class would, of course, be to miss the point. As Jonathan Edmondson has put it: 'Rome was a culture of spectacle, and the spectacle of dress helped to emphasize some of its most important values.'[9] Dress was a central issue in Roman society precisely because it was where fundamental distinctions like status and gender were expressed and negotiated: you were what you wore. It is no coincidence that the shape-shifting nature of such an archaic Roman deity as Vertumnus was symbolized in the variety of dress styles in which he could appear:

Clothe me in silks, and I will become a none too prudish girl:
and who would deny that, wearing the toga, I am a man?
Give me a scythe and bind my forehead with a wisp of
hay: you will swear that my hand has cut grass.

Prop. 4.2.21–26, trans. Goold 1990

It is due to the visual nature of Roman society and its peculiar obsession with dress that Latin is awash with sartorial metaphors: a woman who was respectable was '*stolata*' (from a female garment called the *stola*), whilst '*palliatus*' (from the Greek *pallium* cloak) was a synonym for someone of peregrine status and '*caligatus*' (from the name for soldier's shoes) for a soldier; to 'put on the *sagum*' (a military cloak) meant to prepare for war, whilst to 'change one's shoes' meant to become a senator ('*calceos mutare*' from *calcei senatorii*, the special footwear of senators). The values and identities invested in dress items caused them to eventually stand alone for the things they represented.

Clothing could also hold immense power in real-life situations. In Roman law, if molested on the street, a respectable woman could only sue for injury if she was dressed as such (*Dig.* 47.10.15.15), and Suetonius relates an anecdote in which a slave boy who was dressed in a toga by his slave dealers to avoid customs charges was later able to use that fact to make a plausible claim for freedom (*Rhet.* 1(25)). It is for this reason that clothing was also a matter of legal definition and surveillance, and Roman legal texts include categorizations of garments according to who should be wearing them.[10] The question of legal restrictions on the wearing of the toga will be discussed in Chapter 4.

Moreover, dress was seen to have a direct connection to the personal values of the wearer. Florus' description of Mark Antony at Cleopatra's court is one of many examples:

> Thus, though not for himself, he blatantly began to prepare for rulership; he completely forgot his homeland, his name, his toga and the *fasces*, and soon he became a monster, in character (*mens*) as well as in clothing (*amictus*) and appearance (*cultus*).
>
> 2.21.3

Philosophers like Seneca also frequently spoke about morals and clothing in the same breath (e.g. *Ep.* 114.4–8; 114.21–22), and Cicero made an explicit connection when he stated that the inner workings of the soul expressed themselves in 'outer appearance (*vultus*), voice (*sonus*) and gesture (*gestus*)' (*De or.* 3.216). In a highly visual culture that lacked the identity documents of modern societies, it was down to individual people to actively and visually assert their place in the world, rather than passively to expect to be treated in the correct way. And it wasn't just the garments that spoke: the discourse that arose around the proper appearance of people in public was in itself also a means of social control.[11] Dress – and especially the toga – was a means to articulate social identity, both figuratively and literally.

A great deal of classical scholarship has, in recent decades, focused on questions of identity, partly as a response to discourse in the social sciences surrounding post-colonialism, the changing role of the nation state and globalization. It is clear that in human culture – both ancient and modern – identities do not exist in and of themselves: they are created, are constantly evolving and are lived out by means of specific actions, objects, stories that are told about the past and beliefs about the inherent qualities of the people to whom they apply. In the Roman context the toga played a central role in all of these. But Roman identity was highly complex: in fact, uniquely so for the ancient world, evolving as it did from the customs of a minor Italian city state into the *Leitkultur* of a vast empire. Whilst recent scholarship on identity in both sociology and, increasingly, ancient studies have approached dress as a form of non-verbal language (see below), a similar idea was already formulated by the Romans themselves: in his treatise on language, Varro says that both language and garments were created for the same utilitarian purpose of expression (*Ling*. 9.33.48). The connection also had practical implications: an anecdote of Seneca the Elder describes orators wearing the toga to speak in Latin and changing into a *pallium* to speak in Greek (*Contr*. 9.3.13). The close connection in the Roman mind of both language and dress to identity is also made clear in the *Aeneid*: the scene engraved on Aeneas' shield in book 8 is described as a 'long line of conquered peoples, as varied in their language as in their style of dress (*habitus*) and weapons' (8.722–723),[12] and when, in book 12, Juno tells the Latins not to become Trojans and lose their identity, it is again both language and dress that are singled out as the markers of this: *aut vocem mutare viros aut vertere vestem* (12.825).[13]

The early history of the toga as outlined below in Chapter 2 suggests that it began life as a more or less all-purpose garment of central Italy, worn not only by Romans – both men and women – but also by their neighbours. We do not know at which point it became a male, 'Roman' garment, but it would appear that the process already predated the late fourth-century-CE tomb frescoes in Vulci and Rome.[14] A fragment of Ennius referring to something unknown being the case 'as long as one togate Roman survives'[15] suggests that by the turn of the third century BCE, the link was also explicitly expressed in literature. By the time we start to have more detailed literary evidence, however, Rome was not only already master of a large empire: it was also in the process of trying to formulate what exactly this meant.

For the central period of Rome's history, ideas about what constituted 'Romanness' were characterized by a strange mix of intense bigotry and astonishing inclusiveness. On the one hand, Roman citizenship, although hard-won in the case, for example, of the *socii*, was extending to vast numbers of people in the empire, as well as to freed slaves and their families. At some stage, and certainly by the late Republic, the toga came to be seen as *the* outward symbol of citizen status, and wearing it was a privilege that may also have been protected by law.[16] The Roman citizenship model was unique in the ancient world, and in the late Republic and early Empire this exceptionalism was seen to extend back to Rome's earliest history, when Romulus is said to have supplemented the fledgling Roman population with fugitives, immigrants and refugees from the surrounding area (Livy 1.8.6; Dion. Hal., *Rom. Ant.* 2.15.3–4).[17] Thus a key Roman foundation myth was based in the idea of incorporation, and this went hand-in-hand with expansion, as codified in further foundation myths like the rape of the Sabine women.[18] The mongrel nature of Rome's origins did not always sit comfortably with more high-minded ideas of Roman virtue, but even the superlative snob Cicero drew attention to the fact that Romulus had made Rome out of 'shepherds and immigrants' (*De or.* 1.37)[19] and rebuked Cato the Younger for carrying on in a speech to the senate about Rome's greatness 'as if he were in Plato's *Republic*', when really the Romans were simply 'what Romulus crapped out' (*Att.* 21.8).[20] Both the reality of the expanding franchise – culminating in the bestowal of citizenship to all free inhabitants of the empire in 212 CE – and the idea of generosity that accompanied it continued into the Empire, for example in Claudius' speech arguing for the inclusion of Gauls into the Senate:

> In my own ancestors ... I find encouragement to employ the same policy in my administration, by transferring hither all true excellence, let it be found where it will. For I am not unaware that the Julii came to us from Alba, the Coruncanii from Camerium, the Porcii from Tusculum; that ... members were drafted into the senate from Etruria, from Lucania, from the whole of Italy; and that finally Italy itself was extended to the Alps, in order that not individuals merely but countries and nationalities should form one body under the name of Romans.
>
> Tac., *Ann.* 11.24, trans. Jackson 1937[21]

The implications of such an ideology for the toga are obvious: if Romanness wasn't in the blood, then it could be acquired; it could, like a garment, be 'put on' by those who aspired to it. Remarkably, Roman culture supplied an actual garment with which to signal this. The opportunity to acquire citizenship and display it by means of the toga had enormous repercussions in the Roman provinces, where the franchise was extended only gradually as a special legal privilege, and forms the basis of the discussion in Chapter 6.

On the other hand, Roman identity was marked out at least as much through difference as through inclusiveness. A great deal has traditionally been made of the increasingly Hellenized cultural context of the late Republic and early Empire in which many formative ideas about Romanness were formulated; as the Roman elite increasingly began to incorporate aspects of what many saw as more sophisticated Greek culture into their lives – so the theory goes – they began also to formulate what made them unique as a people; just as the Greeks had used the

Persians as their 'other', so too the Greeks became the contrast the Romans needed to be able to formulate their own identity.[22] And so a series of dichotomies emerged, in which the Greeks were associated, for example, with effeminacy and luxury in contrast to robust Roman masculinity, or as preoccupied by philosophy and learning as against the Roman priorities of war and statecraft.[23] Athenian ideas of autochthony were seen as the polar opposite to the pragmatic Roman attitude to citizenship discussed above. As money began to flood into the centre of the empire and villa estates began to sport Greek-inspired peristyles, art galleries and libraries, the rusticity of the the early Romans came into focus as a paradigm of scholarly discussion, and was held up as the crucible in which the Roman character was forged;[24] as such, Romanness took on a moral flavour: the Roman was sturdy, pious, honest and dutiful, as outlined in more detail in Chapter 3. The toga came to symbolize all of these things, and Andrew Wallace-Hadrill (2008) has argued that it was only at this point in Roman history that the garment acquired special status as a core Roman symbol, as it was seen to embody the *mos maiorum* and everything that set Romans apart from Greeks. Similarly, Matthias Pausch and Paul Zanker have argued that the developments of the Augustan period constituted an exercise in 'Invention of Tradition' in which the toga was effectively created as a Roman garment and given a peculiar new look (the pouch-*umbo*) to set it apart, once and for all, from Greek cloaks.[25]

For the reasons given below in Chapter 2, I believe that the toga became a symbol of Romanness much earlier than any of these scholars suppose, and although the Augustan period was no doubt influential, to see it as some kind of year zero is to deny the existence of any significant ideas that might have fed into the identity process over the hundreds of years that preceded the late Republic.[26] But there is no denying the fundamental and lasting ideological effect of Rome's encounter with Greece. More importantly, the moral dimension of what it meant to be Roman was one that distinguished it from other ethnic identities of antiquity. As Emma Dench has said, '[i]t is significant that we can detect in Roman literature particular kinds of snobbery that are largely absent from the literature of classical Athens'.[27] To be Roman was to be concerned with the acquisition and maintenance of social and political status, as well as with the upholding of the moral codes associated with it. The implications of this for the toga will be a central theme of Chapters 3 and 4.

Very few have criticized the scholarly tendency to see the way Roman culture developed in Italy purely in relation to the Greeks, especially as it focuses attention almost exclusively on the elite.[28] But there are other ways of approaching the issue: Dench has argued for a more home-grown approach to the Romans' ideas about themselves, and has pointed out that there were also streams of Roman thought that saw geographical origin in Italy and long family ancestries as important ingredients in the national character.[29] To this may be added the fact that the Romans also used other ethnic groups apart from the Greeks as a contrast when formulating ideas about themselves, such as the Egyptians when Augustus was fighting Mark Antony,[30] and, on a more enduring basis, the peoples they encountered as they expanded north,[31] such as the marauding Gauls of the opening passage. And yet those very same people 'became Romans'; some of them even ended up wearing the toga, as will be shown in Chapter 6. The question as to whether they did so in spite of or because of the way Roman identity was formulated is to an extent a matter of perspective,[32] but it is important to point out that the 'Romanness' they expressed in their togas is likely to have been a very different one from that embodied in a toga on the streets of Rome, and even the people on the streets of Rome would have had different ideas about what it meant to be Roman. Not all Roman identities were the same, and the toga is an ideal medium through which to better understand the many faces of what 'being Roman' could mean.

There is, however, an elephant in the room when it comes to the toga symbolizing Roman identity. Although, as outlined in Chapter 3 below, young girls and some women could wear it, it was a predominantly male garment for most of its history. As such, there is an obvious conflict between the claims made in this book for its embodiment of Roman identity and the fact that the type of Romanness it conveyed was heavily gendered in nature. There is, of course, no getting around the fact that the way Roman culture was formulated, especially in the public sphere, was also heavily biased toward the ideas and activities of men, and in fact, in many ways the toga stands for this inherent bias. But the toga did not start out as a male garment, it *became* one, and like all gender identities Roman masculinity was something that was constructed, cultivated and contested. For this reason, the strong link between the toga and Roman ideas of gender is explored in detail in Chapter 3. Similarly, the use of the toga was restricted to those of free or freed status, effectively discounting the unfree population from the 'Romanness' it symbolized. But again, we cannot change the fundamental inequalities of Roman society, and Chapter 4 explores, among other things, the extent to which the toga played a role amongst the freed and non-elite population.

As difficult as Roman identity is for us to grasp, what is clear is that by the late Republic, the toga was clearly and explicitly associated with it. Already in Republican coinage the Roman citizen body was symbolized by a figure in a

Figure 1.1 Relief panel on the western side of the Ara Pacis showing Aeneas sacrificing. Ara Pacis Museum, Rome. Photo: Wieslaw Jarek/Alamy Stock Photo.

toga,[33] and poets like Propertius referred to the people of Rome with the epithet '*togata*' (4.2.49–56). When in the Augustan period Romanness was being reformulated, it was not just in new monuments and draping styles, but also in literary works like the *Aeneid* that the toga played a central role; although Vergil chose not to explicitly dress Aeneas in a toga,[34] he is described as wearing an *amictus*, a general covering garment deriving its name from *ambiectum* ('thrown about'), which for Roman readers would have recalled the etymology of the toga (from *tegere*: 'to cover').[35] The *amictus* was clearly intended as a proto-toga because it is worn *capite velato* for sacrifice and Aeneas wears a purple version of it when he arrives in Italy and becomes king (Verg., *Aen.* 3.405). This is reflected in the damaged scene of Aeneas sacrificing on the western side of the Ara Pacis (Fig. 1.1).[36] The implied connection is also clear from book 1, in which Jupiter prophesies Aeneas' fate as a founder of Rome together with that city's future greatness with the words

> Cruel Juno ...
> will with me cherish
> the Romans, masters of the world, and the nation that wears the toga (*gens togata*).
> 1.279–282

The description of the Romans as '*gens togata*' may have gone back even a generation earlier to Laberius (see below), and it went on to display astounding longevity, still being quoted by late-antique writers like Augustine (*De civ. D.* 3.13).[37] In the third century Vergil himself was depicted in a mosaic in Hadrumetum (Africa) surrounded by Muses and wearing a dazzling white tunic and toga (Fig. 1.2). Perhaps one of the most striking demonstrations of the centrality of the toga to Roman identity is the fact that men who were banished from Rome were forbidden from wearing it, and a passage in one of Pliny's letters describing the speech of an exiled senator in Sicily illustrates poignantly the feeling of loss and hurt pride thus created:

> when he entered the chamber dressed in a Greek *pallium* (those who have been exiled are not allowed to wear the toga), he composed himself, looked down at his dress, and announced 'I will deliver my speech in Latin'.
>
> *Ep.* 4.11

Figure 1.2 Detail of a mosaic from Hadrumetum showing Vergil and Muses. Bardo Museum, Tunis. Photo: Musée National du Bardo, Le Bardo, Tunisia/Bridgeman Images.

In addition to the toga being closely associated with Romanness, it could also be used as a metaphor for 'Roman'. Already a fragment of Laberius refers to the Romans as *togata stirps* (*minor. fragm. in aliis scriptis servata* 42), whilst Livy uses the term *turba togata* to mean the citizens of Rome (3.50.10),[38] and Sallust refers in his *Jugurthine War* to a group of assembled Romans as a *multitudo togatorum* (21.2); Cicero frequently uses the term '*togatus*' as shorthand for 'Roman' (e.g. *Phil.* 5.14; *Sull.* 30.85; *De or.* 1.24.111). In this period also, the term Gallia Togata was used for the 'Roman' part of Gaul (i.e. Cisalpine Gaul) in opposition to Gallia Comata ('long-haired') beyond the Alps.[39] The great general Lucullus is said to have been described by a Stoic philosopher as 'Xerxes in a toga' (Plut., *Luc.* 39.3) and the mysterious poet Calpurnius Siculus once referred to Rome-enforced peace as *pax togata* (*Ecl.* 4.8). Valerius Maximus also used the toga as a metaphor for Roman citizens when he referred to civil war as *violentiae togatae* (9.7.1). Many of the dichotomies through which Roman identity came to be articulated also found their expression in toga symbolism, for example in the dividing of dramatic works into (Greek) *fabulae palliatae* and (Roman) *fabulae togatae* (Cic., *Sest.* 118; Varro, *Ling.* 5.25), and in its use as a symbol of Roman expansion into 'barbarian' lands.[40]

As a universal trait of human culture, dress has always been and continues to be closely linked to personal and group identities. And yet, in many ways Roman culture was unique, certainly in the ancient world, for its intense preoccupation with it. No other ancient society was so fixated with the finer details of attire or so sensitive to its potential for symbolism.[41] This mentality of acquirable and outwardly manifesting identity found its ultimate expression in the toga, and it is through this most inherently Roman of all ancient garments that we can explore the myriad facets of what Romanness meant.

Previous scholarship

The earliest studies of the toga are to be found in the works not of classical scholars but of artists keen to faithfully render classical scenes, such as Albert Rubens' (the son of the more famous artist) *De re vestiaria veterum* (1665), as well as those looking to provide a basis for costumes for the theatre, such as Dandré Bardon's *Costume des anciens peuples, a l'usage des artistes* (1784) and Hope's *Costumes of the Greeks and Romans* (1809). It was one such writer, Léon Heuzey, who, albeit somewhat later, first identified the toga as elliptical in shape (1922). Dress was also briefly discussed in the handful of works on Roman private life that appeared in the nineteenth and early twentieth centuries;[42] but otherwise, until the early twentieth century, the toga was largely seen as merely an element of Roman art and is described as such in corpora of specific genres, such as Reinach's *répertoires* of ancient statuary and reliefs (1897/1912) and Altmann's corpus of grave altars (1905).[43]

At the same time, however, some scholars began to see the value of focusing on the toga in its own right from both an art-historical and a text-based angle: Launitz's *Über die Toga der Römer und die Palla der Römerinnen* of 1865 laid some initial groundwork for later studies such as Helbig's 'Toga und Trabea' (1904), Warde-Fowler's studies of the *toga praetexta* of Roman children (1896; 1920) and a host of discussions of the late antique toga, such as Hula's monograph of 1895,[44] which, whilst flawed in many of its conclusions, combined a thorough treatment of the practicalities of the toga with a first attempt at defining the different later fashions in drapery. After initial groundwork by Marquardt (1886), the first overview of the forms and dates of the different toga draping styles across Roman history as a whole was put together by Amelung in 1903 and built on by Albizzati (1922), who for the first time also included iconography on coins. A more systematic and exhaustive approach was achieved in the toga entries in late nineteeth- and early twentieth-century encyclopaedias.[45]

The first monograph dedicated to the toga – and until now the only one in English – was Wilson's *The Roman Toga* of 1924. Her interest in the garment was still, however, largely typological, tracing the evolution of drapery styles in public statuary; but it also broke new ground by attempting to establish – using live models and reconstructed garments – the exact form of the garment and changes in it over time. Many of her conclusions were soon superceded by those of other scholars, and her work made only a cursory attempt at integrating the written material that is so essential for understanding the meaning of the garment, but she was very clear on how central the toga was to Roman identity, and the justification she gave for her book still stands: 'The peculiar place which the toga held in Roman life and affairs, its symbolism, its long existence through many changes, all give it an interest and a significance beyond that of an ordinary article of clothing. Like the letters S.P.Q.R., it was representative of Rome itself' (p. 7).

The next great leap forward was achieved in the 1930s by the German archaeologist Friedrich Wilhelm Goethert. The findings of his doctoral thesis of 1931 on Roman Republican art, which were fleshed out in his toga entry in *Pauly-Wissowa* of 1937 and a journal article of 1939, together presented a thorough survey of all of the major written evidence for the toga, as well as an outline of the main drapery styles. It is his work that formed the primary basis for many subsequent studies. Alföldi's 'Insignien und Tracht der römischen Kaiser' of 1935 also made some headway in getting to grips with evolving toga iconography, albeit only in the context of imperial portraiture. An insightful and often-overlooked article by Zadoks-Jitta in 1939–1940 was unusual in looking squarely at the significance and meaning of the toga as a garment in general, rather than just its formal evolution as an art-historical feature; her attempts to link changes in draping style directly to specific developments in Roman society inevitably strike one today as simplistic, but in its approach the study was nonetheless ahead of its time in recognizing the importance of dress as a reflection of culture.

Of direct relevance to the toga is also Bonfante's pioneering work on Etruscan dress in the 1960s and 1970s[46] arguing for an Etruscan origin of many aspects of Roman dress, including the toga. She was later instrumental in initiating the 'new wave' of dress studies in the 1990s (see below). The 1970s and 1980s saw the publication of two articles by Gabelmann on specific toga forms: the *trabea* of equestrians (1977) and the *toga praetexta* of Roman children (1985). Wrede followed up with further thoughts on the *trabea* in 1988. All of these were immensely valuable contributions to our understanding of the toga, but piecemeal and necessarily limited in scope.

In the mid- to late twentieth century in German-language scholarship there was a growing interest in the development of Roman portrait styles, and especially of imperial iconography, which manifested itself in corpora such as the volumes of *Das römische Herrscherbild*.[47] Of relevance to the toga, also in the same period, again largely in German-language scholarship, is a growing number of catalogue-based studies of specific bodies of material, such as grave reliefs,[48] grave altars[49] and sarcophagi,[50] an approach that continues to this day in works like Wrede (2001) and Reinsberg (2006). As useful as these studies have been, they have tended to treat garments in terms of art-historical 'types' used largely to fulfil dating purposes, although some have included useful short discussions of the significance of the toga in particular genres, such as Kleiner's (1976) monograph on the toga of Roman freedmen.

Very much within the German catalogue-based tradition, but the only recent monograph to have been devoted solely to the toga, is H.-R. Goette's *Studien zu römischen Togadarstellungen* of 1990, building on and significantly expanding Goethert's earlier work. Whilst it contains a compendium of and references to many of the key text passages, Goette's main interest was in the development over time of toga drapery styles, and the result is a complex typology based largely, although not solely, on public statuary art; its methodology was to identify '*Leitstücke*' to exemplify drapery styles, to which other monuments were assigned according to type. The discussion of toga drapery styles in the next chapter is based largely on Goette's thoroughly credible conclusions. But his work only went very briefly into the toga's meaning and role in Roman culture. At this stage, the garment was still primarily viewed by scholars as a feature of elite Roman art, rather than something that was worn by and had significance for real people.

An important sea-change occurred in dress studies in the 1990s. Starting with a conference volume edited by Sebesta and Bonfante (1994), and under the influence – both direct and indirect – of ideas circulating in anthropology and sociology, scholarly focus began to shift from one largely engaged with what ancient dress looked like to one that asked what it meant. It began to be seen as a means by which to better understand ancient societies, rather than as an end in itself, and this led to more integrated methodologies, combining both iconographic and literary evidence. The pioneering work of this volume was built on in further edited volumes in France, Britain, Germany and Canada,[51] which contain a number of excellent discussions of various aspects of the toga, such as its role in patron–client relations,[52] childhood and coming of age,[53] and masculine identity.[54] These studies have gone some way to shifting the focus from art-historical considerations to wider social meaning, thereby creating a new conversation based on the toga as a lived garment. They are, however, all limited to the individual theme under consideration and are largely focused – either implicitly or explicitly – on the elite.

In 1996 Carrie Vout published a short article entitled 'The Myth of the Toga', a deliberately provocative piece that, like Shelley Stone's chapter in the then-recent Sebesta/Bonfante volume, questioned the actual extent to which the toga was ever worn in Roman society, and proposed much greater diversity in clothing than traditional views had allowed for. Whilst the overall exercise in both these works was a fruitful one in terms of bursting some bubbles, the overall effect has been to overly marginalize the toga in terms both of its use in Roman society and its meaning for ordinary Romans, a view that will be challenged in what is to follow.

The past decade has also seen two major works that are of direct relevance to the toga: first, a 2010 article by Melissa Rothfus on the political implications of changes in toga styles in the late Republic and early Empire, which formed part of a larger doctoral dissertation on the toga that was unfortunately never published. Second, a monograph on *Masculinity and Dress in Roman Antiquity* (2017b) by Kelly Olson, one of the main figures in the 'new wave' of dress studies described above. This work sets out to elucidate masculinity in ancient Rome by focusing on dress and appearance, and in this it is highly valuable. But its focus is principally on textual evidence and the elite, and the relatively short discussion of the toga (pp. 23–54) is largely descriptive and based on previous work.

More generally in ancient dress studies, the past two decades have seen increasingly sophisticated attempts to theorize dress as a phenomenon in human culture, and especially to approach it in terms of already long-standing ideas about semiotics and non-verbal language from sociology. Already in 1996 Vout had argued that Roman dress scholarship had been so preoccupied with the precise details of garments in visual depictions that one had made little headway into understanding the meaning of those garments and the ways in which they were used. She suggested seeing the toga 'not as a garment but as a cultural symbol'[55] and invoked the sociologist Alison Lurie's ideas in *The Language of Clothes* (1992) to set out the toga as part of a sartorial conversation, the nature of which was dependent on time and place. More recently, Andrew Wallace-Hadrill's *Rome's Cultural Revolution* (2008) includes an entire chapter on the Roman elite capacity for bilingualism with Greek that addresses it in terms of both language and clothing. Whilst language was more central to Greek and dress more central to Roman identity, he argues that although Greek language and dress became integral to Roman elite culture, they were confined to certain situations, and Romans were able to switch between the two. Similar ideas were developed in Angelika Starbatty's (2010) monograph *Aussehen ist Ansichtssache*. Here, she applies the ancient concept of *aptum* to argue that Romans had a keen sense of what was appropriate to a given person/situation, looking not only at clothes but also personal grooming, shoes and jewellery. Her main thesis is that dress was a central means of communication in Rome, but she does not move outside a view of it as a non-verbal component of ancient rhetorical theory.

None of the recent research has ventured outside elite circles,[56] nor beyond the centre of the empire, and, more importantly, there remains a need for a comprehensive study of the toga that moves beyond the idea of it as an art-historical feature. The purpose of this book is threefold: first, it endeavours to combine the available evidence for the toga, visual, written and artefactual, in order to gain as complete a picture as possible of the history, use and meaning of the garment. Second, whilst necessarily focusing much of its attention on the city of Rome and the elite where ideas about the toga were first formulated, it also seeks to establish the role it played both in non-elite circles and beyond Italy in the provinces, where it developed entirely different, but no less important, values and functions. Third, it aims to swing the pendulum back away from a view of the toga as a mere 'cultural symbol' to one that sees it in its rightful place at the centre, not just of Roman ideas about their own identity, but also the ways in which it was enacted on a daily basis.

2

The Toga

A Brief History

The term 'toga' is almost certainly derived from the Latin word *tegere*, meaning 'to cover' (Nonius 653L; Isid., *Etym.* 19.24.3), which in turn had its origins in an even more ancient Indo-European stem with the same meaning.[1] Whilst the earliest surviving evidence for the word is in Plautus (*Amph.* prol. 68; late third/early second century BCE), its etymology suggests that it began as a very basic cloak of the early Romans. As ancient writers point out, it was distinctive from the beginning in its elliptical shape, setting it apart from the vast array of rectangular cloaks in antiquity such as the Greek *himation*, a rectangle being far easier to create on a loom.[2] There is, however, some controversy surrounding where it originally came from, and like many aspects of Roman culture, the spectrum of opinion is characterized by arguments for a Greek or a local origin.

One school of thought – predominant in German-language scholarship – sees a Greek origin for the toga. Based on two very late sources (Pollux, *Onom.* 7.61; Suidas s.v. *tebennos*), which say the toga developed under Greek influence, and a short passage in Plutarch, *Numa* (7.5), which connects the *laena* – the Latin term for the double toga – with the Greek *chlaina*, scholars such as Amelung, Goette and Zanker have argued that its elliptical form came from the occasionally rounded edge of the *chlaina*.[3] One scholar has even gone so far as to refer to the toga up to the time of Augustus as 'just a modified version' of a Greek cloak.[4]

Far more plausible, however, is an Etruscan origin. The written evidence is admittedly somewhat ambiguous: Livy (1.8), Diodorus of Sicily (5.40), Pliny (*HN* 8.195) and Florus (1.1.5) all say that the *toga praetexta* with its distinctive purple border, along with the *sella curulis* and other insignia of high office, was Etruscan in origin, rather than the toga per se, which has caused some scholars to suggest only the border was Etruscan in origin whilst the round form was

Greek;[5] but a passage in Dionysius of Halicarnassus suggests otherwise, describing the regalia of the Etruscan kings of Rome as:

> a gold-decorated purple robe like those of the kings of Lydia and Persia, except that it was not rectangular in form like theirs, but semicircular. These kinds of garments are called togas by the Romans and tebennas by the Greeks; but I do not know from where the Greeks learned the name, as it does not appear to me to be a Greek word.
>
> *Ant. Rom.* 3.61, trans. Cary 1937

A somewhat baffling passage in Servius' late antique commentary on the *Aeneid* (2.781) suggests there was at some point an idea that the toga made its way to Italy from Asia Minor via the (as yet historically unproven) Lydian connection that was one of several ancient ideas of Etruscan ancestry.[6]

The archaeological evidence provides a clearer picture: already Courby noted that the toga looked more like the curved cloaks in Etruscan art than anything the Greeks wore,[7] and later work on Etruscan bronze figurines,[8] tomb paintings[9] and terracottas,[10] as well as Bonfante's early studies of Etruscan dress,[11] all confirm an unbroken lineage from the semi-circular *tebenna* of the Etruscans to the Roman toga.[12] Some of the earliest images we have of the *tebenna* can be found in sixth-century wall paintings in Tarquinia, such as in the Tomb of the Baron and the Tomb of the Augurs (Fig. 2.1), and already here one can see

Figure 2.1 Detail of a wall painting in the Tomb of the Augurs, Tarquinia. Photo: Tarquinia, Lazio, Italy/Bridgeman Images.

the distinctive curved edge at the bottom and the style of draping diagonally across the upper body and over the left shoulder that was to later characterize the toga.[13]

The 'smoking gun' for an Italian origin has more recently been provided by the textile finds from the Villanovan graves at Verucchio near Rimini. These were discovered during excavation work in the 1970s, but restoration work only began in Cologne in 1994 and was completed within the context of the *DressID* EU project in 2012. Grave 89, dating to around 700 BCE, contained two semi-circular cloaks, circa 280 cm across the straight edge and 90 cm in width to the bottom of the round hem (Fig. 2.2). Further analysis revealed that they had been red in colour with a purple stripe along all the edges (along with an amber bead decoration) and that they showed signs of wear and tear, proving that they were not merely funerary dress.[14] Also found in the Verucchio grave was an ornate throne, suggesting not only that the person buried was of elite status, but also that the bordered cloak and distinctive chair were insignia of high status that went back further into Italian antiquity than writers like Livy and Pliny were evidently aware.

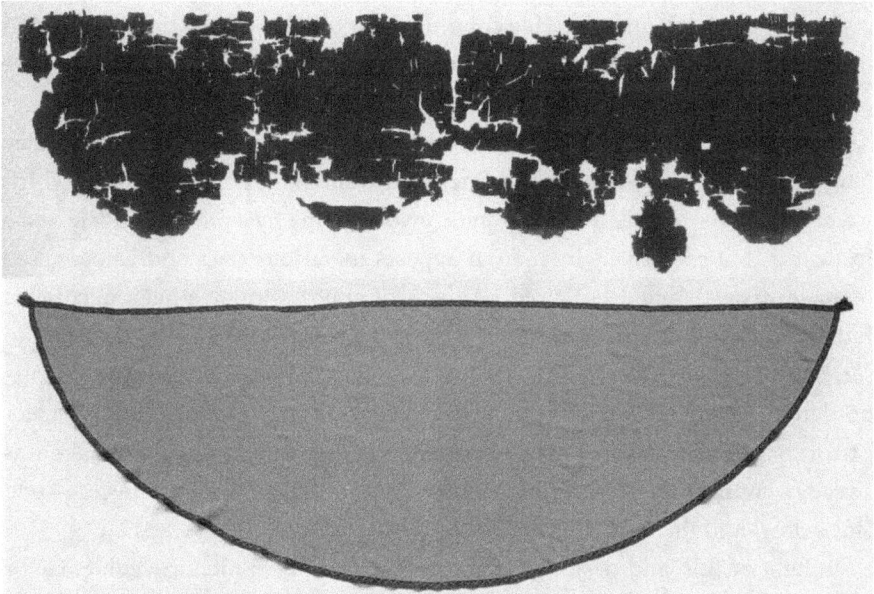

Figure 2.2 Cloak 2 from Grave 89, Verucchio (top) and reconstruction (bottom). Museo Archeologico Verucchio. Photo: Annemarie Stauffer. Verucchio, Museo Archaeologico, Tomba Lippi 89/1972, tebenna 1. © Technical University Cologne. Photo: Ulrich Borowiak.

Etruscan art displays a wide variety of possible draping styles for the *tebenna* over time, and it is more than conceivable that some of these evolved under increased Greek influence from the sixth century onward: it could be fastened at the shoulder with a brooch like a *chlamys*,[15] draped 'back-to-front' with the ends thrown back over the shoulders (especially by youths and people engaged in physical activity)[16] or draped over the left shoulder and across the waist (usually by deities);[17] both the latter draping style and the classic diagonal drape in Fig. 2.1 (along with countless other tomb paintings) bear a striking resemblance to the most common ways of draping the Greek *himation*. Moreover, along with Villanovan-Etruscan inventions like the *bulla* (locket), the *calcei* (closed boots) and the *apex* (hat) of the *flamines*,[18] later Roman dress also contained some Greek dress items that arrived via the Etruscans, such as the *pilleus* hat. However, the Verucchio finds predate the earliest Greek influence on Etruscan dress,[19] and show that both the curved form of the toga and the border decoration must have originated on the Italian peninsula.[20] As Dionysius already pointed out, the term *tebenna* itself is not a Greek word, and etymologists regard it as Etruscan in origin;[21] it is not insignificant that it is this Etruscan word that the Greeks later used for the Roman toga.[22] The Verucchio *tebenna* finds are the only extant textile remains of curved cloaks from the entire territory of the Roman Empire; owing largely to the unfavourable conditions for textile preservation in Italy and most of the empire, no actual toga has ever been found.[23] As a result, we are forced to rely on written and iconographic evidence to trace its origins.

From the sixth century BCE onward, the thread is easier to trace: whilst it may have originally been worn by both men and women,[24] by the period for which we begin to have detailed iconographic evidence, the *tebenna* was widely worn in Etruria, but exclusively by men. It appears in various sizes and colours, and often sports a different-coloured border that appears to have been decorative rather than determined by status.[25] At the same time, however, we also begin to see, in Etruscan art, the *sella curulis*, the *lituus* and the *calcei* paired with purple-bordered *tebennae* that later became the insignia of high office at Rome.[26] Later Etruscan art also features some ways of draping the *tebenna* that show there was already a connection with the toga, such as the *himation*-inspired 'armsling-style' (see below) and the veiling of the head (*capite velato*: see Chapter 3).[27]

In light of this, and despite the non-existence of documentary evidence for early Rome, it is not difficult to understand how the toga became a Roman garment. To start with, any Etruscan rulers of Rome would have worn it, along with the other insignia of rank that evolved in Etruria.[28] It is likely that at this stage the rounded cloak was a more common garment of central Italy in general.

Livy (6.25.6–8) certainly considered it to be appropriate to describe the people of the Latin city of Tusculum as wearing togas when the Romans conquered their territory in 382/381 BCE. The fact that by the third century the register of Rome's Italian allies was called the *formula togatorum* suggests that the *socii* were also toga-wearers;[29] perhaps more generally in Italian communities the toga signified citizen men of military age, as Wrede has suggested.[30] However, already in the late-fourth-century BCE François tomb paintings at Vulci, the Roman nobles are set apart from their Etruscan assailants by wearing distinctive white togas with purple borders,[31] and for the turn of the third century BCE a fragment of Ennius survives that refers to something unknown being the case 'as long as one togate Roman survives',[32] which suggests that by this stage the connection between the toga and the Romans specifically had established itself.

It seems to have been common knowledge – going by later Roman sources (e.g. Gell., *NA* 6.12; Livy 1.8.13) – that originally the Romans wore the toga without a tunic underneath, calling to mind the way it was often worn in Etruscan tomb paintings (see Fig. 2.1). Pliny (*HN* 34.23) mentions archaic statues of Romulus and Tatius allegedly still standing in Rome in his time, in which the figures wore the toga without a tunic underneath,[33] and it was the dress chosen for the figure of Aeneas on the Ara Pacis (Fig. 1.1). But the figure of Q. Fabius in the Esquiline tomb frescoes shows that Roman dignitaries were already wearing a tunic under their toga by the mid Republic;[34] and although we are told that in the late Republic Cato chose to wear the toga without a tunic to signal his adherence to ancient Roman values (Plut., *Cat. Min.* 6.3), by the time Roman statuary began to develop in the second century BCE, a tunic seems to have been customarily worn under the toga, along with closed shoes (*calcei*).[35]

As has also been suggested for the *tebenna*,[36] the early toga may have doubled up as a blanket at night (Varro in Non. 867–868L), and from Arnobius we hear of an old custom in which the bridegroom threw his toga onto the bed on the wedding night to invoke the *genii* of husbands (*Adv. nat.* 2.67). Several later sources state that it was originally worn by both men and women,[37] not implausible given the more generalized character of the early toga, as well as the fact that in later periods female children wore the *toga praetexta*.[38] In Pliny's catalogue of Roman statuary, he mentions an equestrian statue of Cloelia, a heroine of the early Republic, wearing a toga (*HN* 34.28), although it is conceivable that she was so dressed in recognition of her bravery rather than because it being what she was supposed to have worn.

The written evidence we have also makes clear that the toga was originally worn in both peace and war. Livy records that in 205 BCE the Romans asked the

Spanish tribes Ilergetes and Ausetani to provide the army with '*saga et togae*' for the soldiers (29.3), and for 169 BCE that 6,000 togas and 30,000 tunics were ordered to be sent to the army fighting in Macedonia (44.16).[39] Valerius Maximus tells us that during the First Servile War, a cavalry prefect by the name of C. Titius was made to stand on duty wearing an ungirt tunic and a toga which had been stripped of its '*lacinia*' (probably meaning its border) as punishment for being routed by the enemy (2.7.9).[40] Whilst it would have been impossible to do battle in the larger togas of the imperial period, the Etruscan and earliest Roman pictorial evidence suggests the original toga was much smaller and easier to manage.[41] Nonetheless, it would seem that a special style developed that allowed maximum movement: the so-called *cinctus Gabinus* ('Gabine belt'), which involved twisting the toga tightly around the waist and over one shoulder. It was named after the city of Gabii, an early enemy, then ally, of Rome, but it is not clear whether it evolved as a result of combat or under friendly influence; in any case it seems from the outset to have been associated with both war and certain religious rites. Dubourdieu has suggested that it originated in the religious drapery of the people of Gabii, relating to the augurs and especially any activity related to the frontiers,[42] and it seems that the early Romans used it in the context of the foundation of new colonies, the *sacra Ambarvalia* and the opening of the temple of Janus, as well as for battle and actions relating to warfare.[43] It survived in Roman art as the distinctive dress of the *Lares* (Fig. 3.2).[44]

It is difficult to assess the significance of an Etruscan, rather than a Greek, origin for the toga. Dench has recently argued that the tendency to see Etruscan roots as more authentic is a characteristic of modern scholarship, and that the Romans themselves did not regard Etruscan culture as more native to them than Greek culture.[45] The point is well made, and the argument holds to an extent, but one should not ignore the significance of the continuity the toga represents, nor the close geographical proximity of where it originated. It is for these reasons that dress scholars began to characterize it as a native dress of central Italy even before the Verucchio finds were published.[46] Pliny tells us that the *toga praetexta* of the early Roman king Servius Tullius was preserved – like a holy relic – in Rome until 31 CE (*HN* 8.197), and an intriguing column base in the Capitoline Museums dating to the Claudian period but apparently depicting a sacrificial scene from earliest Roman history shows all the male figures bearded and wearing little togas,[47] similarly to Aeneas on the Ara Pacis (Fig. 1.1). In the end what perhaps matters most is that the Romans themselves considered the toga to have been an integral part of their culture from the very beginning, and it is this conscious antiquity that helped to make it such a potent symbol in later Roman history.

Material, production and acquisition

The toga was generally made out of wool, as were most outer garments in antiquity.[48] Sheep herding was widespread in central Italy in the early Roman period, and wool was regularly produced on the *latifundia* of later periods as well. In comparison with their later counterparts, early togas would have been quite rough, and Pliny describes them as *undulata* ('wavy' meaning 'shaggy'?: *HN* 8.195), suggesting they had a long nap. However, the growing empire facilitated access to a wide variety of additional sheep breeds, and by the late Republic increasingly fine wool could be produced from cross-breeding, whilst different types of wool could be sourced from all over the empire, leading to the development of specialist wool production regions aimed at empire-wide export in places like Gaul, Spain and Asia Minor.[49] By the first century CE Martial could include a whole range of regions as possible sources for the wool of a beautiful toga given to him,[50] and both Columella's treatise on agriculture (*Rust.* 7.2.3) and Pliny's *Natural History* (8.190–191) set out in detail the various places in the empire that produced the best wool. Pliny contrasts the earlier *togae undulatae* with the *togae rasae* of his day that came into fashion under Augustus (*HN* 8.74; 8.195), and both the term he uses and a passage in Quintilian's oratory handbook suggest that in the early Empire the cloth was often teased up into a nap and then closely clipped to form a smooth surface.[51] With access to the finest types of wool and refined weaving techniques, the Romans were apparently also capable of producing woollen cloth that was diaphanous (Columella, *Rust.* 7.2.3–5), and Varro apparently wrote about togas through which one could see the stripes of the tunic (in Non. 861L). By the imperial period there seems to have been the option of lighter summer togas and heavier ones for use in winter.[52]

Although many different wool colours and dyes were available in the Roman period,[53] excessive colour was considered inappropriate for men (see, e.g., Mart. 1.96), and the normal colour for the toga appears to have been the natural pale colour of undyed wool from white sheep.[54] The palest wool was the most expensive in antiquity, partly because it was easily dyeable, and the most desirable appearance was as white as possible (Columella, *Rust.* 7.2.4). In the poem already mentioned above, Martial goes on to admire the remarkable whiteness of the new toga he has been given:

> You outdo lilies and privet still unfallen and the ivory that whitens on Tibur's hill. Sparta's swans will yield to you and Paphian doves; the pearl shall yield, dug out from Erythraean shallows. But though this gift challenges fresh snow (*primae*

nives), it is no whiter than Parthenius, its giver. I would not rather have the painted fabrics of proud Babylon, embroidered by Semiramis' needle.

8.28.12–19, trans. Shackleton Bailey 1993[55]

Martial is probably exaggerating somewhat: even the whitest of sheep do not produce wool that is as white as virgin snow, and the existence of the extra-white *toga candida* (see Chapter 5) shows that normal togas were not as white as they could be made to be using artificial means. But what this exaggeration shows is that the togas made of the palest, cleanest undyed wool were the most desirable.

We are at a considerable disadvantage when looking at colours of garments in antiquity in not having the original paintwork on sculpture, nor extant textile objects to help us. But written sources indicate that the additional colour features of special togas were achieved in a variety of ways. The colour of the full purple *toga purpurea* (see Chapter 4) and the stripe on the *toga praetexta* (see Chapters 3 and 4) will ideally have been achieved using authentic Tyrian dye from murex shellfish, but there were various shades and qualities of this, as well as cheaper substitutes.[56]

Whilst Wilson had argued, based on her reconstructions, that it would have been impossible to weave an entire toga on an upright loom,[57] Granger-Taylor has more recently maintained that even the very large imperial togas could have been woven in one go,[58] and Stauffer has shown that the *tebenna* from Verucchio had also been woven in one piece in its final shape.[59] Mary Harlow has been working on time calculations for the production of Roman garments, and her preliminary findings based on experimental work at the Centre for Textile Research in Copenhagen show that the yarn needed for an imperial-style (see below) toga would have taken around 900 hours to spin, whilst the fabric would have taken a further 200 hours for a single person to weave.[60] It is also likely that any coloured borders were woven, rather than sewn, onto the toga[61] and the technical skill involved in weaving an elliptical garment and achieving a curved selvedge no doubt added to the garment's prestige. In light of this, a passage in Quintilian (*Inst.* 11.3.139), in which he says that an orator's toga should be 'round (*rutunda*) and cut to fit (*apte caesa*)', is difficult to make sense of. The usual meaning of *caedo* is 'cut' or 'hew', but there is no evidence that Roman garments were ever generally cut or tailored, in part due to the immense outlay of labour needed to hand-weave cloth. We also have no clear evidence for any tailors, although the exact function of the epigraphically attested *vestifici* is as yet unconfirmed.[62]

In early Roman history, garments were spun and woven by female members of the household. The extent to which this happened in later periods is clouded by the fact that textile work was a long-standing *topos* of female propriety, such that evidence like funerary inscriptions describing deceased women's devotion to wool-work,[63] the inclusion of textile implements in funerary portraits[64] and claims like that made by Suetonius (*Aug.* 73) that Augustus' female family members made his clothes must all be taken with a pinch of salt. Still, in the second century CE Fronto uses wool spinning as an analogy of destiny and says 'surely no spinner (*lanifica*) would be so unskilful and ignorant as to spin for her master's toga a heavy (*solidus*) and knotty (*nodosus*) yarn?' (*Epist.* 2 Naber p.232), suggesting that households might still plausibly include women spinning wool for togas. Some domestic production of textiles certainly continued, as loomweights are found in Italian houses throughout the Roman period and weaving is sometimes mentioned amongst the tasks of household slaves.[65] If one had space, a loom and manpower it would have been cheaper to produce textiles at home, but many people would not have had these at their disposal.

By the late Republic there is considerable evidence for 'proto-industrial'[66] textile production, including inscriptions mentioning people involved in various stages of manufacture.[67] Interestingly, it would seem that when textile production became professionalized it also started to be carried out by men rather than women. For the imperial period we have detailed papyrological evidence for large-scale textile manufacture in Egypt recording a vast array of specialist sub-professions, suggesting workshops tended to be involved in one small part of the process to achieve economies of scale, as well as information on wages and the hiring of apprentices,[68] leading Jones to conclude that in the Empire, weaving was 'in the main a professional occupation, and clothing an object of trade.'[69] It also appears that finishing processes, such as dyeing and fulling, which were conducted by other specialized professionals, may often have been commissioned by the consumer of the garment post-purchase.[70] The textile industry does not then seem to have changed substantially until late antiquity, when we see the additional development of large, state-run textile workshops called *gynaecea* (e.g. *Cod. Just.* 11.9.1).

Considering how one might have acquired a toga, it seems that by the late Republic most people would have bought their garments ready-made. Already Plautus (*Aul.* 508–516) mentions the profession of *vestiarius* (clothes dealer) and *vestiarii* are commonly attested in inscriptions throughout the late Republic and Empire.[71] Trade in garments, like any consumer good, tended to accumulate in certain places in the city, and Claire Holleran has shown how many of the clothes dealers of Rome accumulated in the Vicus Tuscus, whilst others were dotted around the city, such as in the Horrea Agrippiana and the Horrea Volusianis.[72]

Street sellers (*institores*) are known to have sold clothing amongst their other wares,[73] but we also have evidence for merchants dealing in specific garments such as the *sagarii* who traded in *saga*.[74] It is all the more perplexing, then, that we do not have any evidence for toga traders. The literary evidence attests to the fact that already in the late Republic togas were commonly bought as finished products: in Cato the Elder's farming handbook he says that they are best bought at Rome, along with tunics and other textiles (*Agr.* 135.1). Martial and Juvenal also mention budgeting for and buying togas,[75] so there must have been a way to get them quite easily retail, although Martial also mentions them as the kinds of things one might be given by patrons[76] or friends.[77] It is possible that togas were in the remit of the general *vestiarii*, or perhaps the *sagarii* were dealers in cloaks more generally, including togas, rather than just *saga*.

There was also a vigorous trade in second-hand garments,[78] and the frequent mention in inscriptions of professions relating to patching[79] and mending[80] suggests that many people would have held on to garments for as long as possible.[81] For late antiquity, Diocletian's Price Edict is the most valuable source for the clothing industry, and it is again surprising that in the lists itemizing every consumable thing, including a huge number of different garments of every price and quality, there is no mention of a toga, although the pictorial evidence attests that it continued to be worn for some time longer. This document does, however, give us a good indication of the immense financial outlay that was involved in purchasing clothing, largely due to the amount of labour that went into even the most simple textile production. For example, the various cloaks listed in the Price Edict, although much smaller than the toga in size, could cost anything between 2,000 and 12,500 *denarii* (19.51–60), whilst in the same document, the average worker (stonemason, carpenter, blacksmith) earned around 50 *denarii* a day (7.1–14). This means that such a worker would have had to dedicate the wages of around 40 days' work to have bought a simple cloak; a toga would have incurred considerably more expense. It is for this reason that garments were among the valuable items most commonly stolen from bathhouses,[82] and for poor people clothing may have been the most expensive thing they owned. As Ovid exclaims in *Ars Amatoria*, 'What madness it is to carry whole incomes on one's body!' (3.172).

Draping

The basic shape of the toga was a semicircle of cloth, which meant that it produced a distinctive appearance when draped around the body. As a basic principle, it was always wrapped with the straight edge (*balteus*) upwards and the curved edge hanging down; the *balteus* was placed over the left shoulder with the tip (*lacinia*) hanging down the front; the rest of the toga was then draped around the back, under the right arm, diagonally across the chest and then thrown back over the left shoulder (Fig. 2.3: top row). In statuary art a toga can thus be easily recognized based on the rounded hem at the front (with no corner) and at least one *lacinia* hanging between the legs. Variations on this draping principle occurred over time, however, and it is this feature that pushed the toga into the centre of art-historical interest as a result of its dating potential. The first comprehensive survey of toga drapery was Wilson's monograph of 1924, which explicitly set out to identify key changes over time. Her ideas relating to changes also in the *form* of the toga have, however, since been disproved by Goette, and it is his comprehensive 1990 typological work that is now considered the main authority on this matter.[83]

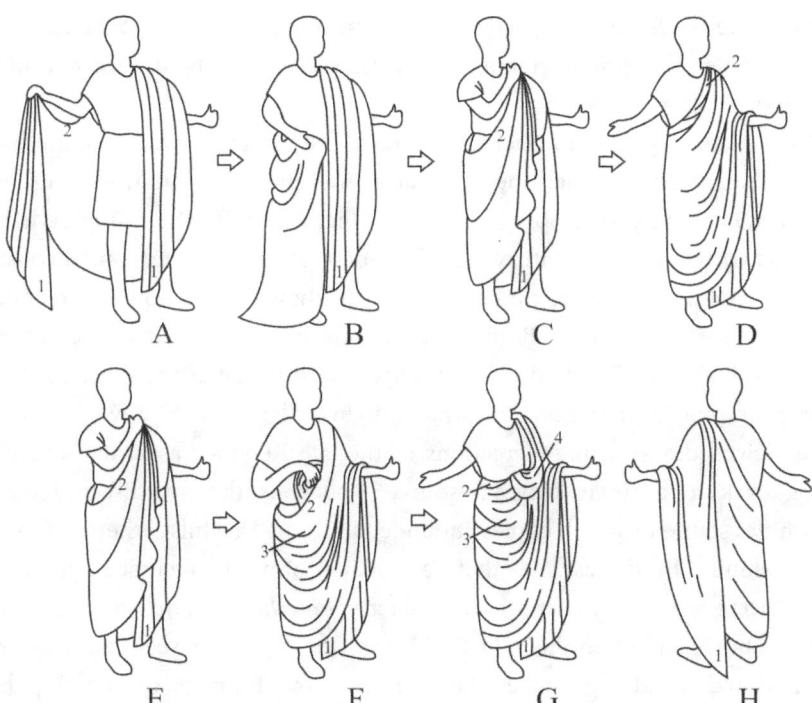

Figure 2.3 How the toga was draped. A–D: basic toga draping style; E–G: imperial toga draping style; H: rear view; 1: *lacinia*; 2: *balteus*; 3: *sinus*; 4: *umbo*. Drawing: U. Rothe.

The earliest images we have of the toga suggest that for much of the Republican period it retained the simple diagonal draping style that had already been a common way of wearing the Etruscan *tebenna* (e.g. Fig. 2.1) and conforms to the basic method described in the previous paragraph.[84] This was the toga in its simplest semi-circular form, and it appears to have been modest in dimension, with estimates as to its width across the *balteus* ranging from 3 to 3.7 metres;[85] based on a passage in Horace, the type is often now referred to as the *toga exigua* ('skimpy toga'),[86] although we have no reason to believe that this was ever a set term. We see it in early Roman frescoes like those in the Esquiline Tomb, which are generally dated to the late fourth/early third century BCE.[87] The reverse of a silver *denarius* of C. Minucius Augurinus from 135 BCE (Fig. 2.4) is particularly interesting as it shows not just two – presumably contemporary – figures wearing the simple Republican toga, but also a similarly dressed statue on a column, apparently for an ancestor who is supposed to have been thus commemorated in 439 BCE.[88] Better-known examples include the statue of the 'Arringatore' (Fig. 2.5) from Perugia and the census relief on the altar of Domitius Ahenobarbus from Rome, both dating to around 100 BCE.[89] Whilst this style seems to have remained relatively unchanged over the course of the Republic, Goette claims to be able to identify a gradual tendency over time toward a slightly larger garment with more elaborate folds.[90]

In the late Republic an alternative draping style came into fashion which, rather than passing under the right arm, was pulled up to the right-hand shoulder, effectively enveloping both arms (Fig. 2.6).[91] This 'armsling' style has been dated to the first century BCE by Goethert and Goette,[92] but Etruscan images from the fourth–second centuries BCE show it was known a great deal earlier, at least in Etruria.[93] Both the Etruscans and the Romans were familiar with Greek art from a relatively early stage, and it is one of the most common ways of draping the *himation* (Latin: *pallium*) in Hellenistic art.[94] Several scholars have viewed the 'armsling' depictions of the late Republic as visual formulae going back to a single original source[95] (such as the fourth-century-BCE 'Aeschines statue' of which copies abounded in Rome[96]), whilst others have seen it as a genuine, lived dress style that was a matter of personal choice.[97] It may be what Cicero referred to in his use of the term '*bracchio cohibito*' when speaking of his youth,[98] and Quintilian (*Inst.* 11.3.138) seems to have seen it as a Greek-inspired old-world style when he wonders how Romans of the Republic gesticulated in oratory as their arms were confined in their togas, 'just like the Greeks' (*sicut Graecorum*) (see below).[99] A certain amount of ink has been spilt over the cultural developments that led to the popularity of the 'armsling' style in

Figure 2.4 Reverse of a silver *denarius* of C. Minucius Augurinus from Rome. *RRC* 242/1. Photo: De Agostini Picture Library/A. De Gregorio/Bridgeman Images.

Figure 2.5 'Arringatore' statue from Lake Trasimeno. Museo Archeologico Nazionale, Florence, inv. 2. Photo: Museo Archeologico Nazionale, Florence, Italy/Alinari/Bridgeman Images.

Figure 2.6 Grave portrait of a Roman couple from the Via Statilia. Musei Capitolini, Centrale Montemartini, inv. MC 2142/S. Photo: U. Rothe © Roma – Sovrintendenza Capitolina ai Beni Culturali.

the late Republic, and it is likely to have been a combination at the time of an intensifying engagement with Greek culture and education, and the visibility of increasing numbers of freedmen, particularly from the Greek East.[100] The similarity of this toga style with the *pallium* has led to some confusion in distinguishing between the two in Roman art, and Olson has recently argued that this ambiguity was intended at the time, and that the overall symbolism was the link to Hellenized ideas of erudition and learning;[101] but whilst this may be true for bust portraits, in full-length depictions where the hemline is visible it is generally clear whether the cloak is a *pallium* or a toga.[102]

The next major change occurred in the Augustan period, when the toga acquired an additional semi-circular section of cloth, making its shape when spread out roughly oval, but retaining its semi-circular shape when draped as it was folded double along the *balteus*.[103] This additional part was called a *sinus* and it formed a second, slightly shorter layer of drapery over the main semi-circular fold. In addition, part of the front-hanging section of *balteus* was pulled out over the diagonal section, forming a pouch-shaped fold called an *umbo* (lit. 'knob') (Fig. 2.7 and Fig. 2.3: bottom row). In part to accommodate the *umbo*, it also appears to have grown in volume, and scholarly estimates of its width range from 4.8 to 6 metres.[104] It seems likely that the new style was related in some way to the beginning of the new political era and Augustus' interest in cultural renewal,[105] and the transition is exemplified on the Ara Pacis, where it is found along with the simpler, older style on the north and south friezes.[106] It held sway for the whole of the Julio-Claudian period, although there may have been fluctuations in the width of the *sinus*.[107]

Figure 2.7 Statue of the 'Togatus Barberini'. Musei Capitolini, Centrale Montemartini, inv. MC 2392/S. Photo: J. Fabiano © Roma – Sovrintendenza Capitolina ai Beni Culturali.

The *sinus* of the imperial toga became a constant feature, but in the late first century a style emerged in which the *umbo* was twisted up into the *balteus* rather than protruding like a pouch (Fig. 2.8: middle right figure).[108] The earliest images we have of it are on the Arch of Titus in Rome.[109] Whilst in many ways a more practical style, as it was fastened more tightly and the entire toga was somewhat shorter, the *sinus* had simultaneously grown longer, which is why many figures hold it in their left hand.[110] (The holding of the elongated *sinus* is something that then goes through into late antiquity – see below.)

In the second century the twisted *umbo* in the *balteus* became gradually more visible again, this time being pulled out at the left shoulder and folded so as to form a kind of triangle (Fig. 1.2).[111] This toga is sometimes called 'partly contabulated'. At the same time, the round edge of the *sinus* was folded over flat, becoming more pronounced.[112] The first indications of the style appeared already in images of Hadrian, such as the *adventus* relief in the Capitoline Museums in Rome,[113] but it became more distinct and more widespread in the later second century,[114] and it is the main type of toga used for portrait reliefs in Noricum when that genre burgeons there in the Severan period.[115]

The so-called 'fully contabulated toga' emerged in the mid-third century and involved the *umbo* now being folded flat in wide bands reaching from under the right arm, this time with visible stitches or staples.[116] The best image we have of it is a statue in the Villa Doria-Pamphilj,[117] but we also find it in private grave reliefs,[118] on the 'Brothers' Sarcophagus' (Fig. 2.8: group of figures on the left) and later on the Arch of Constantine (Fig. 2.9: figures to the left of the emperor),

Figure 2.8 'Brothers' sarcophagus'. Museo Archeologico Nazionale, Naples, inv. 6603. Photo: © Marie-Lan Nguyen/Wikimedia Commons/CC BY-2.5.

Figure 2.9 Detail of the forum frieze, Arch of Constantine, Rome.
Photo: Wikimedia Commons.

showing it was popular in the fourth century as well.[119] In its later forms the *sinus* becomes even longer, whilst the toga as a whole shrinks and is now worn over two tunics – one tight with long sleeves and one loose and sleeveless – that reach to the lower calf. The combination of tunics continues until the end of antiquity. Goette's contention that full contabulation was a result of Greek and Egyptian influence[120] holds some water, as we do find priests of Serapis depicted in a similar way,[121] and Fejfer has more recently argued that it developed as a new status symbol after the *constitutio Antoniniana* granted Roman citizenship to all free inhabitants of the Roman Empire.[122]

From the early fifth century until the time of Justinian another type of contabulated toga was worn in which the earlier band-like *umbo* was loosened to form a large triangle of drapery over the left shoulder;[123] this is often called the 'magistrate type' because by this stage it is chiefly magistrates who wore the toga and they feature heavily in the iconographic evidence, such as two well-known statues in the Centrale Montemartini in Rome (Fig. 2.10).[124] Goette's typology ends with this toga, and other scholars end theirs even earlier,[125] but in reality the toga continued under a different name: *trabea*. This was the dress of late antique consuls and its most well-known depictions are found in the consular diptychs.[126] A more detailed discussion of this late toga will follow in Chapter 7.

Whilst the intricate details and dating of the changes in drapery described above have preoccupied art historians for decades, the fact of these changes is interesting in itself. Olson has recently argued that '[a] series of prevailing styles in male clothing and deportment which rapidly succeeded one another ("fashion"), does not seem to have existed in Roman antiquity'.[127] However, even using the more restrictive definition of fashion provided by sociologists for the

Figure 2.10 Statue of the 'young magistrate'. Musei Capitolini, Centrale Montemartini, inv. MC 895/S. Photo: Stefano Castellani © Roma – Sovrintendenza Capitolina ai Beni Culturali.

modern period, i.e. frequent, conscious change that occurs for its own sake,[128] it is clear that male dress was subject to it. More generally, although the mainstream view from the social sciences sees fashion as a Western phenomenon that began in the late Middle Ages,[129] in ancient Rome it is actually perfectly evident in hair and beard styles[130] (probably because of the ubiquity of coins); but the three main criteria for fashion are clearly represented in the toga as well: as outlined above, it varied markedly in style from one era to the next, and these changes seem to have occurred on aesthetic, rather than any real practical, grounds. We also have every reason to believe that people were aware of these changes: a number of them seem to have been deliberately created by key figures, such as Augustus, and we have some literary evidence for a concept of fashion as well: Pliny goes to some length in the *Natural History* to outline changes in men's dress since the time of the kings (8.194–195), and Quintilian also discusses toga fashion in his oratory handbook:

There are some features of clothing which have changed over time. The ancients wore no *sinus*, and those after them very short ones. Thus, they must have used different gestures from us at the beginning of their speeches, because their arms were contained within their clothing, like the Greeks.... Our ancestors used to let the toga fall down to the feet, like the Greek *pallium*; and Plotius and Nigidius, who wrote on gesture around about that time, recommended this. I therefore wonder at a statement by Pliny the Younger, a man of learning and in this book in any case painstakingly meticulous. He says that Cicero was in the habit of wearing his toga in this way to hide his varicose veins, although this fashion (*amictus genus*) can also be seen in statues of people who lived after Cicero.

Inst. 11.3.137; 143

The basics of the fashion process were already set out in 1899 by Thorstein Veblen in *The Theory of the Leisure Class*, where he argued it needs both a hierarchical society and a certain amount of social mobility to occur: those lower down the social scale emulate the styles of elites, the latter then change their style to distinguish themselves anew, and the whole process starts again. It seems likely that some of the very large and elaborate versions of the toga would have been beyond the means of humbler folk, but the actual draping styles, which seem often to have emerged from the imperial family, or at least influential members of the elite, did always end up working their way out into general use.[131] The enormous social importance attached to the toga meant that it is the only item of Roman clothing clearly to show elements of fashion: no other male garment was subject to the same forces of change, and women's garments also do not appear to have evolved much over the half millennium between the late Republic and late antiquity.[132] The change in toga style over time puts paid to the idea, common in recent scholarship,[133] that the toga was really only ceremonial costume in the imperial period, rather than lived dress. Ceremonial costume is almost by definition characterized by imperviousness to the vagaries of fashion: only clothing that plays a central role in the everyday lives of a significant number of people tends to change as markedly as the toga did.

The fact that fashion existed, and that people were conscious of it, does, however, produce some complications for those wishing to use the toga as a dating method for ancient statuary, because then as now older men often wore earlier styles long after they were fashionable, and people could and did deliberately choose toga types according to taste and situation. For instance, as already mentioned, Cato deliberately adopted what he saw as an early fashion by eschewing the tunic under his toga, and the funerary reliefs of freedpeople in the Augustan period still display a great number of men in older toga styles amongst the fashionable new ones.[134] In imperial iconography it would appear that older styles of toga – especially the first-century draping with pouch-*umbo* – were considered appropriate for the figure of the emperor in later periods: already on the Arch of Trajan at Benevento the businessmen wear the new form of twisted toga, whilst the emperor is depicted in the older pouch-*umbo* style,[135] and on a relief from a lost arch of Marcus Aurelius in the Capitoline Museums the emperor wears the pouch-*umbo* toga whilst the *Genius Senatus* wears the new, partly contabulated style.[136] In fact, the older pouch-*umbo* style continued to be worn for several centuries, including by Septimius Severus in some portraits,[137] imperial figures on the Decennalia Base[138] and the Arch of Constantine,[139] and a statue, probably of an emperor, from Ostia dating to around 400 CE.[140] The so-called 'Brothers' Sarcophagus' (Fig. 2.8) shows especially well how by the mid-third century different toga drapery styles were suited to different occasions. (This monument will be discussed in more detail in Chapter 7 below.) The extent to which such images represent what was actually worn by these people, as opposed to merely acting as image formulae, is, of course, debatable, and difficult to prove either way. But more recent cases of archaic dress being used, such as the wearing of older styles of suits by men in modern British weddings, at least suggest the possibility that older styles of toga could be used in this way.

The fact that the toga was subject to the vagaries of fashion and taste reminds us that it was a living, evolving garment. One of the main purposes of this book is to shift the focus from an idea of the toga as a feature of Roman art to one that gives it its rightful place as an important object in real, everyday Roman social relations. Among other things, the toga expressed uniquely Roman ideas about masculinity, and this is the subject to which we now turn.

3

The Toga and the Roman Man

Vergil proclaimed the Romans as the *gens togata*, but by this stage of Roman history the toga was worn predominantly by men. More than that, it was a garment that symbolized many of the key aspects of what it meant to be a Roman man. This chapter will explore Roman masculinity by tracing various facets of meaning bestowed on the toga in terms both of its role as the dress of public life and its inherent qualities as a garment. But first it is necessary to look at how it is that the toga came to be a male garment in the first place.

The toga as a gendered garment

By the time we have adequate visual evidence for the dress of women – as ever, the late Republic – their normal dress consisted of a sleeveless, foot-length, belted tunic and a large rectangular cloak (*palla*), a virtually identical outfit to that worn by Hellenistic Greek women; a further pinafore-like garment called a *stola* that was worn over the tunic can sometimes also be seen in statuary art, although it features more heavily in Latin literature as a symbol of matronly virtue than it does in images.[1] However, as a garment that came to be seen as the embodiment of Roman masculinity, scholars have understandably found it somewhat perplexing that the toga could also be worn by females,[2] albeit in two specific situations: as the dress associated with prostitutes and adulteresses, and as the *toga praetexta* of Roman children, which could be and was worn also by girls. But, in fact, the association of females with the toga reveals a great deal about the way in which the toga came to be so strongly associated with males, so it is worth exploring in more detail.

First, it is clear from the evidence that girls could also wear the *toga praetexta*, the purple-bordered garment that was a privilege of freeborn children.[3] The purple border signified purity and was supposed to protect the child from witnessing or experiencing obscenity or untoward behaviour.[4] Boys replaced it with the plain white *toga virilis* in a special coming-of-age ceremony in their teens (see below). A handful of text passages mention girls in *togae praetextae*: in the *Verrines*, Cicero accuses Verres of scandalous behaviour toward the daughter of a man whose property he has confiscated: 'Will you, then, seize the *toga praetexta* from a young girl? Will you seize not only the insignia of her fortune, but also of her free birth?' (2.1.44).[5] Several passages reveal that girls, rather than having a coming-of-age ceremony like boys, gave up their *toga praetexta* the night before they married: Propertius, in a poetic sequence, imagines Augustus' stepdaughter Cornelia (who died tragically young) surrounded by wedding flame torches and laying off her *toga praetexta* before her wedding (4.11.33); and the fourth-century writer Arnobius explains that girls dedicated their *togae praetextae* to Fortuna Virginalis on the eve of their weddings (*Adv. nat.* 2.67).[6] Livy's history also contains another little-cited passage (34.7.2), which lists for the year 195 BCE all the people who were allowed to wear the *praetexta*: magistrates, priests and *liberi nostri*; only adult women, the passage says, are not allowed to wear purple, suggesting that both girls and boys were meant in the term *liberi nostri*.[7]

The visual evidence for girls in togas is equally sparse, but, as with the textual evidence, this may have as much to do with the general paucity of evidence for Roman girls as anything else.[8] The earliest is a statue of a mother draped in a *palla* and togate daughter dating to the mid-first century BCE in the Centrale Montemartini (Fig. 3.1)[9] and the latest is a Severan bust of a girl in a *toga contabulata*,[10] with other images dating to various periods in between,[11] proving that it was not a time-limited phenomenon.[12] At least one girl wears a toga on the Ara Pacis: Julia, daughter of Agrippa, on the north frieze.[13] Scholars are undecided about a second figure – Domitia on the south frieze – as her 'toga' has a less distinct curved hem.[14] None of these images, of course, include any indication of a purple stripe, nor can we expect them to, as their original paintwork has not survived; but contrary to what Goette has argued, this is no reason to believe that they are not *togae praetextae*:[15] in the written sources the *praetexta* is the only type of toga mentioned in connection with girls.

To the *toga muliebris*: a handful of passages make a connection between the toga and prostitutes(/adulteresses). Some of these are somewhat opaque in meaning: in Tibullus, for example, Sulpicia refers to the toga of a prostitute (*scortum*) with whom her husband was unfaithful (3.16.3–5), and Juvenal writes of an adulteress (*moecha*) who 'will not put on a toga' if she is found guilty of the crime (2.68–70). Martial criticizes a man by calling him the son of a *mater togata* (6.64.4), and in a separate passage a eunuch in a toga is referred to as a 'convicted adulteress' (*moecha damnata*: 10.52). Some passages are more straightforward:

Figure 3.1 Statue of a mother and daughter. Musei Capitolini, Centrale Montemartini, inv. MC 2176. Photo: U. Rothe © Roma – Sovrintendenza Capitolina ai Beni Culturali.

Horace muses on the fact that a *togata* had more sexual freedom because she didn't have a husband to worry about (*Sat.* 1.2.80–85), and Martial says an infamous adulteress (*famosa moecha*) should be sent a toga to wear instead of fine clothes (2.39). Finally, in the second *Philippic*, Cicero mentions the *toga muliebris* in the sartorial symbolism he uses to chart Mark Antony's ignoble career:

> Let us start from the beginning. Do you remember how you were bankrupt whilst still wearing the *toga praetexta*? … You assumed the *toga virilis* and immediately turned it into a *toga muliebris*. You started out as a common

prostitute (*vulgare scortum*). Your disgrace had a fixed price, and no small one. But soon along came Curio, who removed you from prostitution (*meretricius quaestus*), gave you a *stola*, and settled you down in stable wedlock.

Phil. 2.44

This passage is significant for a number of reasons, and we will keep returning to it, but for now it is important that it shows, along with the other passages cited, that in a female context adultery, prostitution and the toga seem to have gone hand in hand. What none of these authors say, however, is that the women in question were ever required to wear the toga by law (as some scholars have argued[16]), nor indeed that they actually wore the toga in real life. All they do is draw a connection between the two and imply that the adjective '*togata*' was synonymous with 'immoral'. The only authors to explicitly state that prostitutes and adulteresses were forced to wear the toga by law are later scholiasts attempting to explain the situation in the early Empire from a distance of several centuries, and as such very plausibly getting it wrong.[17] There is no mention of it in legal texts like the *codices* of Theodosius and Justinian or the works of Tertullian or Ulpian, and there is also no visual evidence for an adult woman in a toga.

Those few scholars who have looked at the female toga in any detail have rightly argued that its literary deployment held a symbolic meaning that far outstripped its use by women in reality.[18] But I would like to go further and argue, for the girl's *praetexta* as well, that it was not a case of a male garment at some stage being transferred to women – for honour in the case of the *praetexta*, for disgrace in the case of the *toga muliebris*; rather, it was a remnant of an older reality. As we have already seen, the toga started out as a much more general-use garment worn by all groups and strata of society, including both men and women.[19] A late-second/early-third-century scholastic text on Horace's *Satires* states that women who were divorced by their husbands due to adultery were 'barred from the *stola*' and took up the toga as a result, and that freedwomen were often called '*togata*' because they were not allowed to wear the *stola*.[20] Although the latter comment must relate to a much earlier period than Horace, as the *stola* seems to have been allowed at least to freedwomen married to *ingenui* by the time of the Second Punic War,[21] the author's use of the phrase 'barred from the *stola*' perhaps betrays an underlying truth that, at least in an earlier period, the toga was considered the norm for both sexes, and that it was the *stola* that was the special privilege. We know that an equestrian statue depicting the archaic heroine Cloelia in a toga existed in Rome in the Republican period (*HN* 34.28), and although Pliny disapproves of both the clothing and the statue form for a woman, again the toga here could conceivably relate to its earlier unisex role.

We have no way of knowing when the *stola* – an apparently uniquely Roman garment – entered into the equation, but the frequency with which we find it in evidence closely mirrors that of the *toga muliebris*, i.e. a dearth of it in visual art coupled with a much stronger representation in literature, albeit largely as a rhetorical device. The terms '*stolata*' and '*togata*' almost certainly go back to a time long before we have such texts, perhaps reflecting a real-life situation in an earlier period.[22] The fact that women's dress became Hellenized – probably in the mid-late Republic – whilst men retained the ancient toga (at least in public) is a result of the different spheres the two genders inhabited: Roman men would not abandon the toga because of its significance as a symbol of civic identity and the importance of the insignia of rank contained within it. As private, not public, figures, women could take on Greek dress without threatening those structures.

Instead of seeing the toga as naturally male dress, and the *palla* and *stola* as naturally women's dress, it makes more sense to see the toga as the original default garment of all Romans, with the *stola* as a special privilege for some women and the *palla* gradually entering Roman culture through contact with Greece, eventually almost entirely replacing the toga as a female cloak. If we see the toga this way, we can explain the strange situation that togas could be worn by both respectable statesmen and prostitutes, and both boys and girls. It is significant that no distinction is made in the association of women with the toga between prostitutes and adulteresses; rather than seeing the toga as a badge of shame bestowed on certain people engaged in a 'shameful' profession, what we are seeing is the carving out of a clearly defined 'respectable' status for some Roman women: 'togate' women were simply those from whom the outward symbols of respectability, such as the *stola*, were withheld. And togate girls represented an idea – possibly very ancient – of children as in some senses genderless until they assumed their separate adult social and sexual roles.[23]

By the late Republic, however, the toga had indeed evolved into a symbol of masculinity. Like identity more generally, what constitutes maleness in any given society is not a given: it is constructed and it evolves over time; it is subject to negotiation, can be measured, gained and lost, and it is often dependent on the tone set by the elite.[24] In her recent book on Roman masculinity and appearance, Olson has shown that the Romans had a range of different ideas of what constituted masculinity, and that there was 'a wide repertoire from which masculine identities could be assembled'.[25] Although it is puzzling that the military variety of Roman masculinity is never mentioned in her work, her point still stands: it is important not to see the ideal Roman man as a single, monolithic entity. The facet of Roman maleness represented in the toga was only one of several, but it was arguably the most important, as it pertained to a man's civic role.

We do not know when and for how long the toga was linked to citizenship as a legal status,[26] but it is clear that by the late Republic it had come to embody the Roman ideal of the civic-minded, politically engaged Roman man; it was a garment that was worn in public for public roles. As Maud Gleason has pointed out, closely related to the public-oriented nature of ideal Roman masculinity was the concept of *virtus*: '[t]o exhibit courage or excellence (*virtus*) was by definition to exhibit the qualities of a man (*vir*)'.[27] In his study of manliness in Rome, Myles McDonnell attempted to define *virtus*, and showed how although in the early- and mid-Republic it was synonymous with martial prowess and courage, under Hellenistic influence it moved closer to the Greek concept of ἀρετή: general moral and ethical virtue.[28] By the time of Cicero, it had come to mean the 'quality of the good public man', and that statesman used the concept of ἀρετή to redefine the ideal Roman man as less an aristocrat or soldier, and more as one who used his personal integrity and skills to serve the state in a civic capacity.[29] The beginning of the Empire saw some changes as both politics and war were managed by the emperor,[30] but the institutions of public duty remained, and so did the concept of the virtuous public man.[31]

Habitus patrius et civilis

Suetonius characterizes the traditional dress code of Rome as '*patrius et civilis*' (*Calig.* 52.1), and in so doing gives us a neat résumé of the toga's basic symbolism: the ambiguity of both words was almost certainly intended, *patrius* meaning both 'paternal' and 'of the native country', and *civilis* meaning both 'civilian' and 'civic'. These threads of meaning, although interlocked, require some unpicking in order to get to the heart of what made the toga so central to Roman male identity.

First, it was the garment of public life.[32] The Romans considered the public sphere to be the domain of men, and Latin literature abounds in cautionary tales of the dangers of letting women get involved in public life.[33] In the late Republic and Empire the toga seems *only* to have been worn in urban, public situations: in Amedick's collection of Roman sarcophagi, all the main portraits show a toga, whilst none of the private scenes do,[34] and the term *forensia* ('relating to the forum') is sometimes used as a synonym for the toga (e.g. Suet., *Aug.* 73; *Calig.*

17.2), whilst civic life was referred to by Fronto as the *vita togata* (*Epist.* 2.4 (Naber p.106)). Cicero had one set of clothes for home (*domesticus*) and one for public life (*forensis*) (*Fin.* 2.77).

Public life for the Roman man meant civic duty, and the toga was first and foremost the dress code for assemblies, court hearings and state religious ceremonies. One anecdote shows the link clearly: in it, Livy describes how during the Sabine Wars Cincinnatus was working in his fields when a senatorial delegation arrived and asked him to put on his toga to come to the senate for state matters. (He was to be declared dictator.) He asked his wife to go and get his toga. It was only when he had put it on that they greeted him as dictator (3.26.7–10). When at home Augustus is said to have always kept a toga handy in case an urgent public matter should arise for which he needed to be appropriately dressed (Suet., *Aug.* 73); and when the third-century emperor Claudius was declared emperor the senators are described as putting on their togas and heading to the Temple of Apollo (SHA *Claudius* 4.2). Valerius Maximus records the phrase *togata praesentia*, meaning (to show) courage in civic life (3.7.5); and in keeping with that festival's inversion of roles, during the Saturnalia those men who generally wore a toga changed into a *synthesis*, the dress of private banquets (Mart. 14.1; 14.141).

Through its association with civic roles the toga came also to be more narrowly associated with oratory, as this was the main tool of business in courts and political assemblies.[35] Quintilian – whom Martial called 'the glory of the Roman toga' (2.90) for his services to oratory – makes it clear in his oratory handbook that the toga functioned as a prop during speeches (see below). Starbatty has recently shown how Roman rhetorical texts and the concept of '*actio*' reveal an awareness of the role of dress in non-verbal communication, and of an understanding that it functioned in subtler, more ambivalent ways than was possible in speech.[36] It is clear that although all male citizens were ideally involved in the workings of state during the Republic, during the Empire, as opportunities for political involvement diminished, many of those who wore a toga on a daily basis would have belonged to the elite and to professions surrounding the courts and state institutions. The status implications of this will be explored in the next chapter, but it would be wrong to confine the toga to this sphere alone, as some have done.[37] We know that the toga was worn by men, for instance, to conduct business, attend festivals and visit the theatre.[38] But it is no coincidence that these are all urban activities: the toga was a thoroughly urban garment.

There are a whole host of passages in Roman literature that make it clear that the fundamental distinction between *otium* and *negotium* was codified in dress, wherein the toga was very clearly the dress of *negotium* and city life; Martial even uses the phrase '*urbana toga*' in connection with his city-based readership (11.16).³⁹ In Pliny's *Letters*, *togati* are contrasted with men who live in the countryside (6.30.4), and both Pliny and the satirical writers contrast the stresses and strains of city life with the delights of being in the countryside using the toga as a proxy:

> Whilst you, Juvenal, are probably running about restlessly in the noisy Subura or wearing away Diana's hill, whilst you traverse the thresholds of the powerful in your sweaty toga that fans you ... I am enjoying a vast and indecent amount of sleep, often not broken until past the third hour, and am fully paying myself back for thirty years of morning visits. The toga is unknown here, and when I ask for a garment I am given the nearest one to hand from a broken chair.
>
> Mart. 12.18.2–19⁴⁰

Some of the most informative passages of literature for the toga's meaning in the civic sphere are those that describe what happened when things went wrong. Tacitus tells us how the Roman general Caecina shocked the people of the Italian towns when he arrived from campaigning in the north wearing trousers and a brightly coloured cloak;⁴¹ this was inappropriate for a Roman general and is contrasted, in the anecdote, with the orderly togas of the gathered citizens (*Hist.* 2.20). According to Cicero, Antony's return from Gaul was similarly dishonourable, and he contrasts it with his own return from duty in the provinces:

> As to your question, how did I return? To start with, it was by daylight, not darkness; second, it was in *calcei* and a toga, not *gallici* and a *lacerna* (i.e. Gallic dress) ... Of all the disgraceful things I have ever seen and heard, none was more shameful.
>
> *Phil.* 2.76

And in fact, the most famous examples of allegedly inappropriate dress come from Cicero in his speeches relating to the prosecution for misdemeanour of returning provincial governors; a good example are his tirades against Verres, former governor of Sicily, whose alleged wearing of Greek clothing whilst on duty is repeatedly described, such as in the following passage:

> All that our governor saw of the fleet he was supposed to command was when it sailed past the location of his shameful binges; he had actually been invisible for several days, but on this occasion he did momentarily show himself to his sailors. This Roman governor stood there on the shore wearing *soleae* (slippers), a purple *pallium* and a long tunic, whilst leaning on one of his floozies; and before that time many Sicilians and Roman citizens had also seen him dressed in this way.
>
> *Verr.* 5.33⁴²

From the language used in these passages and elsewhere in Roman literature,[43] it is clear that it was the obligation of a representative of the *res publica* to appear in public wearing Roman state dress, and that what was perceived as the reverse of this – Greek dress – was seen to embody a moral code characterized by the opposite of everything a Roman man should possess: effeminacy, vice and self-indulgence. That is not to say that Roman governors only ever wore the toga: some occasions would have called for military dress,[44] and in other speeches, when it suits his needs, Cicero makes (albeit somewhat far-fetched) excuses for the use of Greek dress by Roman officials.[45] But the fact that dress codes could be employed to such rhetorical effect at all suggests they were deeply implicated in the conduct of Roman public life. As Rothfus has said,

> Leaving off appropriate garments was a symbolic action and was seen as such by the jurists, who judged it not a matter of individual dress preference but an abandonment of the values those garments represented and the social role for which those values were essential.
>
> 2010: 429

In this context it is interesting to note the existence of a phrase that comes up several times in Latin literature: *oblitus togae*, literally 'to forget the toga'. What it signified seems to differ slightly depending on the context: when used by Florus to describe Mark Antony at Cleopatra's court (2.21.3), it seems to denote loss of masculine dignity, but when Horace uses it for Crassus' troops captured by the Parthians after the battle of Carrhae it is listed along with Vesta, the Temple of Jupiter and the city of Rome (*Odes* 3.5.8–12), suggesting they had forgotten they were Roman; when Lucan employs it to describe the behaviour of the tribune Metellus as he briefly considered using arms to defend the *aerarium sanctius* from requisition by Caesar (*Phars.* 3.141–143), it seems to mean forgetting the calmness and dignity with which Roman men were expected to behave amongst Roman citizens.

As discussed in Chapter 2, in earlier periods the toga seems to have been a more general-purpose garment and was even worn, it would seem, by Roman soldiers on campaign, reflecting the citizen nature of the Republican army. But by the late Republic it had come to symbolize the civilian, as opposed to the military, sphere. The increasing need to delineate the two was a response to the growing threat posed by the ability of individual men to amass military power. Zanker has pointed out that even in the Republic, victorious generals were depicted togate in official portraits in Rome: never in military dress.[46] In *Pharsalia*, Lucan praises Pompey for returning to the toga immediately after war (8.813–15). The alternation between war and civilian life was soon even codified in language. From Cicero we know that the donning of the military cloak (*saga sumere*) was a symbolic act of preparing for war and could be decreed by the Senate in times of emergency (i.e. the suspension of civic life) (*Phil*. 5.31; 14.1–3; see also Dio Cass. 41.17); and generals returning from command to Rome also ritually laid off the *sagum* and put the toga back on (Cic., *Pis*. 55). It also became an allegory: Latin writers throughout the late Republic and Empire use the word 'toga' as a metaphor for peace, often contrasting it with words like '*castra*' and '*bellum*'.[47] Livy used the phrase 'while they were still in the toga' to mean 'while they had not yet left on military campaign' (3.10) and Cicero praised Caesar for being *clarus in toga* – distinguished in civilian life (*Fam*. 6.6.5).

There is every indication that this ideology continued under the Empire. Emperors were expected to wear the toga when in Rome,[48] as were even praetorian guardsmen, as military dress would have been seen as an affront to civic life, even if they did conceal weapons underneath (Tac., *Hist*. 1.38; *Ann*. 16.27). Tacitus praised 'common people (*plebs*) who have distinguished themselves in the toga' (*Ann*. 11.7) and Tiberius, who had done excellent work 'in the toga' (1.12), i.e. in civil affairs. The connection with civilian life can also be seen in third-century sarcophagi that contrast a portrait of a man in a *sagum* with one in a toga to symbolize achievement in both the military and civic realms.[49]

The final ingredient of the ideal togate Roman man was piety; male virtue was defined by a sense of duty not just in the civic sphere, but also in relation to one's family honour, ancestors and household gods, as well as to the deities who ensured the wellbeing of the state and society as a whole; and this applied both in the Republic and in the Empire.[50] At the same time, Roman political life involved not just holding secular positions, but also serving as priest in one of the main state cults. The latter held obvious significance as a status symbol, but it also enabled leading men to show off their moral credentials. Similarly, the ubiquity of images of religious ceremonies in Roman art signals the central role of religion in the Roman self-image as a whole.

As a general rule, the toga was the dress expected of men for public religious rituals, whether as priests or participants. When performing a sacrifice, the custom was to cover the head with the toga ('*capite velato*': e.g. Fig. 3.2 and cover image: central figure). Whilst men might cover their head with their toga against rain or sun, they would usually go bare-headed, so the covering of the head was a break from normal practice. Moreover, the physical adjustment of the toga required to bring it over the head was a performative act that symbolized a move from the realm of the profane to that of the sacred; it was a bodily preparation for ritual. It appears that the ritual covering of the head was considered – especially

Figure 3.2 *Lararium* painting in the House of the Vettii, Pompeii. Photo: Alamy Stock Photo.

by outsiders – to be a peculiarity of Rome. Aeneas was believed to have been the one who started it (e.g. Plut., *Quaest. Rom.* 10; Festus 432L=322M): the figure thought to be Aeneas on the Ara Pacis is shown thus (Fig. 1.1), and Vergil also makes the connection clear in *Aeneid* 3.403–408:

> Moreover, when your ships have crossed the seas and anchored, and when you then raise altars and pay vows on the shore, veil your hair with the covering of a purple robe (*amictus purpureus*), that in the worship of the gods no hostile face may intrude amid the holy fires and mar the omens. Hold to this mode of sacrifice, you and your company.
>
> Trans. Rushton Fairclough 1916

The idea conveyed here is that Aeneas established not just Rome but also the correct Roman way of honouring the gods. It seems likely that the *Romanus ritus* dated back to Roman history before the advent of solid visual sources, and the first image we have of it is on the Domitius Ahenobarbus relief of the late second century BCE.⁵¹ The fact that Augustus and other leading figures are also depicted *capite velato* elsewhere on the Ara Pacis is intended to visualize the link between the pious founder of Rome and the pious re-founder of the Republic;⁵² henceforth it became one of the main genres of imperial portraiture, symbolizing the emperor's humility and piety.⁵³

So why did the Romans cover their heads to sacrifice? The passage above contains one explanation – it allowed the eyes to be shielded from potential bad portents – but naturally, this may be a retrospective explanation. Plutarch also grappled with the matter in his *Roman Questions*, asking 'Why is it that when they [i.e. the Romans] worship the gods, they cover their heads, but when they meet any of their fellow-men worthy of honour, if they happen to have the toga over the head, they uncover?' He concludes that it was either intended to show the person as humble before the gods, or that it was a way of dampening external, ill-omened sounds, and that the uncovering in the presence of other men was done to avoid incurring the jealousy of the gods (*Quaest. Rom.* 10).⁵⁴

Whilst most of the central Roman state rituals required the covering of the head (e.g. Livy 1.18; 1.36; 2.39.12; 8.9), there were, however, some that required an uncovered head ('*capite aperto*': the so-called *Graecus ritus*), a practice that was apparently already well-established by the mid-Republic (e.g. Cato, *Disc.* frg. 77 Malcovati). It appears to have depended on the deity involved whether covering was required or not, but there is no clear division here between 'Roman' and 'Greek' gods.⁵⁵ On the columns of Trajan and Marcus Aurelius the emperor is shown in some sacrificial scenes in a toga *capite velato*, and in others sacrificing bare-headed and in military gear; the former appears to have been especially expected for the *suovetaurilia*, but there does not appear to be anything Greek about the latter scenes.⁵⁶ *Graecus ritus* was apparently expected for sacrifice to, among others, Hercules, Saturn and the more obscure Honor (Val. Max. 6.3.10; Plut., *Quaest. Rom.* 11–13).⁵⁷ For the latter two, it is again Plutarch who gives us the only insight into why they were honoured in this way, but his explanations are even more dubious than for *Romanus ritus*: for Saturn he suggests that the cult may have predated Aeneas, or that for the god of the earth and truth the gesture was unnecessary; and for Honor he postulates that it was because honour and renown are open and conspicuous by nature (*Quaest. Rom.* 11–13). The true explanations for the differences are likely to be less rational than any of this, and almost certainly date to an earlier period beyond the reach of our sources.

The question of covering the head also relates to family honour, and Roman sons were apparently expected to wear the toga *capite velato* for their parents' funeral processions, whilst their sisters were expected to go bare-headed and with their hair open (Plut., *Quaest. Rom.* 14; Apul., *Flor.* 4.4). Plutarch wonders whether this has to do with sons honouring their fathers as gods, whilst daughters honour them as people, but more likely is his back-up explanation that each represented an inversion of the everyday norm.

Finally, and perhaps relatedly, the toga appears to have been the dress expected of bridegrooms at their wedding. The most illustrative body of evidence for this are the numerous marriage scenes in biographical sarcophagi of the second and third centuries CE.[58] Reinsberg has argued that such scenes, along with others depicting military valour or state service, portray a normative image of elite Romans using visual references to key values and virtues ('*Leitwerte*');[59] in this context, marriage appears not as a private agreement but as a public act, showing the institution of marriage as central to a man's public identity. It could be postulated that, in addition, being married was considered a good, masculine thing to be, and implied stable heterosexuality and (future) control over a family.[60]

The toga statue

The fundamental characteristics of Roman male virtue embodied in the toga discussed in the previous sections rendered standing toga statues the perfect portrait genre for Roman men, ensuring both their popularity over much of Roman history and their ubiquity in Roman cities across the empire. What Goethe once called the 'other population of Rome',[61] and often the first things to spring to mind if one mentions the toga in a modern setting, these statues themselves had a history, and it is one that is inextricably linked to the evolution of the toga as a symbolic garment.

The exact sequence of events surrounding the origins of the toga statue are a matter of some debate, and closely mirror the controversy surrounding the origins of the toga itself. Whilst the marble and other stone statuary of the late Republic and Empire very clearly derived from Hellenistic art, there was a parallel stream of bronze statuary art that made its way to Rome from the Etruscans. The latter, it would seem, produced bronze statues in large numbers,[62] and many of these would have been portraits of leading local figures. Very few of these remain, in part because bronze can be melted down and reused, but Hafner has argued that the Etruscan bronze statuettes and terracottas dating from the fifth to the third century BCE that do survive in large numbers give us an indication of what their larger counterparts would have looked like, and figures wearing togas/*tebennae* feature prominently in this imagery (Hafner's 'Etruskische togati': 1969).

Pliny devoted a large section of his *Natural History* to the development of statuary art in Rome, and to account for some of the older statues that were still standing in his day. In book 34, he confirms that the first images were in bronze, and tells us that they tended to be of deities, but that the practice soon passed from gods to representations of men (34.15). He postulates that originally they were reserved for prominent figures to commemorate an 'illustrious deed' (*inlustris causa*) (34.16). He also says that the practice started at Athens, but that it

> was then adopted by the rest of the world, and statues were erected in public spaces in all the towns. The memory of men was thus preserved, and their honours were collated, inscribed on the bases [of these statues], not just on their tombs. Then a public place was made in private houses in the *atria*: thus clients could honour their patrons.
>
> HN 34.17

So far it is possible to lend broad credence to the framework Pliny provides, although scholars have also added Roman death masks and Etruscan statuary to the influences that resulted in the Roman honorific statue.[63] The passage is followed by a comprehensive account of honorific statues in Rome believed to have been erected in both the Regal and Republican periods and the deeds for which they were bestowed (*HN* 34.20–34.32).[64] From Pliny's description it is clear that the main places in Rome where honorific statues were erected in the Republican period were the Comitium, the Rostra, in front of temples and especially the forum and the Capitol, through which triumphal processions and the *transvectio equitum* passed. Whilst one must be sceptical of the exact dates and locations Pliny provides for the statues, it is significant, first, that he considered them so important as to dedicate a large part of his work to them and, second, that some of the very early statues are described by him as togate. Other Roman authors also mention the existence of older statues still standing in their day[65] and confirm the central role they played in both the development of the Roman state and the formulation of its key values and aspirations.[66]

Whilst it is clear from Pliny's frequent use of words like *tribuo*, *decerno* and *honor* in his survey (e.g. 34.21; 34.24–25) that public statues were generally decreed in some way by a public body like the senate or the *comitia*, it is also evident from his and other accounts of sporadic purges by the authorities of unofficial statues that a form of common law was emerging in which people who held high office were commissioning monuments for themselves (e.g. 34.30–31; Suet., *Iul*. 11; Cic., *Brut*. 168).[67] This is of significance for the types of statues that might have adorned Republican Rome. Pliny's claim (34.28) is entirely plausible that although what he calls '*pedestres*' – i.e. standing statues – were around for a long time in Rome, of even greater antiquity were equestrian statues: McDonnell has recently argued that the ultimate manifestation of masculine virtue in the Republic was the military triumph, and the equestrian statue was its lasting visual representation. Both were, however, fraught with danger to the ideals of the Republic, and had to be meted out carefully by the authorities.[68] It is odd that McDonnell does not mention toga statues at all in his discussion of visual representations of *virtus* in the Republic, as it seems clear that such images not only existed, but that their gradual increase in popularity was a result of the restrictions placed on the bestowal of equestrian statues.[69] The peaceful and civic nature of the standing toga statue rendered it both less threatening and within the realm of plausible aspiration for a larger number of people. Moreover, by the late Republic, key figures like Cicero were carving out the possibility of illustrious public careers that did not involve military victories and were arguing that 'triumphs in the toga' (i.e. civic accomplishments) should be valued as highly as military ones.[70]

The oldest honorific toga statue that survives today is the so-called 'Arringatore', albeit not from Rome itself, but Lake Trasimeno in the region of Perugia (Fig. 2.5). It is made of bronze and depicts a man standing and raising his right arm. He is wearing a ring on his finger, senatorial-style *calcei*, a tunic with a narrow stripe and a simple, Republican-style toga with a border along the curved hem.[71] An inscription in the border says: 'To Aulus Metellus, son of Vel and Vesi, Tenine(?) set up this statue as an offering to Sans, by deliberation of the people.' There has been some debate about its date, and views on this depend largely on the artistic tradition in which it is placed: Etruscologists like Prayon see it as late Etruscan in character and date it to the second century BCE,[72] whilst classical archaeologists like Fittschen see it as a Hellenistic sculpture and date it to around 100.[73] This is not the place to enter into a discussion of this, but Dohrn's original and more nuanced appraisal of the piece as combining both Hellenistic and central Italian styles and dating it to the early first century BCE still appears the most plausible.[74]

What is of significance for our study is who the statue represents. Metellus was evidently a prominent man in his local community (probably Perugia), and the fact that he is depicted with such a uniquely Roman combination of status markers – the border of the toga, the finger ring, the stripe on the tunic and the senatorial shoes – means he must, in fact, have been a Roman citizen of some standing;[75] Metellus' raised arm gesture is somewhat unusual for a toga statue of an ordinary civilian: Davies has recently shown that it is later only seen in images of the emperor addressing troops or civilians,[76] and it may be that it was a more common gesture in the period in which the 'Arringatore' statue was produced; we simply don't have the visual evidence to know for sure. It is possible that Metellus gained his citizenship when all free residents of Italy did in 89 BCE, and if, as seems likely from the style of the monument, he was a municipal magistrate, that would explain his use of the *toga praetexta* and senatorial shoes, as these were allowed to men of such standing in Roman towns without having to belong to the *ordo senatorius*.[77] Despite the fact that art-historical discussions of the toga statue give the impression that the Metellus statue stands at the start of the genre,[78] the historical evidence shows that the city of Rome must already have been awash with honorific monuments long before Metellus was born (see above), as also illustrated on coin images like the silver *denarius* of C. Minucius Augurinus from 135 BCE (Fig. 2.4). What his statue does indicate, however, is that the practice was not confined to Rome.

From the first century BCE onward, it is especially the standing toga statue that became the main method of commemoration for leading Roman citizens, and by this stage the practice of inscribing the careers and great deeds of such men on the statue base and nearby inscriptions seems also to have been well established.[79] In this same period we see the transition from bronze to marble statuary: although marble was not unknown in Rome in the second century BCE, it only began to be quarried in Italy after 100 BCE.[80] It seems likely that this is the main reason why the vast majority of extant statues date from the late Republic onward:[81] unlike bronze, marble cannot be melted down and reused. The dawn of the imperial period did bring some changes to the possibilities for commemoration: military and political power was concentrated in the figure of the *princeps*, and Augustus may have been responsible for the removal of many of the statues that stood in Rome in the late Republic; at the very least, we know that he moved large numbers of them out to the Campus Martius,[82] where, according to Suetonius, they were later destroyed by Caligula (*Calig.* 34.1), and it is clear from the many monuments to members of Augustus' family that any that remained would quickly have been swamped by new ones. However, the practice did continue: Augustus himself set up statues to other leading men in his regime like Agrippa (Suet., *Aug.* 59; Dio Cass. 53.27.2-3),[83] and the *summi viri* in his forum were clearly meant to represent a continuation of the idea, albeit under his close control (Suet., *Aug.* 31.5). Moreover, whilst it may be true that certain emperors forbade the practice (e.g. Suet., *Calig.* 34.1), it is clear from the sheer number of objects that have survived that effigies of prominent men continued to be dedicated in large numbers, accounting for what one scholar has described as the 'forests of statues' that adorned the public places of both Rome and other cities across the empire in the first two centuries CE.[84] It was only in the third century with the decline of the senatorial elite that the practice began to wane.[85]

The most important concepts that were expressed in the honorific toga statue were *memoria* and *exemplum*: it was a deeply Roman trait to memorialize and venerate prominent men, and sometimes the statues and their inscriptions were used to draw attention to a man's esteemed ancestors as well. This is most clearly, albeit uniquely, illustrated in the busts held by the so-called 'Togatus Barberini' (Fig. 2.7).[86] The location of honorific statues in the city meant that they served as ideal visual reminders of the model lives to which all men should aspire.[87] It is this ideology Horace was mocking when he described people who were 'struck with admiration' by the inscriptions and statues of famous men (*Sat.* 1.6.15), and we have it illustrated in a fresco from the House of Julia Felix in Pompeii (albeit with equestrian statues: Fig. 3.3). In other words, although there was an individual motivation for statuary in the deeply ingrained Roman elite ideology that commemoration in a public place was something to aspire to, it also served the more general purpose of visualizing the power relations and values of Rome as a

Figure 3.3 Fresco from the House of Julia Felix in Pompeii, Museo Archeologico Nazionale, Naples, inv. 9068. Photo: Museo Archeologico Nazionale, Naples © Samuel Magal, Sites & Photos Ltd/Bridgeman Images.

whole.[88] Such statuary was, of course, not confined to the public sphere, and especially from the first century BCE onward we see much of the iconography appearing in funerary art as well, encompassing a greater spectrum of social levels, including freedpeople and even such low-status people as actors.[89]

Central to the purpose of these statues was, however, the image of the Roman man they conveyed, and central to that was the toga. Moreover, it was an idealized image: whilst the heads of the statues themselves were usually intended as individual portraits, they were often attached to prefabricated toga bodies with standardized gestures.[90] This is the reason why we do not see corpulent, skinny, small or hunched toga figures: the perfect male body draped in the toga was an archetype to which a man could literally attach himself.[91] Quintilian's phrase that an orator's dress should be *splendidus* and *virilis* (*Inst.* 11.3.137) expresses the key elements: it should not only be impressive to behold, but also manly. The dress historian Hollander's description of the Western suit as symbolizing 'diplomacy, compromise, civility and physical self-control'[92] resonates for the toga as well. Davies has argued for the imperial style of toga that the key ingredients were twofold: on the one hand, the complex and voluminous drapery of the toga made the body appear wide; on the other, the way the arms are held away from the body suggests control, as they were not needed to hold the complex folds in place:[93] the *splendor* of the toga was tempered by the *virilitas* of the man's nonchalance toward it.[94] Christ has argued for a more nuanced understanding of its visual qualities, pointing out that it revealed parts of the torso that were meant to look manly and concealed other parts of the body.[95] Whilst these theories may apply to official art in the imperial period, they are less applicable to Republican statues, such as those depicting the 'armsling' style, or the many hundreds of images of more modest individuals. As Davies has recently shown, the body language of these statues conveys a different, more introverted and modest message from those depicting the elaborate imperial toga.[96] But the constant in all public statuary of this kind is that it is the toga itself that communicates the main message. This was peculiar to Rome and contrasts sharply with the heroic nudity of ideal Greek masculinity:[97] it was not the male body that was the main *locus* of virility, but the clothing in which it was draped.

Wearing the toga

Toga statues have created an image of how Roman men looked that persists to the present day in both scholarship and the popular imagination, and it is important to point out just how unrealistic an ideal they represent. Even in its simplest forms, the toga would have been a difficult garment to wear. To start with, it was draped rather than tailored to fit around the body. This is a fundamental distinction, not just in the scholarly classification of dress, but also in the ideas surrounding what it conveys.[98] In more recent history the draped/tailored divide also played a role, for example in colonial India in the relationship between the local culture and that of the imperial power: in striking resemblance to expectations of Roman provincial governors, in spite of the hot climate, British officers and Indian employees of the ICS were expected at all times to wear neatly tailored Western-style suits that embodied adherence to the duties and norms of what they perceived to be superior British civilization. A great deal of Indian dress, in contrast, was based on draping, most clearly embodied in India's national garment, the sari. The British viewed such garments as primitive and showing a lack of technical sophistication, whilst Indian people saw them as beautiful and dignified, and tailored Western garments as ugly and functional.[99] Hence it was not just for economic reasons that the boycott of Western textiles was a central part of the independence movement: when Gandhi adopted the *dhoti* and shawl as his signature outfit and wore it on his visit to England in 1931, he was deliberately mobilizing dress to assert Indian national pride and challenge British notions of what constituted civilization. Interestingly, in the Roman Empire it was the imperial power that viewed draped clothing as the epitome of dignified appearance: it is for this reason that the Romans held such disproportionate disdain for the trousers and sleeved tunics of their northern and eastern neighbours.[100]

Draped clothing is by definition more difficult to wear than tailored clothing in that it takes skill to keep it in place. This was, and still is, a key element of the dignity with which it is associated. In India, young women devote a great deal of effort and all manner of helpful devices like safety pins to gradually acquire the posture, gestures and gait needed to wear a sari with dignity. One young woman in Banerjee and Miller's 2003 study of the garment said:

> When I first started to wear a sari, my mother helped me for a couple of days. People used to laugh at me and say, 'look at her, she is going to fall down, the way she has worn her sari.' And I did fall down sometimes, because the sari used to get caught in my legs. I couldn't walk properly.
>
> 2003: 69

This means that, unlike tailored garments, which after they are put on do not require any further thought or skill until they are taken off again, draped garments like the toga require a constant dialogue with their wearer. As Banerjee and Miller explain, for the sari wearer 'to achieve social respectability, she must learn to move, drape, sit, fold, pleat and swirl the sari in an appropriate way.... But this requires a constant, more or less unconscious responsiveness to the way the sari moves with every gesture that she makes' (2003: 70–71). The fact that the sari is often considered the most appropriate dress for the upper classes and for formal occasions relates not just to the appearance of the garment itself but also the skill and poise required to wear it.[101] Something similar would have been understood by Roman viewers when looking at a toga statue or a man wearing his toga with grace. Quintilian provides some detail as to the the correct drapery of the toga and how its wearer could achieve it:

> The toga itself should be round and cut to fit;[102] otherwise, there are many ways in which it will be out of shape (*enormis*). The front should reach to the mid-shin, while the back should be higher.... The *sinus* is most becoming if it sits a bit above the lower hem of the toga:[103] it should certainly never hang below it. The *balteus* should be neither too tight nor too loose. The part of the toga that is set in place last should be lower; that way it sits better and is held in place. Part of the tunic should also be drawn back ...; then the *sinus* should be thrown over the shoulder, and it is not unseemly to turn back its outermost edge. However, it is not becoming to cover the shoulder and the whole throat, as the garment will be tight and lose the dignity of the broad chest. The left arm should be lifted up at a right angle, and over that the double edge of the toga should sit evenly.... As the speech proper begins, ... it is quite fitting for the *sinus* to slip off the shoulder; ... And when the speech is almost over, ... almost anything is acceptable: sweat, fatigue, neglected clothing, a loose toga falling down all over the place.... But if the toga falls down at the beginning or early on in the speech, failure to put it back in place signifies neglect, tardiness and ignorance of the way clothes should be worn.
>
> Inst. 11.3.139–149

Even though Quintilian is relating here what was expected of a Roman orator, it is nonetheless also indicative of the many things a Roman man had to bear in mind, not just when he was putting on the toga, but also the whole time he was wearing it.[104] In addition, as the toga was a white or off-white colour, its wearers would have had to avoid walking styles and situations in which it might have become dirty. Indeed, Davies has recently argued that much of Quintilian's advice on how a young orator should behave would have related to more general expectations of the way young elite men should walk, move and gesture, constituting a learned body language that affirmed both the high status and the masculinity of the person in question.[105]

Central to this was the idea of control: self-control was expressed in the avoidance of overly emotional, dramatic or crude gestures, but control over the surrounding environment was equally important, and conveyed in ways of walking, standing and gesticulating that were dignified and decisive.[106] Craig Williams has shown how Roman ideas of sexuality were defined not by the sex of the partner but by whether a person was the penetrator or the one penetrated in the sexual act.[107] Proper men were expected always to play the active role: in bed as in life, Roman masculinity meant always being the one in control. All of this is of fundamental importance to the role of the toga in articulating Roman masculinity: as a difficult and unwieldy garment, it required dignity and restraint of gesture to keep it in place, but effortlessly controlling it conveyed a sense that its wearer was more generally in command of his situation.[108] This is one of the reasons the garment was, as discussed in a previous section, loathed by the Roman satirists who longed to escape to the countryside where they didn't have to wear it. As Tertullian says in his speech advocating the replacement of the toga with the *pallium*:

> How do you feel in a toga: dressed or oppressed? Like you are wearing clothes or lugging them around? If you refute this, I will follow you home; I will observe what you do as soon as you cross the threshold of your house. Surely there is no garment that a man takes off with more relief than a toga!
>
> *De pall.* 5.2.1–2[109]

This should not, however, be used as evidence that the toga would rarely have been worn in real life, as several scholars have argued.[110] The widespread use of, for example, the sari in India and the Western suit and tie in most of the global business world is modern testimony to the fact that ease and comfort are not always decisive factors in an outfit's popularity. In fact, in both of these modern examples as well as in the case of the toga, the skill required to put on and wear the clothing properly is part of its allure.[111] Awkward or not, the symbolism embodied in the toga and its correct use cannot but have rendered it a powerful tool in the way at least certain classes of men interacted with one another and with wider society on a daily basis.

The toga reflected high social status not just in the dignity and skill required to wear it, but also in the fact that a man needed at least one other person – usually a slave – to maintain it and to help him put it on. Tertullian gives us some insight into this, when he says that the toga requires

> a specialist, who, the day before use, forms the plies at the beginning and leads them in pleats, assigning the whole formation of the contracted *umbo* to the custody of the pincers; who, at daybreak, having first shortened the tunic (which

had better been woven at a moderate length!) with a belt, checks the *umbo* again and if anything has gone out of the track, rearranges it, lets a part of the garment hang down on the left, draws back from the shoulders the surrounding part (from which stem the foils), with its folds now ending, and leaving free the right shoulder piles it on the left shoulder yet again, with another mass of folds destined for the back, thereby imposing a burden upon the man.

De Pall 5.1.3–4 trans. Hunink 1995

Mastering the skill of wearing a garment that was so prone to slipping or sitting incorrectly was, evidently, no mean feat. But the real-life corollary of this is, of course, that it was possible to wear the toga badly. As with the countless examples of people making barbed comments about women wearing their saris poorly in Banerjee and Miller's study such as in the quote further above,[112] Roman literature also abounds in examples of people being ridiculed for displaying ineptitude in wearing their togas: Horace, for example, describes both himself and other people being laughed at for appearing in public with their toga lop-sided ('*dissidet impar*": *Epist.* 1.1.94–97) or falling off ('*defluit*': *Sat.* 1.3.31), and Valerius Maximus mentions the Republican orator Sempronius Tuditanus' tendency to drag his toga on the ground in the same breath as his alleged *insania* (7.8.1); similarly, according to Macrobius, Cicero criticized as womanish Caesar's habit of draping his toga in such a way that it dragged along the ground (*Sat.* 2.3.9). Even emperors could be the object of scorn for wearing their togas badly: according to Suetonius, Claudius was reproached for letting his left arm escape from his toga when he got excited at games (*Claud.* 21.5), and Caligula is said to have once tripped over his toga when he stormed out of a theatre (*Calig.* 35).

Recent work by Olson has, however, revealed that some of these apparent oversights might actually have been intentional when practised by what she describes as Roman 'dandies': young, elite, urban men who indulged in a certain amount of what was usually considered effeminate sartorial behaviour, such as colourful dress, loose belting of the tunic and draping of the toga, long sleeves and overt care of the hair, of which the young Caesar is a notable example.[113] Sterner senior figures of Roman literature would have us believe there was a golden mean that Roman men needed to strike between too much care for their appearance (= effeminacy) and too little (= boorishness):[114] Quintilian, for example, tells us that it was reprehensible to display 'both too much care and neglect' (*nimia cura quam negligentia*) for one's toga, shoes and hair (*Inst.* 11.3.137). There is, of course, some disingenuity here. Whilst Quintilian evidently would agree with Ovid that 'simplicity in dress is what best befits a man' (*Am.* 1.508), the vast amount of care and skill needed to achieve the required look in evidence in his copious advice on how to wear the toga belied its desired uncomplicated appearance. Aulus Gellius, to take another example, has nothing but disdain for the dandified appearance ascribed to the Republican orator Quintus Hortensius:

> Because he dressed with extreme foppishness, arranged the folds of his toga with great care and exactness, and in speaking used his hands to excess in lively gestures, (he) was assailed with gibes and shameful charges; and many taunts were hurled at him, even while he was pleading in court, for appearing like an actor.
>
> NA 1.5.2, trans. Rolfe 1927[115]

It is clear that there was a spectrum of opinion as to how far one could go, which Starbatty has argued was encapsulated in the Roman concept of '*aptum*'.[116] But whilst Gellius clearly disapproved of overly flamboyant dress and behaviour, and Quintilian opined that throwing part of the toga over the right shoulder whilst orating was sloppy (*solutus*) and effeminate (*delicatus*) (*Inst.* 11.3.146), a young man and his peers might have thought otherwise.

Nonetheless, the mainstream view is clear: the toga was a garment that should be worn with dignity and grace. This meant that young Roman boys, like young women in India with the sari today, would have needed to *learn* how to wear it.[117] Indeed, Quintilian's work was intended as a handbook for young Roman men embarking on careers involving oratory, for which reason Martial described him as the 'supreme guide of wayward youth and the glory of the Roman toga' (2.90). The 'trainer' garment with which such youths would have started their toga-wearing lives was the *toga praetexta*.

Toga praetexta

The distinguishing feature of the *toga praetexta* was its purple border (Fig. 3.2 and cover image: central figure). Borders of a colour different from that of the main garment were a key feature of Etruscan dress, and especially the rounded *tebenna* from which the toga almost certainly evolved, but there is little evidence that they held the symbolic significance in Etruscan culture that they later acquired in Roman dress.[118] Ancient accounts of the origins of the *toga praetexta* are somewhat contradictory, and are additionally confounded by the fact that it was also the dress of Roman magistrates. As we saw in Chapter 2, Roman writers of various eras and backgrounds certainly believed that the *toga praetexta*, along with the *sella curulis* and other insignia of high office, was Etruscan in origin,[119] and most scholars agree that this must be the case.[120]

How the garment came to be the dress of Roman children is less certain. In the fourth century, Macrobius attempted to make some sense of it, citing various stories in circulation in his time: one that the garment was introduced for boys by Romulus, another that it was introduced under Tullus Hostilius as an honour for magistrates, and only later bestowed on children, and yet another that Tarquinius Priscus let his 14-year-old son wear it with the *bulla* at the celebration of the triumph over the Sabines as an honour for having killed an enemy in battle (*Sat.* 1.6.7–17).[121] The *bulla* in this context came from the triumphal costume, the *toga praetexta* from that of magistrates. According to Macrobius, the same king introduced a dress reform that allowed all the sons of curule magistrates to wear both. He suggests that the wearing of the *toga praetexta* was gradually widened to other parts of society, for example citing the augur M. Laelius who said that at a celebration after the Second Punic War all freeborn sons were allowed to attend wearing the *toga praetexta*, even those of freed parents. The earliest image we have of a boy in a *toga praetexta* is a bronze statue in the Louvre dated by Gabelmann to the second century BCE: although no border is visible, a *toga praetexta* is strongly suggested by the fact that he is clearly a child and is wearing a *bulla*.[122] Valerius Maximus mentions an equestrian statue of Aemilius Lepidus as a boy on horseback wearing a *toga praetexta* and *bulla* (3.1.1). We don't know which Aemilius Lepidus is meant, but it could plausibly be the one who was consul in 187 BCE.[123] In summary, then, whatever the precise sequence of events, it seems likely that the Etruscan-inspired purple border on the toga of early Roman magistrates was gradually at some stage transferred as an honour to Roman citizen children, first those of the elite and then wider circles.

Further controversy surrounds the location and construction of the purple stripe. Whilst the Verucchio cloak has a border all the way around (Fig. 2.2), older images of Etruscan cloaks[124] and the 'Arringatore' statue (Fig. 2.5) have it at the bottom on the round hem.[125] It seems that with the advent of the imperial toga with its distinctive *sinus* the border gradually moved onto this feature, as can be seen, for example, in the *lararium* frescoes in Pompeii (Fig. 3.2 and cover image: central figure).[126] On the newly found Tetrarchic-era reliefs from Nicomedia on which some paintwork still survives, on the other hand, the border is found on every edge (Fig. 3.4: figures on the right). Some scholars have argued that the border must have been sewn on because it would have been impossible to dye it in this way,[127] but it seems clear that, like the *clavi* of the

Figure 3.4 Relief from Çukurbağ (Nicomedia) showing part of an *adventus* scene. Kocaeli Museum, Izmit, Turkey. Photo © Carole Raddato/Wikimedia Commons/CC 2.0.

tunic, the border was woven into the fabric using a different colour thread.[128] This is, indeed, the way the border on the Verucchio cloak is constructed.[129] Several scholars have, moreover, pointed out that the term '*praetexta*' is likely to come from the fact that the band was 'woven first' in the sense that it formed the first lines of weaving on the warp-weighted loom, before the weft was transferred to white thread.[130]

The border of the *toga praetexta* marked it out as a garment designed to protect the child from danger and inappropriate behaviour: Persius referred to it as the '*custos purpura*' (5.30). Whilst it was the most expensive dyestuff in antiquity, purple also appears to have been related more generally in Roman culture with purity, as purple borders also adorned the clothing of sacrificial attendants (Serv., *Aen.* 12.120), Vestal Virgins (Paulus ex Festus 475L), prominent mourners (Festus 272–3L; 342L) and some deities (e.g. Pliny, *HN* 8.197 and *genii* in *lararium* paintings in Pompeii: Fig. 3.2 and cover image[131]), as well as priests and magistrates.[132] Much of what a praetextate child was shielded from was sexual in nature: a passage in Catullus implies that the garment protected a boy from sexual advances (61), and Cicero invites condemnation from his audience in accusing Verres of having allowed his praetextate son to recline on a couch, witness suggestive dancing and see his father drinking and cavorting with women (*Verr.* 3.23; 5.137). Paulus defined *praetextus sermo* as language which is lacking in obscenity and said that it contravened divine law (*nefas*) to utter obscenities around a *praetextatus* (283).¹³³ *Stuprum* was the act of desecrating the sanctity of childhood, and Roman law made allowance for a wide spectrum of misdemeanour of this kind: the *Digest* says that anyone who persuaded a praetextate boy to commit *stuprum* or any other crime would receive capital punishment if the crime was actually committed, and otherwise banishment (47.11.1.2; cf. Gaius, *Inst.* 3.220). *Stuprum* also involved taking advantage of a child's naivety for financial gain, and the emotional currency of such an act is best encapsulated in a passage of Cicero, in which a young boy has been swindled out of his family fortune by Verres and appears in court in his *toga praetexta*:

> He was the son of a plebeian Roman called Publius Iunius, whose dying father believed that he had entrusted him, not only to his guardians and kinsmen, but also to the law, the integrity of the magistrates, and to your administration of justice.... For we have little children, and it is uncertain how long any of us will live: while we are alive we need to reflect and make provision that their vulnerable state of childhood is protected by the strongest possible defences.
>
> Verr. 2.1.151; 153¹³⁴

It is difficult to gain a picture of just how widespread the wearing of the *toga praetexta* was by children in real life. For much of Roman history the term *praetextatus* was shorthand for 'boy' or 'youth' (e.g. Cic., *Arch.* 3; *Sest.* 144; Livy 42.34.4), so its symbolism was certainly common knowledge. We also know that by the first century BCE at the latest, all freeborn children were entitled to wear it (Cic., *Verr.* 2.1.152), which is why it features so prominently in images of children on the gravestones of freedpeople,¹³⁵ but of course not all families would have been able to afford one. There is some evidence that at least in Rome in the Republic, boys further down the social scale did wear it, as Cicero complained about having to attend the *toga virilis* ceremonies of his humbler associates (*Mur.* 69) and Phaedrus tells a story from his own time involving a boy from a relatively humble family about to gain his *toga virilis* (3.10.10). (For the *toga virilis*, see the next section.) It seems likely that, as with the toga itself, there were classes of society who never wore it, and others for whom it was the dress of special occasions, such as court cases (e.g. Cic., *Verr.* 2.1.58) and religious rituals (e.g. the boys on the south frieze of the Ara Pacis; Macrob., *Sat.* 1.6.13–14; Suet., *Aug.* 94.8). During weddings, according to Festus (282L), three boys whose parents were still alive customarily led the bride to the groom's house holding flame-torches and shouting lewd words, before which they removed their *togae praetextae*, temporarily leaving the protective cover of the garment.

Although girls also wore the *toga praetexta*, it was elite boys who were destined to go on to social roles and professions for which the toga was the requisite dress, and for them the *toga praetexta* may have been a relatively frequent imposition. Children's sarcophagi decorated with scenes of them engaging in everyday activities portray them in a variety of dress styles, but the toga is the dress commonly worn in scenes in which the boy is receiving lessons (in oratory).[136] On one sarcophagus a boy even wears a toga whilst playing with a toy chariot.[137] It is these children for whom it would have been most important to master the wearing of the garment. Quintilian mentions some of the people who might be involved in training a young boy in correct body movement, such as gymnastics instructors, teachers and actors (*Inst.* 1.11–12),[138] and Seneca also writes about *paedagogi* and even grandmothers teaching boys how to behave (*Ep.* 94.8–9). Albeit in a Greek setting, Plutarch lists as the remit of domestic tutors teaching a boy how to behave at the table, walk in the street, sit up straight and, importantly, wear the *himation* properly (*Mor.* 439f–440a/*An virtus doceri possit* 2). But in the aforementioned letter, Seneca also speaks of bringing up children as the father's responsibility (*Ep.* 94.1) and it seems likely that it was ultimately fathers who oversaw this 'training', just as it is mothers for the sari in India.[139] As McDonnell has pointed out, the relationship between elite Roman fathers and sons was both peculiar and intense:[140] Plutarch's account of the Elder Cato is an oft-cited but extreme case of a father spending a great deal of time with his sons and supervising their education (e.g. *Cat. Mai.* 20.4–9), but other, more incidental passages reveal how common and important it was, for example, for fathers to keep an eye on their boys' education and psychological development, as well as to spend time with them dining and bathing to teach them how to behave (e.g. Plut., *Quaes. Rom.* 33; Val. Max. 2.1.7; Cic., *Orat.* 2.224; *Att.* 6.1.12).[141] It is surely not too much of a leap to suggest that the acquisition of toga proficiency was part of this.

And it wasn't just the attainment of a physical skill: like the toga in general, the *toga praetexta* was more than a reflection of certain values and responsibilities; it was a tool for shaping a child's character with the hope that its symbolism – pride in freeborn status, future social and political responsibility[142] – would be internalized by the child who wore it.[143] This is best illustrated in grave monuments set up by parents for boys who died young, often including portraits of the youngsters expertly mastering their togas.[144] The imagery should be seen in the same light as the accounts of precocious intellect and skills that are sometimes included in the inscriptions: both point to the roles and expertise the boy – so their parents hoped – would have assumed had they made it to adulthood.

Togam virilem sumere

The entry into manhood was marked, in Roman culture, by a special ceremony in which the boy laid aside his *toga praetexta* and assumed the plain white *toga virilis* – also sometimes called the *toga pura*[145] – of the adult man. We have snippets of evidence that give us some idea of what this entailed: it would seem the occasion began in the family *lararium*, where relatives, household slaves, friends and important people associated with the family would gather.[146] The boy's *bulla* was first removed from around his neck and dedicated to the household gods by hanging it up on the figure of the *lar*, after which he laid aside his *toga praetexta* (Pers. 5.30–31; Prop. 4.1.131–132) and put on a *tunica recta/regilla*.[147] His father then handed him a *toga virilis*, which he put on (Val. Max. 5.4.4; Apul., *Apol.* 73.9; Stat., *Silv.* 5.2.64–67; Cic., *Sest.* 144). Next the party would process to the Capitol where the boy performed sacrifices at the temple of Jupiter Optimus Maximus (App., *B Civ.* 4.5.30; Val. Max. 5.4.4).[148] The procession then left the temple, perhaps through the forum, and money and food would be distributed to onlookers.[149] Some scholars have suggested, based on an ambiguous passage of Dio (55.10.2), that in the imperial period in Rome the procession also visited the Forum Augustum.[150]

Ovid tells us that the coming-of-age often happened on the Liberalia (March 17) (*Fasti* 3.771–788), but the evidence we have for the dates for famous men show it could be any time of the year.[151] The age at which it happened seems to have been at the family's discretion, and although it was not a celebration of puberty per se, fathers watched their sons closely for signs of both physical and psychological maturity,[152] arranging the ceremony for when this maturity was believed to have set in.[153] The usual age seems to have been 15 or 16,[154] and although a passage in Livy (22.57.9) presumes it usually happened before the age of 17, we are told that Caligula received his *toga virilis* when he was 19 (Suet., *Calig.* 10).[155] The existence of the ceremony and what it symbolized reveals a Roman concept of the transition from childhood to adulthood as a sudden step, rather than a gradual process. (For girls this happened with marriage: the night before their wedding they laid aside the *toga praetexta* and, in the morning, assumed bridal dress.[156]) In concrete terms, the assumption of the *toga virilis* signalled the beginning of a man's career (Val. Max. 5.4.4). Consequently, in imperial biographies the ceremony is usually followed by an immediate assignment to a political task.[157] In the Republic this meant the right to vote, to appear in the courts and to start military training (see below). In legal terms, although it did not mean complete freedom from parental control – that came only with the death of the *paterfamilias* – it meant the right to inherit, preside over assets and make a will.[158] It also bestowed social licence, such as the right to recline at *convivia*, and sexual freedom, including the right to marry.[159] Some authors also mention intellectual autonomy, at least for elite boys: in other words, freedom to eschew school lessons and explore new and more creative intellectual avenues.[160] Several writers list the assumption of the adult toga as one of the joys of one's life, and it is sometimes referred to as the *toga libera* due to the newfound freedom it bestowed.[161]

Together, though, these new rights and responsibilities also reveal a great deal about the nature of Roman masculinity. As McDonnell has said, 'in most cultures manhood is regarded not as a status gained merely by coming of age, but as something that must be demonstrated or won, a concept that is precarious, elusive, and exclusionary'.[162] In Roman culture this meant the beginning of life as a civic figure and the expectation of masculine forms of behaviour.[163] The distinctive Roman notion of manhood was evidently not lost on Tacitus, who compared it to the initiation ceremony of Germanic boys, which involved being presented to the tribe and given weapons when they were deemed old enough to bear arms for the first time (*Germ.* 13). Tacitus' characterization of the ceremony as the passage from the private to the public sphere was evidently intended to resound with his Roman readership; however, whilst the assumption of the *toga virilis* may originally also have related to the age at which boys were considered old enough to fight in the army,[164] by the late Republic, at least for the elite, civic responsibilities were at least as important as military ones, and by the time of Tacitus, the contrast between Roman manhood and its much more martial Germanic counterpart was seemingly clear.[165] By this stage, the toga was not a military garment, but one of peace and civic duty, and *togam virilem sumere* was not a biological threshold, but one that was defined and affirmed by the community. Whilst Roman manhood was not unrelated to sexual maturity, far more important was the cultural and political role that the young man assumed with his first *toga virilis*.[166]

Ad cohibendum bracchium toga

The assumption of the *toga virilis* turned a boy instantaneously into a man. Nonetheless, it would seem that the event was often followed by a period of several years in which the young man was still considered to be vulnerable. Older relatives worrying about the behaviour of newly initiated young men is almost a commonplace of Roman literature,[167] and a passage in Plutarch's *Moralia* is particularly illuminating:

> The discourse which I gave on the subject of listening to lectures I have written out and sent to you, dear Nicander, so that you may know how rightly to listen to the voice of persuasion, now that you are no longer subject to authority, having assumed the garb of man. Now the absence of control, which some of the young men, for want of an education, think to be freedom, establishes the sway of a set of masters, harsher than the teachers and attendants of childhood, in the form of desires which are now, as it were, unchained. And just as Herodotus says that women put off their modesty along with their undergarments, so some of our young men, as soon as they lay aside the garb of childhood, lay aside also their sense of modesty and fear, and, undoing the habit that invests them, straightaway become full of unruliness. But ... I ask you to believe that in persons of good sense the passing from childhood to manhood is not a casting off of control, but a recasting of the controlling agent, since instead of some hired person or slave purchased with money they now take reason as the divine guide of their life.
>
> Plut., *Mor.* 37c-e/*De aud.* 1, trans. Cole Babbit 1960

The emphasis here is on unchained desires and immoral behaviour, which should be countered by reason and common sense. Further details of what could go wrong in this phase of a young man's life are given by Apuleius:

> While he was under our guardianship, he used to go to school: now he has bidden a long farewell to study and betaken himself to the delights of the tavern. He despises serious friends, and ... spends his tender years reveling with the most abandoned youths among harlots and wine-cups. He rules your house, orders your slaves, directs your banquets.... He never speaks any language save Punic, and though he may occasionally use a Greek word picked up from his mother, he neither will nor can speak Latin.
>
> *Apol.* 98, trans. Butler 1909

Here, the temptations of drink and sex are accompanied by neglect of intellectual training, undignified pastimes and arrogance toward other members of the household. Persius gives us some insight into what it was like to be going through this phase when he describes it as 'the age when the route is unclear and perplexity ignorant of life splits the agitated mind at the branching crossroads' (5.3–35).[168] Cicero characterized it as a time that barely any young man escaped without scandal, but that if he did, it led to eternal esteem (*Cael.* 5.11).[169]

The way in which dangers were countered appears to have been to entrust the young man to the watchful eye of older male relatives and friends. In one of his letters to Atticus (113.9), Cicero promises, having given his nephew Quintus the *toga virilis*, to keep him on a tight rein, and far from being entirely free, a passage of Gellius makes it clear that newly initiated young men could still expect to be reprimanded by their elders for poor behaviour: he recounts a story in which the oratory teacher Titus Castricius, seeing some former pupils on holiday, castigated them for wearing *lacernae* and sandals rather than togas, and reminded them that they were now senators of the Roman people (*NA* 13.22.1).

Some young men, it would appear, went out to seek guidance and learning off their own bat. Gellius tells us that when he was a young man in Rome and had just laid aside the *toga praetexta*, he independently sought out 'masters of deeper knowledge' among the booksellers of the Via Sandaliaria (*NA* 18.4.1). But at least in the Republic the mentoring of new initiates appears often to have been a more formal arrangement in which young men would undergo a kind of internship with an established jurist or rhetor.[170] The best description we have of this *tirocinium fori* comes from Tacitus:

> In the old days a youth who was being prepared for oratory, after basic schooling at home ... was taken by his father or relations to an orator who held a leading position in the city. He assumed the habit of accompanying his patron in public and supporting him in all his speeches, whether in the law courts or the assembly; in this way, hearing his debates first-hand, standing nearby, he learned to fight on the frontline.
>
> *Dial.* 34.1–6[171]

Cicero's patron was Scaevola, and he tells us that as part of his training he also memorized some of the old man's sayings and arguments for later use (*Amic.* 1.1). The arrangement may have involved some socializing with the patron as well, as Persius describes not just intellectual training from his teacher, but also feasting with him in the evening and arranging both work and leisure activities together, creating a friend for life (5.41–44).

Another Cicero passage suggests that the period of internship was usually one year, that it also involved physical/military training[172] and that it may have been associated with a particular way of wearing the toga:

> In those days, by custom, we spent one year with our arms confined in our toga (*ad cohibendum bracchium toga*), and in tunics we took advantage of physical training in the Campus Martius, and if we were immediately entitled to begin military service, the same practice was used in the camp and in the army.
>
> *Cael.* 5.11

Scholarly opinions diverge as to what exactly is meant here. Christ has suggested that the restrained arms were a reference to the 'armsling' style of draping the toga that was common in the late Republic,[173] whereas Richardson and Richardson argued that this cannot be what was meant, as the 'armsling' fashion was worn by fully fledged adults as well; they suggested that the phrase was primarily intended to be metaphorical, meaning that young men were expected to show restraint and be passive students of what was going on around them, rather than taking the initiative or playing an active part in public life.[174] A comment of Seneca the Elder shows, however, that a real clothing practice was meant: in the context of an anecdote explicitly about inappropriate clothing, he says that in the old days it was considered outrageous for young men starting out on their careers to let an arm poke out from under their toga (*Contr.* 5.6). It seems likely that the 'armsling' drape was *both* the style in which young men were expected to wear their togas *and* a more widespread fashion of the late Republic that was chosen by those who wished to convey an image of restraint and modesty more generally.[175] After all, an alternative style of draping was available in this period in which the right arm was free.

The *tirocinium fori* appears to have gradually died out as a custom, as both Gellius (*NA* 1.23) and Tacitus (*Dial.* 35) write of it as a thing of the past. At what point it disappeared is not clear: according to Suetonius, Augustus was responsible for reviving the custom in Rome (*Aug.* 38), but Seneca the Younger might be alluding to it as something that was still a custom when he was a youth as he describes being 'escorted to the forum' (*in forum deductus*) after acquiring his *toga virilis* (*Epist.* 1.4); it may, however, be that he is here simply referring to the procession of the coming-of-age ceremony.

Conclusion

Although originally a garment of both sexes, the toga eventually became central to what it meant to be a Roman man. Masculinity was defined not merely by physiological sex, but by the acquisition and maintenance of a particular set of rights, responsibilities and behaviours; in the mid–late Republic these became especially focused on civic duty. The toga was both the canvas on which this was reflected and the tool by which it was enforced. Thus, when young male children learned to wear the difficult garment, they were also learning the bearing and control expected of them later in life; when they came of age, their *toga virilis* meant not just sexual and social freedom, but also the beginning of public life and, in the elite, a career in service to the *res publica*. The ultimate visual embodiment of these ideals was the toga statue: with their standardized bodies masterfully controlling the copious, dignified folds of the unwieldy garment, they represented both the roles and the capabilities to which Roman men were expected to aspire. The fact that such attributes were not an automatic given, and that in reality there would have been a wide spectrum of behaviour from the exemplary to the inept to the downright scandalous, is evident in the many tales of things going wrong: men showing too little care over their appearance, tripping over their togas or allowing them to slip off; representatives of the state in foreign lands lounging around in louche Greek clothing instead of togas; and new initiates to the *toga virilis* going off the rails. Being a Roman man was something that one could do both very well and very badly, and the toga was its ultimate test.

4

The Toga and Social Status

Rome did not have a legally binding sartorial order,[1] and some scholars have suggested that the fact that dress could so easily be usurped and manipulated reduced its effectiveness as a signifier of status.[2] But it is precisely this fluidity that gave clothing symbolism its currency. In this chapter, it will be shown that the toga was in fact central not only to the outward communication of rank distinctions, but also to the process of negotiating them. Roman society was characterized by a curious combination of, on the one hand, steeply structured hierarchies and deep-seated inequality and prejudice, and, on the other, social mobility on a scale unknown in other pre-modern cultures.[3] However, rather than presenting a dichotomy, this chapter aims to show that the two were inextricably linked, and, in fact, the corollary of social mobility was a disproportionate level of angst surrounding rank and status, and especially its outer manifestations. Moreover, it was not enough to have achieved a certain social position: in order to be treated appropriately, one had to *show* it, and the prime means of doing this was through dress. As Rothfus has said, 'in Roman society, the burden of proof rested on the holder of rank'.[4] It is for this reason that the toga became a prime locus for the enactment and negotiation of status. The following will show that, as was the case with masculine identity in the previous chapter, the toga was not just a passive canvas on which status identity was reflected: it was also a tool used actively to assert and challenge it.

In this chapter, 'status' relates to a wide variety of social classifications: it begins by looking at formal positions of power within the Roman state and the status that different roles and occupations bestowed, but then moves on to patron–client relations, legal status (freed, citizen etc.) and the subtler nuances of wealth differentiation with which eagle-eyed satirists were particularly fixated. None of these existed in isolation from one another, and it seems befitting to discuss them together, although some teasing out of the strands is necessary to structure the discussion. The term 'elite' will generally be used to denote persons of senatorial and equestrian rank. But in contrast to most previous scholarship,[5] this chapter intends to show that it was not just the elite who were concerned with their place in society and the outward means of displaying it: in a culture that was marked by social mobility at all levels, clothing status markers became especially important amongst the non-elite, and the toga played a central role here as well.

Magistrates, priests and triumphant generals

Polybius, as both an outsider to and keen observer of Roman society, was especially impressed by the pageantry of elite funerals, in which men bearing the closest resemblance to various illustrious ancestors were fitted out with masks representing their faces to wear in the procession, along with the requisite togas. The passage in which he describes them illustrates especially well the Roman preoccupation with the display of rank and its role in creating *exempla* for others to follow:

> The men representing the ancestors wear togas, with a purple border if he was a consul or praetor, whole purple if he was a censor, and decorated with gold if he had celebrated a triumph or something similar. Together they ride in chariots led by the fasces, axes, and other insignia of rank by which the different magistrates are accompanied according to their rank during their lifetimes; and when they arrive at the Rostra they sit down in a row on ivory chairs. There can be no more ennobling a spectacle for a young man who aspires to fame and virtue. Who would not be inspired by the sight of the images of men distinguished by excellence, all together and as if alive and breathing?
>
> Polyb. 6.53[6]

As laid out in the previous chapter, the ideal Roman man was a public being, and his funeral was, accordingly, a public event. Within the elite it was especially the pursuit of honour in the form of magistracies and priesthoods that was the aim of one's public life. And whilst during the Republic such roles were the prime means by which the state was run, they did not disappear under the Principate, and, irrespective of the real power relations, competition for honour and status by means of the *cursus honorum* remained undiminished. Moreover, the number of people who might aspire to positions of rank actually increased under the emperors to include not just a whole host of new magistracies but also what Dench has termed 'paramagistracies' like the *seviri Augustales* popular with freedmen, meaning that a large number of men could now plausibly aspire to office of some kind.[7] Such roles, as Polybius makes clear, were associated with different types of dress, and especially different forms of toga, the right to which was generally decreed by the senate, although in the Principate it could be directly ordered by the emperor. In the discussion of toga statues in the previous chapter the issue of polychromy was not yet raised, but it now becomes relevant: both honorific and funerary marble portraits were originally painted with the colours befitting the highest rank achieved by the person commemorated.[8]

At the lowest magisterial level this meant the *toga praetexta*: the garment of Roman freeborn children was also the symbol of magisterial power, possibly again because of the sanctity and purity it symbolized.[9] Originally the dress of curule magistrates in Rome,[10] it was eventually conferred also on those of *coloniae* and *municipia* (Hor., *Sat.* 1.5.34–36; Livy 34.7.2; *lex Ursonensis*: CIL 2.5439) and the *magistri* of urban neighbourhoods in Rome (Livy 34.7.2–3). In some cases, the *toga praetexta* was only allowed for special occasions: former magistrates were allowed to wear it to events like the *ludi Circenses* and for their funerals (Livy 5.41; 34.7.1) and, according to Pliny, centurions sometimes wore it when sacrificing on campaign (*HN* 22.11). It was also the special gala dress sometimes granted to those – apart from the *triumphator* – processing in triumphal celebrations (Suet., *Claud.* 17.3; Dio Cass. 51.20). Recently discovered fragments of a relief from Nicomedia (Turkey) with some paintwork still intact seem to illustrate this still being the practice in the Tetrarchic era as they show various members of the processional party in an *adventus* scene wearing *togae praetextae* (Fig. 3.4: figures on the right). Curiously, the *toga praetexta* is also the garment commonly worn by the *genius familiaris* in fresco paintings in *lararia* in Pompeii (Fig. 3.2 and cover image: central figure),[11] perhaps signalling the sanctity of the *genius* or the high office held by the *paterfamilias* or his ancestors. This may have been general practice throughout the empire, as *genii* are routinely depicted in a toga in statues and reliefs, but it is only in frescoes like those in the Vesuvian towns that we have the colour detail.

As well as being a synonym for childhood, the *toga praetexta* was also used as a metaphor for political power in Roman texts from the late Republic through to the third century: in the *Historia Augusta*, for example, when Elagabulus signals he is finally willing to take control of affairs he is described as putting on the *toga praetexta* and heading to the senate (*Elag.* 15.6–7); similarly, in Plutarch's biography of Cicero (19.2), when Lentulus, implicated in the Catilinarian conspiracy, resigns from his office as praetor, he lays aside his *toga praetexta*. In one text it even symbolizes Roman rule per se, when the Roman annexation of Egypt is described as the *fasces* and *toga praetexta* entering the country (SHA *Tyr. Trig.* 22.14). In the *Historia Augusta* biography of Probus (24.2), a lightning strike that changed the colour of the *toga praetexta* on a portrait of that emperor was said to be an omen signalling great political careers for future members of his family. And the bordered toga did not only symbolize magisterial office, it also stood – like the child's *toga praetexta* – for the inviolability of those who wore it: in 68/67 BCE there was outrage when two praetors were captured by pirates whilst wearing their *togae praetextae* (Cic., *Leg. Man.* 32–33; App., *Mith.* 93),[12] and in 89 BCE a similarly shocking event occurred when the urban praetor A. Sempronius Asellio was attacked and killed – again, those who wrote about it explicitly mentioned that he was wearing his *toga praetexta* at the time, suggesting this made it all the more despicable (App., *B Civ.* 1.54).[13]

The *toga praetexta* also reflects perfectly the elision of the religious and the political in high Roman office, as it was also the traditional garment of members of the highest priestly colleges (Livy 27.37.13; 33.42.1). Here again, the number of people allowed to wear it extended over time: Tiberius, for example, bestowed it as a privilege on the *seviri Augustales*, many of whom were freedmen (which has implications for the view that the toga was only ever worn by the elite as discussed in the section on the non-elite toga below).[14]

Priestly dress in Rome also sometimes involved another type of toga: the *laena*. The name is evidently derived from the Greek *chlaina*,[15] and, like this cloak, it was sometimes fastened with a brooch (Suetonius, fr. 167), but its rounded edge clearly puts it in the toga family, and in fact both Varro (*Ling.* 5.133) and a fragment of Suetonius (fr. 167) characterize it as a '*toga duplex*',[16] which, when laid on the ground, would make it elliptical in shape. The few images that we have of what seem to be *laenae* suggest that in the imperial period it was worn draped around the whole body in a more or less symmetrical fashion[17] over the *toga praetexta*, a good example being the *flamines* on the south frieze of the Ara Pacis (Fig. 4.1).[18] This monument gives us a clue as to its use as well, as it is here worn along with other garments like the *albogalerus* cap by certain priests for sacrifice.[19] At least as much as the *toga praetexta*, it seems to have conferred on its wearer an air of divine authority, and Cicero tells a story in which in 359 BCE the sight of one of the consuls in a *laena* was enough to quell a riot (*Brut.* 56).[20]

Another special toga form associated with sacrificial ceremonies was the *cinctus Gabinus*, in which the toga was tied tightly across the upper body and waist. In earlier times associated with battle and physical exertion,[21] it was also the appropriate dress for the more strenuous parts of sacrificial ceremonies; it seems also to be what the *Lares* wear in fresco depictions from the Vesuvian cities, perhaps because they are shown dancing (Fig. 3.2 and cover image: left and right figures).[22]

Figure 4.1 Detail of the south frieze of the Ara Pacis. Ara Pacis Museum, Rome. Photo: B. Malter, arachne.uni-koeln.de/item/marbilder/404143

As an extremely expensive dye made from crushing thousands of marine molluscs, and a colour closely associated with kingship, purple was both expensive and heavily controlled in antiquity.[23] It is this that gave the *toga praetexta* its distinctive aura, and it is also the reason why the toga next in rank up from it – the *toga purpurea* or full-purple toga – was reserved for only the very highest offices. Originally – or so the Romans believed – worn by the Etruscan kings of Rome,[24] the *toga purpurea* became the ceremonial and funeral dress of censors (Polybius 6.53.7) and perhaps also consuls on specific occasions such as the opening of the Temple of Janus.[25] But it never lost its association with kingship, rendering it the ultimate symbol of power when usurped, for example, by Tryphon, leader of the Slave Revolt in 104–101 BCE (Diod. Sic. 36.7.4), and when worn later by Julius Caesar as an honour bestowed by the Senate (Cic., *Phil.* 2.85–86; Dio Cass. 44.6.1). In the Empire it was mainly associated with the emperor,[26] although it was also granted as special dress to certain magistrates by this date (Dio Cass. 49.16),[27] and this seems to have continued, because in an episode in Apuleius' *Metamorphoses* a man wears a *toga purpurea* to dress up as a magistrate in a fancy-dress parade (11.8).

The most exclusive toga type was, however, the *toga picta*. Although we do not have any confirmed images of it surviving from antiquity[28] – probably due to the lack of surviving paintwork on statues – a handful of text passages attest that it was purple and decorated with gold.[29] It was usually worn over the top of a *tunica palmata* (a tunic decorated with gold palm leaves), which is why the whole ensemble is sometimes condensed to '*toga palmata*' (e.g. Martial 7.2.8; Apul., *Apol*. 22; Servius, *Ad Bucol* 10.27; Isid., *Etym*. 19.24.5).[30] It was predominantly associated with the triumph, and the right to wear it was bestowed by the senate on victorious generals for the occasion of the triumphal procession, although it would seem such men were henceforth also sometimes allowed to wear it for special occasions such as the *ludi Circenses*.[31]

Ancient texts also draw a connection between the *toga picta* and both Etruscan kings and Jupiter O.M. This has resulted in a great deal of scholarly debate surrounding the garment's origins, which closely mirrors that of the toga in general: some see it as an originally Etruscan garment,[32] others see it as originating from Greece,[33] while yet others have argued that it was based on the dress worn by the statue of Jupiter in his temple on the Capitol.[34] Most recently, Beard has dismissed all later written accounts of early origins as 'much more likely to be the outcome of … antiquarian fantasy and invented tradition',[35] effectively arguing that absence of evidence for the early period is evidence of its absence. Piecing the data together carefully, however, it is possible to suggest a likely scenario.

A fourth-century BCE painting in the François Tomb at Vulci shows a prominent local man called Vel Saties in a purple cloak with figurative decoration, and Bonfante has argued that this is a *toga/tebenna picta*;[36] but it is clearly a rectangular garment,[37] and the style in which it is draped is not known for depictions of the *tebenna*. It seems likely, as Lesky has argued, that the cloak depicted had Greek/Hellenistic origins if we consider Plutarch's description of the *chlamys* of Demetrios decorated with stars (*Demetr*. 41), cult statues[38] and vase paintings[39] from southern Italy showing similarly decorated cloaks, as well as the unknown author of *De mirabilibus auscultationibus*' description of an expensive purple *himation* decorated with deities and personifications (96.838a). In fact, the connection seems indisputable given that there are also several Etruscan tomb paintings of famous Greek figures wearing ornately decorated cloaks.[40] Already Pliny pointed to a Greek origin when he said the decoration of the *toga picta* dated back as far as Homer (*HN* 8.195).[41]

On the other hand, whilst we do not have direct evidence for the dress of the early kings, we have no reason to doubt that the *toga purpurea* was, as Roman writers believed, indeed Etruscan in origin, like the other insignia of power such as the *sella curulis* and the *fasces* often mentioned in the same breath and which we find in Etruscan iconography.[42] The *toga picta* was, like the *toga purpurea*, entirely purple (save for the decoration), and it seems likely that the two terms were sometimes used interchangeably, or, in fact, confused. This would explain ancient references to both as the dress of the early Roman kings.[43] In other words, whilst the purple toga itself might have had early Etruscan origins, the decoration of it is a separate phenomenon and may have come somewhat later under either direct or indirect influence from the Greek world. This is, in fact, the scenario already suggested by Festus in the second century CE (228L). In the Regal period it would have been the kings who celebrated triumphs, as later written sources state,[44] and whilst they may have done so in their normal gala dress – the *toga purpurea* – it is not difficult to see how such clothing might have evolved into the dress of the triumphant general in the Republic: it was the one occasion on which a man was allowed to elevate himself above his peers. The first historical figure described as wearing a *toga picta* in extant written sources is Scipio Africanus in Appian *Pun.* 66, which has led some to believe that the decoration only evolved in the third century BCE.[45] It is impossible to know for sure, but by the Augustan period it seems that some liked to think of it as going back to deepest Roman history, because Vergil includes a mantle 'stiff with gold figures' (*signis auroque rigentem*: *Aen.* 1.648) as one of the presents brought from Aeneas' ship to Dido's court.

Regarding the link between triumphal dress and Jupiter O.M., two passages simply describe the dress as 'of Jupiter': in Suetonius' biography of Augustus, for example, triumphal dress is simply referred to as *exuviae Iovis optimi maximi* (94.6), while Juvenal calls it the *tunica Iovis* with *toga picta* (10.38).[46] It seems unlikely that this means triumphant generals were explicitly dressed *as the god Jupiter* because such characterizations of triumphal dress are very rare (these and the passages further below are the only such references), and especially so in comparison with the number that connect it with the early Roman kings. Moreover, the *triumphator* is also described as wearing a *bulla* (e.g. Macrob., *Sat.* 1.6.9): why would he need a protective amulet if he were a god? The painting of the face in red of both Jupiter and the triumphator almost certainly go back to an archaic practice relating to religiosity in general.[47] And whilst the practice of a slave whispering in a triumphant general's ear to 'remember that you are a mortal' does suggest a temporarily deified state, the passages that mention this are late in date (Tert., *Apol.* 33; Jer., *Ep.* 39.2.8), and it may be that by this stage the connection with Jupiter was indeed conceived of in a more explicit way (see below).

The most plausible explanation is that – possibly quite early in Roman history – Jupiter O.M., as the king of the gods, was dressed in his statue in the Capitoline temple in the clothing associated with kingship, which happened also to have evolved into the dress of triumphant generals.[48] After all, according to Dio, when Caesar was offered kingly robes and a diadem by Mark Antony, he is said to have responded that 'Jupiter alone is king of the Romans' before sending the diadem to his temple on the Capitol (44.11.2). A number of (relatively late) passages suggest that triumphal dress was conventionally stored in the Capitoline temple; for example, Tertullian describes the dress being 'taken from Jupiter' (*ab Iove insignes*: *De cor.* 13.1), and Prudentius refers to Jupiter as the one who has conferred (*donavit*) on the Romans the gold-decorated toga (*C Symm.* 1.622–623). Two passages in the *Historia Augusta* enlighten us further: Gordian I is described as 'the first Roman to possess his own private *tunica palmata* and *toga picta*', going on to explain that previously the emperors had got them 'either from the Capitol or the Palatine' (*Gord. Tr.* 4.4), whilst in a description of Severus Alexander's humble behaviour, the emperor is described as having only worn the *toga picta* when consul, and then 'only the one that was brought from the temple of Jupiter and used by all the other praetors and consuls' (*Alex. Sev.* 40.8). Leaving aside what these passages reveal about the wide use to which the *toga picta* was put by the third century, they make it clear that such robes were traditionally state-owned and kept in Jupiter's temple on the Capitol, to which was later added – presumably as a result of increasing use by the emperors – a set on the Palatine as well.[49] There were probably a number of official *togae pictae* in working order at any given time, and they would have been replaced by new ones when they got old and shabby.[50]

What is important to take away from this is that the dress of the *triumphator* was part of what Versnel has called a 'Kreislauf der Macht',[51] in which the power embodied in the dress of the Roman kings was in a constant feedback loop with that of Jupiter O.M. and (on a temporary basis) the triumphant general. Each served to heighten the symbolic power of the other, and integration between the three probably increased over time. Central to this was the *toga picta*: the fact that it was an object that could only be conferred by the senate, was apparently state-owned and kept in the temple of Jupiter on the Capitol for most of its history illustrates the immense symbolic value of this particular form of toga in the Roman state system.

Equestrians

Amongst the Roman elite, there were several items of dress that distinguished men of senatorial from those of equestrian rank: senators were entitled to wear a broad purple stripe (*latus clavus*) on their tunics, along with a special type of *calcei*; equestrians wore a narrower purple stripe (*angustus clavus*) on their tunics, also special *calcei* and a gold ring (*anulus aureus*).[52] There was, however, also a specific form of toga that was especially associated with equestrians: a somewhat mysterious garment called the *trabea*. Linguists suggest it is a Sabine word,[53] but Wilson argued the name came from the Latin word for beams or rafters (*trabes*), meaning the cloak must have been striped.[54] Dionysius of Halicarnassus' description of the *trabea* as πορφύρεος φοινικοπάρυφος (*Ant. Rom.* 6.13.4–5) suggests, however, that its key feature was actually a different-coloured border.[55] It would certainly seem to have been decorated in some way, as of one of the few tantalizing fragments we have of Suetonius' lost work on Roman dress, preserved in Servius' commentary on the *Aeneid*, reveals:

> In his dress book, Suetonius says there are three types of *trabea*:
> The first is sacred to the gods and is entirely purple;
> The second is associated with the kings (*regum*) and is purple with some white on it
> And the third is (worn by) augurs and is purple and red.
> (It's called) 'Quirinal' because it was royal.
>
> Serv., *Aen.* 7.612[56]

Like the *laena*, the *trabea* was apparently sometimes fastened with a brooch (Dion. Hal., *Ant. Rom.* 2.70.2).[57] Several other text passages reveal a belief that the *trabea* was originally worn by the Roman kings,[58] although the Suetonius passage also mentions a sacred version and one worn by augurs, and in the *Aeneid* Vergil has a consul open the Temple of Janus wearing a *trabea* (7.612).[59]

Whatever its precise origins, by the early Empire the *trabea* had become so closely associated with the equestrian order that it was used in literature as shorthand for that status (e.g. Mart. 5.41.5). Gabelmann's suggestion that it developed out of the special dress worn by the mounted bodyguard of the Etruscan kings is plausible, if necessarily conjectural.[60] As difficult as it is to define what constituted equestrian status at any given time[61] – an issue that is not helped by emphasis in the Principate on the property qualification of 400,000 sesterces – it is clear that the original idea was that equestrians were a state cavalry defined by possession of a public horse, and that their major annual event was the *transvectio equitum* on 15 July: what by the time of the Principate was almost certainly an elite group amongst the *ordo equester* would parade on horseback through the city, and this continued to be a significant exhibition of (increasingly symbolic) status until late antiquity. The parade uniform for this occasion was the *trabea*,[62] and visual evidence for the *transvectio*, such as a relief on the base of the lost Column of Antoninus Pius, shows its basic form to be a short style of toga, complete with *umbo*, that was suitable for riding on horseback (Fig. 4.2: top row, second and fifth figures from left and bottom row, first and fifth figures from left).[63] For those who held the privilege of taking part in the *transvectio* it is clear that it was central to their identity, as their gravestones often depict a figure on horseback wearing a *trabea*;[64] when, in the early third century, equestrian status became hereditary, the iconography of horse and *trabea* became the perfect way to commemorate boys from equestrian families who had died before they were old enough to hold any kind of public office.[65]

The existence of the *trabea* as a dress for horse riding illustrates yet again the basic fact that the toga started out as an all-purpose garment, and the longevity of this and other of its more specialized forms is testament to its enduring utility and versatility for embodying status distinctions. But these special toga types were only ever of direct significance to a tiny minority of the Roman population,

Figure 4.2 *Transvectio equitum* scene on the base of a column of Antoninus Pius. Vatican Museums, inv 5115. Photo: Vatican Museums and Galleries, Vatican City/ Bridgeman Images.

and an arguably more interesting story is the role the toga played in the negotiation of status within the wider population.

Citizens

One reason for the central importance of the toga in Roman society – and its near ubiquity in funerary portraits – was its association with citizenship. It is unclear whether non-citizens were ever actually forbidden from wearing the toga in law.[66] There are no passages in surviving legal texts that explicitly state this, and there is some indication that the toga *could* sometimes be worn by non-citizens: for example, the *Digesta* stipulates that hostages taken, if they wore the toga and behaved like Roman citizens, should henceforth be treated as Roman citizens (49.14.32), and two passages in Strabo's *Geography* suggest peregrine inhabitants in early Roman Spain might have worn it to signal their allegiance to Rome (3.2.15; 3.4.20). Non-citizen inhabitants of the provinces sometimes wore a toga on their gravestones (see below Chapter 6), and some very few grave monuments even depict slaves wearing togas, such as the *servi publici* on the grave *ara* of Grania Faustina in Rome[67] and a marble urn in Berlin,[68] or the ill-fated *verna* Eutyches depicted with his freeborn friend Nico.[69] The scrolls they also hold point to the depiction as one of aspiration, rather than reality, as they are both only one year old, and it may be that depictions on gravestones constituted somewhat of a legal loophole in any case.

But a law is certainly suggested by several passages, such as Suetonius' anecdote in which a slave boy dressed in a toga by his dealers to avoid customs charges was able to use it later in court to make a bid for his freedom (*Rhet.* 1(25)), and the passage in the same author's biography of Claudius (15.2), in which a man accused of usurping citizenship was allowed to wear the toga when his defence was speaking, but had to change into a *pallium* for the prosecution. It is also strongly insinuated in the fact that Romans sent into exile had the right to wear the toga taken away from them (Pliny, *Ep.* 4.11.3), and the custom in which citizens removed their togas for the Saturnalia (Sen., *Ep.* 18.2), when everything was inverted. A passage in Seneca's spoof funerary oration for Claudius, in which the Fate Clotho speaks to Mercury about how much time Claudius has had on earth, is also telling:

'By Hercules, I did want to give him a bit more time, so he could give Roman citizenship to those few remaining people without it. (He wanted, namely, to see all Greeks, Gauls, Spaniards, Britons in the toga.) But since you want to leave a few foreigners for seed, and because you are commanding me, so be it.'

Apoc. 3

What *is* evident from these passages is that by the first century CE, the toga had come to be widely seen as, at the very least, a key symbol of Roman citizenship. At what point this began is unclear. As we have seen, the toga started out as a general garment of central Italy, and it must have gained this narrower symbolism over time.[70] It would certainly help if we knew what *formula togatorum*, the name used to denote the register of Rome's Italian allies in the third century BCE, actually signified. Rothfus has suggested it was so-called because the allies were doing service *to Rome*,[71] but it seems more likely that it indicated an alliance of toga-wearers, whether the population of central Italy in general, or military-age citizens of the Italian towns more specifically, as suggested by Wrede.[72] Toga-wearing was, in any case, also associated with Latin citizenship, so a wider use in central Italy does not necessarily preclude a legal distinction.[73] It seems likely that the connection of the toga with citizenship went hand in hand with Roman expansion and the subsequent crystallization of ideas surrounding what constituted Romanness and who was defined as 'other'.

None of the above means, of course, that the toga and what it symbolized could not, in fact, be usurped. With inadequate formal means of documenting citizenship,[74] all the authorities could do was mete out ever harsher punishments to those who transgressed, such as the *Lex Licinia Mucia* of 95 BC that established citizenship usurpation as a crime, or Claudius' order that false holders of Roman citizenship be executed (Suet., *Claud.* 25).[75] In Italy, the toga's association with citizen status gradually elided with that of being free/freed and this played an especially important role in the late Republic as large numbers of slaves were being manumitted and made into Roman citizens.

The toga amongst the non-elite

As *the* iconic Roman garment, older scholarship tended to assume that the toga was the most common apparel in Rome, a view that continues to the present day in schoolbooks and popular culture. However, since the 1990s the trend in scholarly literature has been to downplay its significance, starting with the work of Stone and Vout in their articles of 1994 and 1996 respectively: they argued that the public- and status-oriented nature of public art (Stone) and the elite bias of written texts (Vout) have skewed our vision, and that even though the toga was more commonly worn in earlier centuries, by the late Republic it was too big, expensive and difficult to wear for everyday use, and that it quickly became a kind of 'costume' (Stone) reserved for festive occasions.[76] A passage in Suetonius' biography of Augustus is central to this argument:

> He wanted also to bring back (*reduco*) the traditional fashion of dress (*habitus vestitusque pristinus*), and once when he saw in an assembly a horde (of men) in dark cloaks (*turba pullatorum*), he was incensed and cried out 'Behold the Romans, lords of the world, the nation clad in the toga,'[77] and he told the aediles from then on not to allow anyone to go in or near the forum except in the toga and without a cloak (*lacerna*).
>
> *Aug.* 40.5

Some have used the above passage, along with the centrality of the toga in Augustan art, to argue that it was only in this period that the toga gained currency as a visual symbol and 'Staatsgewand' at all, and that its use declined again rapidly after Augustus' death.[78] One scholar has even claimed that by the time of Vespasian the toga was merely a 'Bildformel' rather than a real garment.[79] The rest of this chapter aims to show that such a view is both incompatible with the evidence and serves to perpetuate precisely the elite-centred view of Roman society from which such scholars seek to have departed.

We have already seen in the discussion of the toga's origins that it was a general garment of central Italy in the early Roman period, but also that the Etruscans already associated certain versions of it with the Romans in the late fourth century BCE;[80] it is worn by Roman figures in frescoes of this period in Rome itself to distinguish them from people of other cultural groups.[81] For the middle Republic both contemporary historical sources like Polybius and later ones like Livy and Appian leave no room for doubt that the toga was the main garment worn in public not just by Roman statesmen (Polyb. 3.33.2; 6.53.7; 10.4.8–10.5.2; App., *Samn.* 7.2), but also by ordinary civilians and soldiers (Livy 6.25.7; 29.3.5; 44.16.4), and manumitted slaves (Polyb. 30.18). Moreover, the fact that the third-century BCE register of *socii* was called the *formula togatorum* means the toga must have held currency as a general dress of men of military age, either in Rome alone or indeed more widely in Italy.[82]

In the late Republic the evidence grows apace, but again, statues, coins, reliefs and written evidence give the unmistakable impression that the toga was the main public dress worn not just by statesmen like Cato and Cicero,[83] but also civilians and soldiers as well.[84] In fact, in Lucan's version of a speech to his troops,

Caesar describes the toga as '*plebeia*' and associates it with ordinary civilian life (*Phars.* 7.267). There are a good number of toga-wearers in the scenes on the Tomb of the Baker in Rome, some of whom may represent Eurysaces (the dedicatee) himself, but most of whom are usually interpreted as public officials overseeing the weighing of his bread products;[85] a grave relief in Capua from the late first century BCE also shows men at work weighing and recording merchandise wearing togas.[86] It was also not only reserved for public duties: Cicero tells us he wore a toga to the bathhouse (*Vat.* 30), and several everyday life scenes on funerary monuments from the late Republic and early Empire show that some, perhaps wealthier, men wore it when out shopping.[87]

On the face of it, Suetonius referring to the toga as a '*pristinus habitus*' and Augustus apparently having to revive and enforce it seems quite damning, but aside from the fact that we have no corroborating evidence for this episode, neither the verb '*reducere*' nor the adjective '*pristinus*' rule out that the toga, though considered long-standing and traditional, continued to be worn; and the clothing regulation he cites – if enacted at all – does not prove that the toga was nowhere to be seen, only that it was too sparse in Rome's central district for Augustus' liking. Similarly, the term '*habitus*' denotes not a specific garment (that would be '*vestis*') but a way of dressing, and Augustus' ruling may, in fact, simply have meant that people were expected to take off their *lacernae* when in the forum to reveal their togas in a way similar to that of some schools in the UK and Australia that forbid their students from wearing a coat over their school blazers in public. The overwhelming impression from other written and visual evidence is that the toga was alive and well in the period in which this incident is supposed to have occurred. For example, whilst Horace's poetry of the same period does paint a picture of the *plebs urbana* in Rome dressed in tunics (Hor., *Epist* 1.7.65) – of which more below – he also mentions non-elite people wearing the toga in the street in a way that conveys that this was not overly unusual (e.g. *Epod.* 4.7–8; *Epist.* 1.1.94–97; *Sat.* 1.3.31–32), and a large number of grave monuments for non-elite people, such as *liberti*, in which the male figures wear togas, date to the late Republic, as discussed further below.[88]

For the first century CE we have a significant amount of evidence that the toga was a common sight on the streets of Rome, much of which will form the basis of more detailed discussion below. The satirists mention some of the occasions on which Roman men commonly wore a toga, such as during the morning visit to the patron and to the theatre or amphitheatre (Mart. 2.29; 2.39; 13.98; Juv. 1.95; 11.204). Martial recommends putting a *lacerna* on over the toga in the amphitheatre to stay warm (14.135), although there are also plenty of references to the toga being used to keep out the cold (e.g. Hor., *Sat.* 1.3.13–15; Mart. 10.15; Suet., *Verg.* 43). He also mentions a man who wore a short toga (*brevis toga*) day and night, suggesting it may even sometimes have been worn at home (11.56.6). We have some reason to believe that the toga was less widely worn in everyday life in Italy outside Rome. In fact, Juvenal famously wrote that 'there are large parts of Italy, to tell you the truth, where no one wears a toga unless he is dead' (3.171–172). Whilst this has generally been taken to mean that people were buried in togas, it is more likely that he is referring to portraits on gravestones, and this has obvious implications for the kinds of information we seek to derive from such monuments. Both Martial (3.4; 4.66.1–4; 10.47; 10.96) and Pliny (*Ep.* 5.6.45) describe not having to wear a toga as one of the joys of escaping to the countryside (see previous chapter), but they are talking about spending time in private pursuits on villa estates where the toga, as a garment of business and public life, was of course worn less often. This may have been the case for much of Rome's history: the Livy anecdote in which during the Sabine Wars Cincinnatus is out working his fields when a senatorial delegation arrives and asks him to put on his toga to come to the senate (3.26.7–10)[89] is but one key example. But when Juvenal tells us that in Italian provincial cities even the aediles get around in just a white tunic without a toga over the top (3.179–180), he is surely exaggerating for comic effect. The central squares of Italian cities were full of honorific toga statues portraying leading local men in the garb that would have been expected of them at least for important public occasions.[90]

The closest thing we have to a snapshot of Roman street life in the first century is, in fact, not from Rome itself but from Pompeii: the fresco series from the House of Julia Felix depicting scenes in the local forum. It is useful at this stage to look at these paintings in detail, as they provide a visual framework for the discussion in the rest of this chapter. They depict a wide range of activities involving different types of people, from beggars soliciting cash, through street sellers of various kinds to magistrates engaged in legal proceedings.[91] It is true that the first thing that strikes one is just how colourful and diverse the dress is; however, whilst some scholars have been quick to point out how few togas we see in the scenes,[92] the fact that we do see a considerable number of them is significant in light of the current trend to deny the toga's use in everyday life. Hartnett, in his recent study of Roman street life, counted five toga-wearers amongst the sixty-seven discernible figures,[93] but in fact there may be more: in one scene, a man in a white toga leads a young woman toward a seated magistrate wearing a red/purple toga (*toga purpurea*?) and his attendant wearing a white toga.[94] In another, several figures read a notice fastened to the front of a gallery of equestrian statues (Fig. 3.3). One of these clearly wears a white toga – the *lacinia* is visible hanging down the back – and the three further figures seem also to be wearing togas, but the fact that they are in shades of orange and red and less clearly defined means that this must remain uncertain. Another man in a white toga appears in a very damaged scene involving some kind of transaction with men in tunics leading a mule.[95] Interesting in this context is also the so-called 'bread-seller' scene,[96] depicting not a baker selling his wares, as often assumed,[97] but a local elite man sitting on a stage and handing out bread to townspeople,[98] his gleaming white toga and tunic standing out amongst the dark colours of the tunics worn by the bread recipients. By contrast, street sellers and the men engaged in physical work mostly wear tunics on their own.[99] Several other figures, including most of the male customers of the street vendors, clearly wear *pallia*.[100] The scenes involving togate men give us an insight into the everyday situations that might involve a toga, as well as the kinds of people one might have seen wearing one on the street: that the magistrate and his attendant wear it is perhaps unsurprising, but it would seem from the figures who approach them that it was also the appropriate dress for men when appearing in front of a judge; the figures reading the notice in the gallery are likely to be men engaged in local political matters, and the man in the mule scene is a businessman of some sort.

In this context it is useful to think of the toga in terms of the modern suit and tie, which the dress historian Anne Hollander has defined as 'the uniform of official power, not manifest force or physical labour'.[101] It is clear that the toga, like the suit, would not have been practical clothing for any kind of physical work, and those men who did wear it on a daily basis tended to be employed in the Roman equivalent of 'desk jobs': administrative clerks, politicians and attendees of political assemblies, some businessmen and those involved in the judicial system, such as magistrates and court assistants.[102] On the other hand, again like the suit today, there would have been many ordinary folk who donned it only for certain occasions, such as to appear in court, or to attend a wedding, funeral or important religious ceremony.[103] Martial, for example, describes his friend Linus shaking out his only toga for the Ides and Kalends (4.66). Likewise – and this is something that is often forgotten in modern scholarship – at any given time there would have been people who deliberately bucked the trend, like the lovably eccentric fresco artist mentioned by Pliny, who always wore a toga whilst painting, even when he had to get up onto scaffolding (*HN* 35.120).

It is striking that none of the togas depicted in the forum frescoes are of the large, elaborate, imperial style. One of the reasons cited by earlier scholars for a very limited use of the toga in everyday life is its impracticality,[104] but smaller, more functional togas that were presumably also a great deal cheaper existed as well. (Further discussion of these can be found later in this chapter.) Besides, a certain amount of discomfort has never stopped an outfit from being everyday dress: very few modern men enjoy wearing a tie, but millions do so for work every day. It may be that some of the most elaborate draping fashions, especially of the early imperial period, passed many people by who didn't belong to the elite,[105] but for toga drapery to have evolved at all in the ways described in Chapter 2, the new fashions must have been worn by at least some real people on a regular basis.

Perhaps one of the most eloquent, if less direct, testimonies to the role of the toga in the lives of everyday people is the fact that throughout Roman history, the protective deities of individual people and families were consistently depicted wearing a toga. *Genii* were venerated along with *Lares* and *Penates* (deities of the house and its contents) in small shrines in the house, ideally every day (Plaut., *Aul.* prol.; SHA *Alex. Sev.* 29.2–3), and the focus of these shrines was an image of the deities on the wall (Fig. 3.2 and cover image). The fact that they are found in both luxurious and humble houses, in *atria* and service quarters, reveals that they must have been venerated by the full spectrum of the population,[106] hence they are often referred to as '*arte plebeia*'.[107] It is significant that while all the main Roman deities were dressed in various versions of archaizing Greek dress, the gods who played the most important role in the everyday lives of ordinary people were invariably dressed in a toga, perhaps because it represented the 'Sunday best' of the non-elite population.[108]

The use of the toga may have declined gradually from the second century onward – for example, Hadrian allegedly found it necessary to legislate for its use in public by senators and equestrians (SHA *Hadr.* 22.2) – but it appears still to have been the common garb of spectators in the arena in the late second century, as Commodus reportedly caused a minor scandal when he ordered people to wear hooded cloaks instead (SHA *Comm.* 16); and in 200 CE Tertullian was able to draw rhetorical value from railing against the use of the toga by ordinary people in Carthage in his speech in favour of the *pallium*, incidentally at one point also giving us his impression of the many areas of life in which the toga was still worn in his day:[109]

> So much in defence of the pallium, in so far as you libelled it by name. But now it makes an appeal on account of its activity. 'I owe nothing to the forum,' it says, 'nothing to the Campus Martius, nothing to the Senate-house. I do not watch for a magistrate's function, do not occupy any platform for speakers, do not attend

to the governor's office; I do not smell the gutters, nor adore the bar in court, nor wear out benches, nor disturb proceedings, nor bark pleas; I do not act as a judge, a soldier, or a king: I have withdrawn from public life.'

De pall. 5.4.1–2, trans. Hunink 1995

The extent to which the toga was worn from the third century onward and beyond Italy in the provinces are subjects for later chapters, but the fact that it figured as largely as it did in both only adds to the overall impression of its widespread and enduring importance in Roman life. Far from being a mere 'Bildformel', or elite fad of the Augustan era, the toga was, in fact, central to what it meant to be Roman.

Freedmen

The idea that the toga played an important role in the self-definition of Roman freedmen, especially in the late Republic and early Empire, is not new: from Susan Treggiari's and Diana Kleiner's ground-breaking studies of the 1960s and 1970s[110] to more recent work by Lauren Hackworth Petersen,[111] in the past half-century scholars have increasingly recognized the importance of this class for understanding Roman society, as well as the role that self-presentation played for them.[112] It is thus somewhat baffling that previous studies of the toga have tended to focus so squarely on the elite. The large numbers of slaves who came to Rome and its environs as a result of expansion, especially to the east, in the mid–late Republic, and their subsequent manumission and bestowal with Roman citizenship, constituted a seismic shift in Roman demographics; and the fact that many of them became quite successful in trade and commerce – sectors traditionally spurned by the elite[113] – resulted in a certain amount of status anxiety amongst the freeborn population.[114] This is typified most memorably in Petronius' *Satyricon*, with its characterization of the central character Trimalchio as an ostentatious and comically insecure *nouveau riche* freedman. But, as Hackworth Petersen has argued, to see the freed class through 'Trimalchio vision' is to side with the Roman elite, resulting in a failure to appreciate the achievements and characteristics of this group of people in their own right, as well as the considerable obstacles they encountered.[115] If we leave Petronius and the elite to one side, it becomes clear that although Roman 'freedmen art' tended to borrow its status symbolism, especially in dress, from those higher up in society, its main aim was to assert an identity in relation not to the elite, but to other *liberti*.

Large family funerary monuments provided a perfect means by which freedpeople could display their hard-won status and achievements. Officially, they had no ancestry, and the right to marry legally and to bear legitimate and freeborn children was a much-valued new privilege that was manifested in funerary art in the form of family portraits. The very earliest phase of 'freedmen art', as collected by Kleiner, was characterized by relief family portraits in which all figures were depicted in the style of known statue types,[116] with most men depicted in the toga 'armsling style'.[117] Nonetheless, there were also individual depictions of freedmen in this style, some of whom, incidentally, were from professions quite far down the occupational hierarchy, such as the actor C. Fundilius Doctus complete with *scrinium* at his feet from near the Temple of Diana at Nemi.[118]

Whilst the choice of the toga itself for these monuments is unsurprising as a symbol of freedom and citizenship, the choice of 'armsling' drapery, which by the latter part of this period was distinctly old-fashioned, is somewhat curious. Various scholars have posited explanations: Kleiner saw it as reflecting an inherent conservatism in the freed class;[119] Davies views it from a body-language perspective and argues that it expresses subordination and the idea that 'one knows ones place';[120] Giuliani and Hertel have argued that it signalled restraint, modesty and *antiqua severitas* to which, as a result of their background, freedmen were more likely to be attracted.[121] German scholarship tends, as so often, to emphasize the eastern connection, arguing that the fact that the 'armsling' style copying the drapery of the Greek *pallium* came to Rome in precisely the era in which so many eastern slaves were being manumitted was no coincidence.[122] Although it would be hard to believe, given their low status, that freed slaves were responsible for the introduction of the fashion to Rome, it is more than likely that easterners would have felt particularly at home in a drapery style that so closely resembled what they wore earlier in their lives, and this may indeed have contributed to its popularity. Rothfus has argued that the new, fuller, *umbo* style of toga of the Augustan era was deliberately designed to visually elevate the elite, and as such was out of bounds for freedmen,[123] but it is difficult to see how this could have been policed; in any case, it didn't last long, as freedmen were already wearing the new style of toga on their gravestones by the reign of Tiberius.[124] None of the factors suggested above are mutually exclusive, and it seems likely that a combination of them was responsible for the popularity of the 'armsling' style with late Republican and early Imperial freedmen.

The *toga praetexta* also played a central role in early funerary portraits of freed families. It is often worn by the children,[125] typically accompanied by a

Figure 4.3 Funerary relief of a family. Chiaramonti Museum, Vatican Museums. Photo: Agnete/Wikimedia Commons.

bulla, and the symbolism in this context is clear: as the privilege of freeborn children,[126] the *toga praetexta* and *bulla* stood for the legitimacy of the marriage and its resulting children, as well as the upward status trajectory of the family in the next generation.[127] It is for this reason that some portraits show the children almost full-figure when the rest of the family is depicted half-figure (Fig. 4.3).[128] It is also the reason why almost all of the images we have of boys wearing *togae* and *bullae* are either members of the imperial household or children of *liberti*. The importance of the garment attested in funerary art suggests that some children of freed parents would have possessed togas in real life to wear in public, perhaps on special occasions.[129] We may also assume, despite the lack of paintwork, that the togas worn by freedmen who were *seviri Augustales* were originally *toga praetextae*, because, as mentioned earlier in this chapter, membership of this new priesthood opened the door to this prestigious garment. The image given by Petronius of Trimalchio's chosen funerary depiction, in which he wears a *toga praetexta* (he was a *sevir*) and several finger-rings, sits on a tribune and hands out cash (*Sat.* 71.9.), is intended to come across as hilariously over the top, but the real-life monuments of freedmen *seviri*, such as those of Sex. Titius Primus from Ancona[130] and Asiaticus from Brescia,[131] are far from vulgar, displaying instead a quiet dignity in their portrayal of the men as stern figures, wearing their togas with grace and dutifully engaging in pious or euergetistic activities. The fact that Roman freedmen tended to deliberately include mention of their libertine status in their funerary inscriptions shows that they were not ashamed of it, and their use of a specific and almost repetitive repertoire of status symbols, of which various toga types formed a central part, reveals not an absurd aspiration to an elite lifestyle but proud membership of a group of successful peers who managed to take full advantage of the limited opportunities at their disposal.

'The dark side of the toga'

One everyday activity in which large numbers of Roman men were involved and which required the wearing of the toga was the *salutatio*: the morning visit of clients to the house of the patron.[132] Clients were also expected to accompany the patron – often in a litter – through the city and give vocal support in law courts and political assemblies (Juv. 7.141–143). For all of these activities, clients were expected to wear a toga, and this could constitute a considerable imposition, one that some clients could barely afford: the 'dark side of the toga', as coined by Michele George in 2008.[133]

It is especially in the works of Martial and Juvenal that we get an insight into this from the clients' perspective. In humorous and often poignant anecdotes, we learn, first of all, what a financial burden it could be to buy and maintain a presentable toga. Although some patrons evidently bought them for their less wealthy clients (Mart. 10.29; 12.36), it seems that clients were more commonly expected to buy their togas themselves, for example from the *sportula* – the money handed out to them by their patrons on a regular basis. The satirists unsurprisingly characterize this as a pittance and hardly worth the effort.[134] Martial tells us that it was barely enough to cover the necessities of life – listed as a toga, the rent, entrance to the bathhouse and a prostitute's fee (3.30)[135] – and suggests some clients actually got into financial difficulty trying to pay for their togas (7.10.11).[136] At one point he addresses his patron directly:

> You give me three *denarii* and tell me, Bassus, to come to your place in the morning, wearing a toga; then to stay by your side, walk in front of your chair, and accompany you on your visits to ten widows, more or less. My poor toga is worn and cheap and old, but, Bassus, I didn't buy it for three *denarii*.
>
> 9.100

But the toga was not just a financial imposition: it was also a physical one. It was difficult to walk in, very heavy and hot in warm weather and as a white garment was almost impossible to keep clean on the dirty streets of Rome, especially if one had to go on foot (Mart. 8.28; 9.49; 12.18.5). Martial paints a colourful picture of the discomfort and humiliation a trip to the patron could entail:

> I must climb the road up from Subura with its dirty stones and wet steps, and I can barely get through the long trains of mules and marble blocks being hauled by ropes. What is worse: worn out after a thousand labours, Paulus, I am told by your slave that you are not home. This is all I have to show for my vain efforts and my soaked little toga (*togula madentis*).
>
> 5.22.5–12[137]

The toga became so closely associated with the travails of patronage that the word '*togatus*' was sometimes used as a synonym for 'client' (e.g. Juv. 7.141–143; Mart. 2.74; 10.10; 10.19; 10.74), and Martial refers to the duties of the client as *opera togata* – toga work – adding that, like the empire granted to the *gens togata* in the *Aeneid*, it was *sine fine* (3.46.1). For both Martial and Juvenal, one of the joys of leaving Rome for the countryside was not having to endure the toga and the obligations it entailed (Mart. 10.51.6; 12.18.17–18; Juv. 3.171–172). This is the reason why Martial, when making fun of people trying to get gifts out of a tight-fisted patron, says: 'Oh Rome, how foolish are your togas!' (10.18).

Naturally, in the anecdotes related here some details would have been exaggerated for comic purposes, but for them to have had the desired effect, they must also have contained a grain of truth. We can, therefore, accept in good faith that clients wore togas for the *salutatio* and that poorer clients would have struggled to buy and maintain them. Thus, at the hands of satirists like Martial and Juvenal, the dignified toga is transformed into an instrument of subjugation and indignity for a class of people who were too well-off to be able to eschew the toga, but too poor to maintain and wear it without hardship and inconvenience. For some the toga could, in other words, be both a privilege and a burden.

Imperfect togas

In ancient Rome status distinctions were often also reflected in the material, shape and condition of the toga itself. Because our main mental image of the garment comes from gleaming white marble statuary, it can be difficult to envisage the many dirty and shabby togas that would have been visible on the streets of Rome at any given time. Due to the nature of the genre, it is mainly in satirical works that we get an insight into this, and they abound with references to togas in various qualities and states of decay. In a passage already cited above, Martial describes his own toga as worn (*trita*), cheap (*vilis*) and old (*vetus*) (9.100), and Juvenal, lamenting the fact that people in Rome had become preoccupied with wealth at the expense of character, says of a poor man:

> Then what do you make of the fact that the same man provides everyone with the material and cause for amusement when his outdoor cloak (*lacerna*) is dirty and ripped (*foeda et scissa*), when his toga is grubby (*sordidula*) and when one shoe is gaping where the leather has torn?
>
> 3.147–151

Martial also describes dirty togas, including one that was 'filthier than mud' (*sordidior caeno*) (7.33; 6.50), and indeed many people's togas must have had a grimy appearance, not just because of their impractical white colour, but also because washing them worsened their condition and removed the colour of any details like borders (see Mart. 10.11.6). Martial's frequent use of the adjective *trita* (e.g. 2.46; 2.58; 3.36; 9.100; 12.72) to describe the togas of the less well-off is especially interesting, as it reminds us that they eventually became threadbare and worn from over use. Even his own beloved toga, the splendour and whiteness of which he described in such extravagant detail when it was first given to him by a wealthy friend (8.28),[138] went the way of all things:

> This is the toga much sung of in my little books, the one my readers got to know and love. Once upon a time it was Parthenius' toga. . . . I used to go about in it . . . when it was new and its bright and shimmering wool shone (*nitida fulgebat splendida lana*), when it was worthy of its giver's name. Now it is an old woman not even worthy of a rickety pauper. Now it is in every sense '*nivea*'.[139] Days, years, what do you not destroy? This toga is no longer Parthenius's. It is mine.
>
> 9.49

Another word used by Martial to describe a worn-out toga is '*pallens*' (e.g. Mart. 9.57): although ostensibly meaning 'pale', in the context of this passage, in which things are described as having become shiny with wear, it could relate to a sheen on the surface of the textile caused by rubbing through a long period of use. Togas could also acquire holes, either through wear and tear or moths (e.g. Mart. 2.43; 2.46), and less wealthy citizens would have had no choice but to patch and repair them.

There are several other reasons why the well-to-do would have been able to take to the streets in smarter-looking togas than those lower down the social scale: added to the expense of buying a toga was that of being able to maintain it properly, which ideally involved, according to Tertullian, a slave (*vestiplicus*) to make sure the folds were correct using tools – '*tabulae*' and '*forcipes*' – to dress the person so that the toga hung correctly, and to hang it up at the end of the day on a special cross-shaped stand.[140] (One's mind inevitably turns to the way in which until relatively recently European aristocratic clothes required servants to put them on.) In the absence of such a *vestiplicus*, the requisite equipment and the space to hang such a large garment, many togas would have ended up shoved into chests and cupboards and may have appeared creased and worn as a result. Moreover, wealthier citizens could afford to have several togas, including perhaps workaday ones and 'Sunday bests', whilst poorer people could only afford to own one at any given time, as the Martial passage above illustrates.[141]

A toga that was poorly draped could also give someone away as low in status, either because they could not afford the fine cloth that hung well, or the *vestiplicus* to help them put it on properly, or indeed because they came from a social background in which less time was dedicated to learning how to arrange it and move in it gracefully. Social status is also reflected in the degree of dignity with which the sari is draped and worn in modern India. In Banerjee and Miller's study, one woman's aunt said to her: 'Piya, darling, why do you tie your sari so high, you might get mistaken for the maid!'[142] Davies has recently argued that the body language and comportment in which elite Roman boys were trained throughout their childhood constituted an important part of the way their high status was conveyed to those around them.[143] Central to this was, of course, the 'correct' way of wearing the toga.[144] Horace several times describes the attributes of a poor man as a bad haircut and an ill-fitting, badly draped toga (*Epist.* 1.1.94–97; *Sat.* 1.3.31–32).

But of course, again like the modern business suit, the quality of a toga also depended on the material it was made from in the first place, and from the written evidence it is clear that togas could come in a wide variety of fabrics. On the one hand, Horace, for example, writes of a 'fine' (*tenua*) toga (*Epist.* 1.14.32), Ovid of a toga 'of the finest thread' (*filo tenuissima*: *Am.* 3.445) and Martial of a particularly desirable toga as 'smooth' (*levis*: 7.86). On the other, the cheaper togas of poorer people are described as *crassa* ('coarse') and darker in colour ('*pulla*').[145] As discussed in Chapter 2, the quality of the wool had a lot to do with where it came from, and Martial writes of a fine toga that was 'washed in warm Galaesus' (4.28), a river that flows into the Gulf of Tarentum – a region which produced some of the most prized wool in antiquity (see Livy 25.11).[146]

Finally, the size and shape of the toga were also indicators of status: only the very wealthiest Romans would have been able to afford the massive togas on display in monuments like the Ara Pacis, and the larger and more involved the drapery was, the more skill, practice and ultimately dedicated education was required to wear it. As mentioned above, none of those worn in everyday life scenes like the forum friezes in Pompeii are particularly large. But we also have reason to believe that the togas of poorer citizens could sometimes be particularly small. Several authors use the term '*togula*',[147] and although it is clear that this was sometimes simply a term of affection, in Cicero's speech against Piso, lictors don '*togulae*' to appear inconspicuous and humble (23.55) and in Martial, '*togulae*' are primarily associated with poor people and stingy presents.[148] We get some rare glimpses of particularly small togas in secondary figures on a handful of monuments, like the flute player in the sacrificial scene on the arch of Marcus Aurelius,[149] one of the figures on the *Liberalitas* panel on the Arch of Constantine[150] and a man and his son on a sarcophagus in the Louvre.[151] These appear similar in dimension to the *trabeae* of Roman equestrians in *transvectio* scenes (see the earlier section on this), but presumably their colour and decoration would have been different, a detail lost to us because we do not have the original paintwork. For all we know from our elite-centred evidence, smaller togas may in fact have been a relatively common sight on the streets of Rome.

The insights we gain from the satirists and the handful of artworks mentioned above as to the different possible sizes and qualities of the toga are immensely valuable because they allow us to see another world beyond the large, cumbersome togas of elite artworks. More importantly, the fact that such variations existed at all means that there must have been a correspondingly wide spectrum of social status groups wearing them.

The status game

The discussion hitherto has followed a predominantly linear trajectory from the most prestigious togas to the most ordinary, but of course in a social system as complex as that of Rome, things weren't always quite so simple, and again it is the works of the satirists, with their emphasis on the less edifying aspects of Roman society, that shed light on the subtler nuances. For example, as well as being a sign of high breeding, a large, conspicuously white toga could, in the wrong hands, also be a sign of low birth coupled with new wealth.[152] Martial describes a rich parvenu wearing a toga that was so ridiculously white that it 'outdid untrodden snow' (2.29), and in one of his *Epodes*, Horace berates an ostentatious freedman for his oversized toga: 'Do you see how, as you strut down the Via Sacra in your toga that is six *ulnae* wide, people turn to face you with the utmost indignation?'

(*Epod.* 4.7). As we saw in the previous section, poorer folk were mocked by the satirists for their deficient clothing; but they were also subject to ridicule if they dressed too well. The margin of acceptable dress choice appears from these authors to have been vanishingly small for those who could not fall back on high birth to give them standing, but acceptability was very much in the eye of the beholder. For learned men like these writers who socialized with the elite but had to rely on patronage to earn their way, it is not hard to see how the sight of an uneducated freedman in fine clothes could be vexing. As the son of a freedman himself, it is perhaps surprising that Horace is often the least forgiving in this respect. In a letter to Lollius, he relates an anecdote in which a man criticizes a client for attempting to copy his high-quality dress; the patron says, 'Do not compete with me. Whilst my wealth allows for stupidity, your means are small. A narrow (*arta*) toga befits a sensible (*sanus*) client' (*Epist.* 1.18.28–31). High-born people fallen on hard times did not escape the satirists' attention either: Juvenal tells of an old impoverished nobleman who hired expensive clothes to give the impression of continued wealth when he went to the theatre (6.350–352).

On the other hand, satirical writers also held in contempt those who dressed below their means. For example, Horace wrote disapprovingly of a rich miser who hid his money away and dressed like a slave (*Sat.* 1.1.95–97), and in Martial we find a similar story of a newly wealthy man who dressed in a dirtier (*sordidior*) toga than before (1.103). Evidently, at least in the eyes of people like Horace and Juvenal, there was a very fine line between the conspicuous plainness of the wealthy and miserly appearance on the one hand, and dressing with dignity and appearing ostentatious on the other.[153] Naturally, when in their works these same authors wear shabby clothes themselves, it is invariably associated with virtue and integrity. Martial, for example, rebukes someone for laughing at his threadbare toga, saying that at least he paid for it himself (2.58), and in another passage he tells his readers that if they can be content with a modest toga like his, they can live a life free from obligation and clientship (2.53).[154] It is clear that even within the confines of the toga-wearing demographic, the Roman fixation with status meant that there were numerous potential pitfalls in choosing how to dress, as well as an infinite number of views on what was acceptable.

Tunicatus populus

For the final section of this chapter, we turn to a group of people who did not wear the toga. Whilst it may seem strange to devote space in a study of the toga to its absence, in this case its absence speaks volumes about what the toga itself represented. In 1982, Gerhard Zimmer published a woefully under-cited study of 200 Roman workshop scenes from funerary monuments, votive stones and shop signs in central and northern Italy.[155] In it, he highlighted among other things the curious fact that the men in such scenes, even when they constituted the main portrait, tended to wear a *tunica* on its own without a toga or other cloak. We have, of course, already established that the toga was an unsuitable garment for physical activity, and it may seem logical that the dress chosen for men depicted at work in their *fabricae* was the ubiquitous and practical tunic, but the stones themselves suggest there was more to it than that. To start with, the choice of a work scene as a main portrait is remarkable in itself, and reveals a mentality in which hard work and successful enterprise formed the main element of the identity and self-worth of those commemorated. Moreover, it was a dress choice that emerged in a particular period (the early–mid first century), before which men of the artisan class were usually depicted in togas.[156] In the workshop scenes in which the men wear tunics, the wives of such men are often depicted in the workshop as well, but dressed in fine clothes with elaborate hairstyles showing that realism was not the main object of the exercise (Fig. 4.4).[157] Finally, the *tria nomina* in the inscriptions for these monuments, when extant, reveal that they were Roman citizens, and thus allowed to wear the toga.[158] In other words, it is clear that these people made a conscious decision to have themselves depicted *in the tunica* and *at work*, rather than in a toga like most other grave portraits hitherto.

So who were these people and what did their dress choice mean? The range of occupations represented (e.g. butchers, bakers, carpenters, shipbuilders, stonemasons, surveyors, potters and shoemakers) reveals them to belong to a class of skilled artisans who would normally have run their own operations from fixed workshop locations in city centres, and were thus a cut above mere unskilled day labourers and those engaged in the most strenuous work.[159] A third of the monuments for which the legal status is clear involve freeborn people, whilst for the rest it is either stated or strongly implied in their Greek names that they are freedpeople.[160] Of some significance is also the fact that these monuments all date to the period from the early–mid first century to the end of the second century CE: this was a period of exceptional stability and economic prosperity, and one in which savvy and hard-working people could expect to do well.[161] Taking these factors together, a picture emerges in which, in contrast to the 'first wave' of *liberti*, who in their grave monuments were so keen to show off their freedom and citizenship in their togas, and who, as outlined in a previous section, derived their status markers, like the *toga praetexta* and *bulla*, from the elite,

Figure 4.4 Funerary relief of a potter and his wife. Virginia Museum of Fine Arts, Richmond. Adolph D. and Wilkins C. Williams Fund. Photo: Katherine Wetzel ©Virginia Museum of Fine Arts.

many later freedmen were absorbed into a wider artisanal class in which such distinctions no longer signified.[162] Free or freed, what mattered to these people was membership of a class of small businessmen, where respect was derived from hard work and commercial success.[163] These are the people Tacitus and other authors had in mind when they referred to ordinary Romans as the *tunicatus populus*;[164] for Zimmer they represent the Roman 'middle class', and the tunic was their 'standesspezifische Tracht'.[165]

Numerous subsequent studies have established similar scenarios in related bodies of evidence, such as Amedick's 1991 work on the so-called *vita privata* sarcophagi and Joshel's on occupational inscriptions (1992). However, much of the discussion surrounding the pride in work evidenced in the monuments of the artisan class assumes these people still looked to the elite for confirmation, such as, for example, the idea that occupation was used as an inferior proxy for real social standing,[166] or that pride in one's business resulted from having wealthy elite customers and patrons.[167] Those very few funerary depictions that show (wealthy?) togate customers buying their goods from tunicate artisans are far more likely to be pointing to the quality of the products (i.e. respectable people pay good money for them), rather than any kind of desperate attempt to connect themselves socially with the elite.

What the monuments under discussion here, with their eschewing of the toga, show us is that this group of people had constructed a parallel world for themselves, in which it was membership of the group that mattered, not their relation to the elite. It is no coincidence that the period covered by these monuments was also one which saw a massive increase in the number, size and importance of professional *collegia*.[168] For our tunic-clad artisans, membership of such colleges bestowed not just respectability and a sense of belonging, but also the ability to exert indirect but real political power in their own terms. These monuments are testimony to the limits of the power of the toga. They remind us not only that not everyone wore a toga, but also that by the second century CE, significant numbers of citizens no longer wanted to.

Conclusion

The toga embodies the fundamental paradox at the heart of Roman society: whilst as a general garment it symbolized the unity and equality of the citizen body that comprised the *res publica*, its more elaborate forms reflect the fact that throughout Roman history, some men were considered to be above their fellow citizens, even if in many cases this was on a temporary and heavily controlled basis. The demarcation and enactment of an intricate ladder of ranks and honours was, in fact, fundamental to Roman self-definition. Moreover, the different types of toga that reflected these ranks and honours were actively used as tools to enforce power relations and even to influence behaviour: it is only in this context that we can understand the *laena*'s alleged ability to quell a riot, or the immense significance of Tryphon's and Caesar's assumption of the *toga purpurea*, or the outrage generated by attacks on men wearing *togae praetextae*. It is also the reason why Polybius went into such detail in his description of the elite Roman funeral: the different types of toga worn by actors in the procession served not only to reflect the honours achieved by the family itself, but also to provide a visual representation of the codified power which all citizens should respect, and to which all young men should aspire.

But the significance of the garment for status distinctions was not confined to the elite, as most recent scholars assume. The central importance of citizen status, especially to the earliest waves of freedpeople, meant that it served as an important symbol of their newfound respectability and the potential for upward status mobility of their children. And for the wider Roman population, the fact that the toga was requisite dress for certain jobs and occasions meant that rather than there being a clearly demarcated toga-wearing class, the members of which always wore the toga, and a non-toga-wearing one, whose members never did, there were, in fact, a whole host of gradations in between. For every elite statesman who wore the toga at all times in public (even – in the case of Cicero – to the bathhouse), there would have been a multitude of men like Martial's friend Linus who only dragged their dusty old togas out when the occasion demanded it. As the work scenes collated by Zimmer show, however, by the second century, some non-elite men were also deliberately formulating an alternative sartorial language to that of the toga and expressing pride in the values it symbolized. Finally, the copious literary evidence for the vast array of qualities, sizes and states of repair in which the toga could appear when worn by real people means that rather than seeing it merely as the idealized garment of an exclusive class, we instead need to view it as a dynamic, everyday object that embodied a whole host of nuanced status distinctions for a significant number of Roman men, and could be employed or rejected depending on context and personal preference.

5

The Toga and Politics

Roman politics was a world of spectacle. From the bombast and drama of debate in the Republican senate to the stage-managed public appearances of the Roman emperors, the visual element was always key. Emblematic objects, special garments and symbolic acts were crucial to the enactment of state procedures and the way political discourse was conducted. Accordingly, dress – and as the garment of public business this meant the toga – played a central role in Roman political life; so important, in fact, that many aspects of its use were closely regulated by senatorial or consular decree, even several generations into imperial rule.

The toga could be used in political iconography, such as in Republican coinage where a figure of a togate man was used to symbolize the Roman citizen body,[1] but also in political discourse itself: the highly visual nature of dress and clothing gestures meant that they were deliberately employed by key players in major political events, or at least the way these were later narrated by biographers. According to Plutarch, for example, on the day he was assassinated, Gaius Gracchus deliberately set out for central Rome dressed in a toga to signal his reluctance to fight (Plut., *C. Gracch.* 15.1), whilst in the case of his brother Tiberius' death some years earlier, his opponent Scipio Nasica symbolized the beginning of combat by winding his toga around his head and exclaiming, 'everyone who wants to uphold the laws (τοῖς νόμοις βοηθεῖν) follow me!' (Plut., *Ti. Gracch.* 19.3–4);[2] in this way he could be seen to be arming himself not with weapons but with the rule of law. The toga also plays a part in accounts of Caesar's assassination: in Suetonius, Cimber's grabbing of Caesar's toga signals the beginning of the violence (*Iul.* 82.1), whilst Valerius Maximus' almost panegyric narrative describes Caesar's final moments thus:

> At the very moment when his divine spirit was departing from his mortal body, not even his twenty-three stab wounds could deter him from obeying the laws of decency. With both hands he pushed his toga down so that the lower part of his

body was covered as he collapsed to the ground. This is the gesture not of a mortal man dying, but an immortal god returning home.

4.5.6

According to Quintilian, Caesar's blood-spattered toga would go on to be used by Mark Antony to elicit anger at his death from the crowd (*Inst.* 6.2), and indeed the blood-stained toga became almost a *topos* of Roman civil strife, symbolizing, as it did, the incongruity of violence and civic order. In Plutarch, for example, Pompey's wife miscarries when she sees his bloodied toga[3] (Plut., *Pomp.* 53.3), and in Prudentius, the blood-stained toga is used to symbolize civil war itself, when he expresses the wish that Rome never again 'tolerate the staining of the togas of great men with smoke and blood' (*C. Symm.* 1.1–8).

Whether or not the stories discussed above represent *topoi* rather than reality, it is clear that the toga did indeed play an important role in real political life in Rome. As discussed in Chapter 3, the dress code for political assemblies, court hearings and other official civic occasions, was, for most of Roman history, the toga. In Chapter 4 we saw how the different magistracies were symbolized in specific types and colours of toga. But there were also more subtle and ad hoc messages for which the toga was used and it became a powerful tool in the hands of Roman statesmen in the way they conducted themselves in the political sphere. This, roughly chronological, chapter will follow the development of the toga as a political symbol from the Republic to the third century in a range of areas of state life, including political assemblies and meetings, the behaviour of key parties in the context of civil unrest, the image management programmes of political figures and the courtroom, which became a political space when important state figures were involved.

Political uses

In the Republic, there was a whole range of political occasions on which the wearing of a special toga was a matter of protocol. Men standing for any political office, for example, wore a toga that, rather than being the normal off-white of the *toga pura*, was bleached or coloured extra white, apparently using chalk according to Isidore of Seville (*Etym.* 19.24.6). It was called a *toga candida*, whence the Latin term *candidatus* and its variants in later European languages, and it signalled the candidate's political intentions whilst also rendering them a focal point when canvassing.[4] Although we don't know much about what it entailed, the whitening process evidently involved some cost, so it was one of the core expenses of any political campaign, and had to be arranged at short notice when the decision to stand for office was made on the spur of the moment (see, e.g., Polyb. 10.4–5). Whilst Persius referred poetically to the striving for political glory as *cretata ambitio* – 'chalky ambition' (5.177), it would seem that the phrase *in toga candida* was also commonly used in more prosaic literary settings as shorthand for a period of political campaigning, such as when Pliny describes Scipio Nasica as having experienced defeat twice '*in toga candida*' (*HN* 7.120), and more famously in Cicero's lost election campaign speech *Oratio in Toga Candida*, in which he first hinted at the secret manoeuvrings of Catiline. In keeping with the visual drama of Roman political life, a *toga candida* could also be physically discarded in public to signal abandonment of one's election campaign (e.g. Val. Max. 4.5).[5]

From Plutarch we learn that at some early stage in the Republic, candidates for political office had also appeared in public in the toga without a tunic. This forms the basis of one of his moral questions, to which the answer, he suggests, is one of three possibilities: either they wished to show that bribery money couldn't be hidden on their person, or it allowed them to draw political capital from showing off war scars, or it was simply a sign of humility (*Quaest. Rom.* 49).[6] The same author also tells us that tribunes refrained from wearing *togae praetextae* like other magistrates because they wanted to show, through their normal togas, their affinity with the people they represented, although as this is not mentioned elsewhere it is impossible to say whether it was general practice (*Quaest. Rom.* 81).

Another special type of toga that was required on certain occasions was the *toga pulla*. The main characteristic of this garment was its dark appearance, but it is unclear exactly what colour it was.[7] *Pullus* was an adjective associated with poverty, and the humility and lack of self-care associated with it meant that it was the main garment associated with mourning.[8] It had a religious connection by being the dress worn for the annual festival of the dead (Parentalia) (Lydus, *Mens.* 4.29), and it was a matter of protocol usually decreed by the senate to don it ('*vestem mutare*') for periods of public bereavement, such as the passing of a respected statesman, or in the time of Augustus the deaths of his sister and grandsons.[9] If what Cicero says is correct, it was, however, only supposed to be worn to the actual burial, as he is able to attack a political opponent (the tribune Vatinius) for appearing at both the funerary banquet and in the Temple of Castor still dressed *pullatus* (*Vat.* 30–32). *Vestis mutatio* did not only apply to the *toga pulla*; as a ritualized 'dressing down', it could mean, for example, that magistrates temporarily eschewed the *toga praetexta* for the plain *toga pura*, such as when the state was in mourning for Augustus (Dio Cass. 56.31.2), or that the opportunity to wear triumphal garb was passed up in favour of the simpler *toga praetexta*, as practised by Tiberius to mark the loss of Varus' legions (Suet., *Tib.* 12.2). After a *vestis mutatio* had been declared, it could only be terminated by a formal act of the senate or consul (Cic., *Sest.* 32).

The symbolism of *vestis mutatio* was applied to times of national emergency as well, and this again involved a senatorial decree, although the cloak one usually changed into on such occasions was the military *sagum*, hence the official term '*saga sumere*'. Again, rather than being a simple matter of appropriate dress code, the practice was central to the way political crises were managed and responses to current events debated and formulated, as a passage in Cicero's *Philippics* demonstrates:

> Members of the Senate, the dispatches which have been read out have told me that an army of very wicked enemies has been cut to pieces and routed. If those dispatches had also told me that Decimus Brutus has already been liberated from the siege of Mutina, . . . then I would have no hesitation in moving a return to our previous dress. . . . But until the news which the community is so impatiently awaiting arrives, it is enough to enjoy the happy knowledge of a great and glorious battle. Reserve a return to normal dress for final victory. . . . What sort of proposal do we have here, that we change our dress only for today and reappear tomorrow in military cloaks? No, when once we have returned to the dress we want and pray for, let us make sure we keep it forever.
>
> Cic., *Phil.* 14.1–3, trans. Shackleton Bailey/Ramsay/Manuwald 2010

Both the *toga pulla* and the so-called *toga sordida* ('soiled, dirty') were also worn by the accused and their family in high-profile court cases to evoke sympathy,[10] a practice described as an '*institutum*' by Quintilian (*Inst.* 6.1.30). It could have even more rhetorical effect when lawyers like Cicero used it to paint a dramatic visual image of a person's change in circumstances, such as when in *Pro Sestio* he points to Lentulus in his mourning dress when only last year he had cut a resplendent figure as augur in his *toga praetexta* (144). But the use or not of the *toga pulla/sordida* in court was a matter that required careful navigation: the lack of it could be used as an effective symbolic assertion of innocence,[11] or as a sign that one was too stoical to stoop to such pathetic display (Cic., *Mil.* 101), but it could also be read as arrogance (Plut., *Cic.* 35).[12] The presiding judges at such trials also customarily engaged in staged sartorial drama when they reversed their toga ('*toga perversa*'[13]) or changed into a *toga pulla* before announcing a capital sentence, a gesture so powerful that on at least one occasion it caused the defendant to take his own life (Val. Max. 9.12.7).

Political protest

The institution of *vestis mutatio* could also be used in a more spontaneous manner to signal dissent at an action or situation. It could be used by anyone, from individual people, like the son of a disgraced statesman who used it to protest against his father's banishment (Diod. Sic. 36.16.1.),[14] to special interest groups as a means to lobby a particular case, like the propertied men who entered the forum in *togae pullae* to symbolize their opposition to the agrarian reforms of Tiberius Gracchus in 133 BCE (Plut., *Ti. Gracch.* 10.7). Earlier, in 169 BCE, leading men of the state (*principes civitatis*) had used it to contest their indictment and to entreat the common people to show mercy (Livy 43.16.14). The Senate also sometimes decreed *vestem mutare* as a means of protest, for example to express outrage at an infringement of its authority, and in such cases it came close to a declaration of national emergency, such as in 56 BCE when the plebeian tribune C. Cato vetoed elections to aid the cause of Pompey and Crassus (Livy, *Per.* 105; Dio Cass. 39.28.2). Unsurprisingly given the period of turmoil they cover, we find several instances of *vestis-mutatio*-as-dissent in the works of Cicero, such as in 58 BCE when his friends – amongst them even sitting magistrates – protested against a bill condemning to exile anyone who had been responsible for the execution of Roman citizens without trial, which was clearly aimed at Cicero for his suppression of the Catilinarian conspiracy (Cic., *Sest.* 26; *Red. Sen.* 12). On this occasion, the consuls apparently attempted to stifle the protest by forbidding the senators from changing their clothes, and this is the subject of a lengthy diatribe by Cicero that is informative of the political dimension of *vestis mutatio*:

> The citizen body, by public decree, had enacted *vestis mutatio*; in Italy there was no *municipium, colonia*, prefecture, society of tax collectors, club, association or council that had not passed a motion expressing concern for my welfare. Then, suddenly, the consuls decreed that the senators should return to usual dress. What consul ever prohibited the senate from obeying its own orders? What tyrant ever forbade the unfortunate to mourn? Are you not content, Piso (let alone Gabinius), that you have thwarted the public will by ignoring a decree of the senate, that you have belittled the views of the citizens, betrayed the republic, and brought shame on the office of consul? Do you dare to declare that people

should not lament my, their, the whole state's calamity? that they should not show their pain in their dress? Whether *vestis mutatio* is used to express individual grief or as an act of deprecation, what kind of person is so cruel as to prevent someone from mourning for himself or for others?

Sest. 32–33

Despite the obvious hyperbole, it is clear from this passage that in the practice of *vestem mutare*, the realms of private mourning and public calamity could be closely intertwined. Perhaps even more telling is the fact that the consuls felt the need to officially ban the act at all: it is further proof that what may on the surface appear as a purely symbolic undertaking could be feared to have real political consequences.

Diplomacy

Like domestic politics, Roman foreign policy was also characterized by symbolism and highly visual statements, and the toga also played a key role in the diplomatic sphere. In the Republic, and perhaps even as early as the sixth century BCE (Dion. Hal., *Ant. Rom.* 5.35.1), foreign dignitaries and kings were bestowed with a *toga picta* or *praetexta* as an honour and a sign that they were considered allies of the Roman people. Examples of this include the sending of a senatorial delegation in 210 BCE to Syphax of Numidia with gifts of an ivory chair, a tunic and a purple toga to thank him for his help in the war against Carthage (Livy 27.4), or the bestowal of the same, along with triumphal insignia, on Masinissa to keep him on side in the same conflict (Livy 31.11; see also 30.15). The sources make clear that the reason such togas were gifted, rather than, say, money or jewels, was because they were considered to be the highest honours the Roman senate, as a civic body, could conceive. It is possible that along with the idea of high honour, there was an element of political programme here as well: after all, Rome was a republic, and self-consciously so, and the recipients were petty monarchs. The custom of giving special togas to friendly foreign kings seems to have waned by the late Republic: when during the reign of Tiberius, Ptolemy of Numidia was given an ivory sceptre and *toga picta* by a senatorial delegate and greeted as 'king, ally and friend', Tacitus describes it as a revival of an old tradition ('*vetus mos*': Tac., *Ann.* 4.26). As King Prusias II's clothing gesture on his visit to Rome discussed in Chapter 1 (Polyb. 30.19.2–5) shows, foreign and client kings also themselves sometimes availed themselves of the toga to signal allegiance (if in this case with mixed success), and it appears to still have been common practice during the time of Augustus (Suet., *Aug.* 60).

Diplomacy sometimes also required more spontaneous action. One example of this is an anecdote recorded by Suetonius in which the first emperor is seen to display a remarkable degree of savoir-faire:

> As Augustus sailed past the bay of Puteoli, it happened that an Alexandrian ship had just arrived, and the passengers and sailors, dressed in white, crowned with garlands and offering incense, lavished him with praise and good wishes.... Augustus was gratified by this and gave forty gold pieces to each of his travelling companions, making them promise not to spend the money on anything other than goods from Alexandria. What's more, for the remaining days of his stay, he handed out togas and *pallia*, among other gifts, saying that the Romans should use the Greek dress and language and the Greeks the Roman.
>
> *Aug.* 98.4.1–3[15]

It is particularly interesting that here, the toga is considered to be on a par with the *pallium*, and the incident reveals a relaxed attitude to the fact that, whilst also inhabitants of the Roman Empire, the Alexandrians belonged to an 'other' cultural sphere, in which Greek dress and language held sway (see Chapter 6).

Political ideology

In the highly visual arena of Roman domestic politics, the toga – as the garment of Roman public life – was variously and frequently employed as a means to express political ideologies. In some cases, it was individual politicians who applied specific toga practices to communicate their doctrine or their stance on particular issues. Cato the Younger, for example, is famously said to have worn his toga in the old-fashioned way without a tunic underneath to symbolize his adherence to the *mos maiorum* (Plut., *Cato Min.* 44.1; Val. Max. 3.6.7),[16] whilst according to Sallust, during a famine riot in the early first century BCE, the consul C. Cotta donned the toga of mourning to address the plebs in order to communicate his sympathy with their plight (*Hist.* 2.47 A). The toga was also used by individuals for the opposite purpose: to lay claim to higher power. Tryphon's brazenly unlawful adoption of the *toga purpurea* to lead the rebellious slaves in the Second Servile War is a case in point (Diodorus 36.7.4), as is Julius Caesar's use of the same garment, along with the high red shoes of the Kings of Alba and the laurel crown, to assert his authority (Dio Cass. 43.43; 44.6.1; Cic., *Phil.* 2.85); in the latter case, the fact that he had acquired senatorial dispensation to appear as a king did not, in the end, stop him from being assassinated for that very reason: the *toga purpurea* was the outward visual manifestation of a personal political ideology that his assassins (rightly) considered a danger to the Republic.

In more general political struggles, the toga could find itself at the centre of negotiations between conflicting factions, as was the case in the fifth century BCE, when (at least according to Livy) the apparently expensive process of rendering a toga *candida* was declared by the plebs to be an unfair advantage of wealthier patricians when canvassing, and the tribunes proposed a law 'prohibiting anyone from whitening their toga to announce themselves a candidate' (4.25.13). As late as the third century BCE the *toga candida* was subject to sumptuary legislation,[17] but it was evidently no longer an issue later on in the Republic, as Livy goes on to say: 'This may now seem like a trivial matter..., but at the time it caused considerable discord between patricians and plebs' (4.25.13).

As we have seen in previous chapters, Cicero used the symbolic properties of clothing to full rhetorical effect in his legal and political speeches to cast aspersions on his opponents' moral and political integrity,[18] like when he lambasted Verres' habit of dressing in Greek clothes whilst governor of Sicily,[19] or when he portrayed the allies of his political enemy Catiline as louche and effeminate because of their 'well-trimmed beards, sleeved tunics reaching to the ankles, and the fact that they wear mantles (*amicti*), not togas' (*Cat.* 2.10.22).[20] But the most significant role the toga played in the ideology of the late Republic was in Cicero's concept of the 'new man'.[21] Whereas traditionally in the Republic the tenor of political glory had related to pedigree and military prowess, Cicero promoted (to his own ends, of course) a new ideology of public virtue that centred on the skills and accomplishments of individuals in the civic domain. The dire political unrest of the era provided the perfect setting, allowing him to reinvent weaponry as a symbol of disorder and civil war, and contrast it with the toga as the symbol of peace and order.[22] A line of one of his poems reads

> *Cedant arma togae,*
> *concedat laurea laudi*
> ('Yield, ye arms, to the toga; to civic praises, ye laurels')
>
> *Pis.* 29.72–73, trans. Miller 1913

Cicero spoke of his major legal victories as if they were military ones and used the term *consul togatus*, i.e. non-military consul, to denote the pinnacle of public honour (e.g. *Cat.* 3.23). This ideology also allowed him to lay claim to the moral high ground for his treatment of the Catilinarian conspirators:

Aside from various other instances, did arms not yield to the toga when I led the state? The republic was never in more serious danger, stability was never more greatly needed. But on this occasion, as a result of my advice and diligence, the weapons quickly fell from the hands of these shameless citizens.... What achievements in war were ever so great? What triumph can compare?

Off. 1.77–78

Not everyone was convinced: in the section previous to the passage above, Cicero himself tells us that there were people who found his poem about arms yielding to the toga reprehensible, and some later Roman writers took a less than favourable stance toward his claims to innocence, his use of political cases as proxy military victories and, indeed, the quality of his poetry;[23] but, on the whole, the idea that a well-rounded career could consist mainly or wholly of accomplishment in the civic sphere persisted and was forever associated with Cicero (see, e.g., Juv. 8.237–243; Pliny, *HN* 7.117). Valerius Maximus, for example, frequently employed the sartorial metaphor of the toga (standing for the senate and as such legitimate power) as opposed to weapons (standing for that bestowed by the army) in his narrative of Republican history (e.g. 8.15.1), claiming at one stage both that Scipio Nasica earned as much glory in the toga as either of the Africani did with their weapons (5.3.2e), and that 'bravery in the toga should be counted among military achievements, as courage deserves the same praise whether shown in the forum or the army camp' (3.17).

The 'togate' ideology of Cicero, of course, ultimately failed, and in the end it was real weapons in the hands of powerful individuals that decided the fate of the republic. But even here, it could come in handy in masking the extent of the changes that were befalling the state. In Republican coinage, for example, where traditionally mortal men had only rarely been depicted (the togate figure usually representing the whole citizen body[24]), the triumviral period saw the first contemporary political figures depicted, and the dress chosen by those who wished to appear peaceful and loyal to the state (however far this may have been from the truth) was the toga. The general Q. Cornuficius, for example, chose to have himself portrayed on coins togate rather than in the more obvious military dress (*RRC* 509/1–5). The sartorial imagery in Dio's portrayal of Mark Antony and his allies in the final days of the Republic provides a striking metaphor for what was to come:

For there was as yet no consul or praetor, and while Antony, in so far as his costume went, which was the purple-bordered toga, and his lictors, of whom he had only the usual six, and his convening of the senate, furnished some semblance of the republic, yet the sword with which he was girded, and the throng of soldiers that accompanied him, and his very actions in particular indicated the existence of a monarchy.

42.27.1–2, trans. Cary 1916

Augustus' cultural revolution

The Augustan era saw the continuation, and in many ways intensification, of the use of the toga for ideological purposes. The restoration of social order was central to the *princeps*' programme of renewal after the chaos of the civil wars (in which, of course, he was heavily implicated), and according to Suetonius this manifested itself, among other things, in a number of directives relating to dress in public places. We already saw in the previous chapter that Augustus was said, at the sight of men in dark cloaks, to have cried out the lines from Vergil about the Romans as the *gens togata* (*Aen.* 1.282) and to have ordered that only men wearing togas be allowed in or near the forum (*Aug.* 40.5). His attempts to address the manner of viewing theatre and games that had, according to Suetonius, become 'shambolic and highly disordered' also included a strict seating code by gender and class, and he decreed that no one in a dark cloak (*pullatus*) should be allowed to sit in the centre of the auditorium (*Aug.* 44.1–2). (An unmistakable characteristic of the toga was its light colour, and it is clear that it is the required dress here.)

Whilst it is curious that we find no mention of these or any other clothing laws in the various *leges Iuliae*, we have no reason to doubt the basic veracity of Suetonius' account. In general terms, both the clothing laws and the invocation of the garment in Vergil's patriotic poem suggest that Augustus intended the toga to act as a symbol of renewed national pride, and its more widespread and regulated use was part of his vision to 'make Rome great again'.[25] It is no coincidence that in the same era, Horace, in his *Odes*, lists the toga as one of the main features of Roman national identity that Crassus' 'gone-native' soldiers have tragically forgotten (3.5.8–12).

But it was not just the wearing of the toga per se that was the focus of attention; the Augustan era heralded an entirely new type of toga as well: the large, double-layered style with *sinus* and pouch-like *umbo* (Fig. 2.3 E–G; Fig. 2.7).[26] Whilst most scholars agree that it must have been devised by Augustus or those in his inner circle,[27] the inspiration for its distinctive form has been a matter of some scholarly disagreement. Stone suggested it was influenced by the overfold of some *himation* statues,[28] whilst Hafner, Gabelmann and others have more convincingly argued the opposite: that it developed as a deliberate contrast to the more Hellenized 'armsling' form of toga, and thus represented both a means by which the elite could distinguish itself from the masses, and a conscious 're-Romanizing' of the garment as a focus of national pride.[29] Goette and Rothfus suggest the *sinus* was a nod to the double layering of the priestly *laena*,[30] through which the new toga would have acquired a sacred air, and in fact the pious element may have been twofold, as several scholars have pointed out: the *umbo* made it easier to loosen the toga out to draw it over the head for sacrifice.[31] Consequently, the new toga may plausibly be seen as going hand-in-hand both with Augustus' temple rebuilding programme[32] and the multitude of images in which Augustus and his family are depicted *capite velato*;[33] they were all part of a wider policy to restore the *pax deorum* after the transgressions of the civil wars. Like most things Augustan, however, the new toga was above all a shrewd political device: as Zanker has pointed out, it 'obviated entirely the delicate question of Augustus' political power and the problem of its visual expression'.[34] It also struck a delicate balance between the idea of a fresh new beginning and the restoration of the old ways.

The role of the toga in Augustus' cultural policy is best illustrated in the image programme of the Ara Pacis:[35] on it, associations with the *mos maiorum* and Rome's past are provided by figures like that of Aeneas sacrificing, bearded and in the archaic style of toga without a tunic (Fig. 1.1), and the *flamines maiores* in the south procession in their time-honoured *laenae* and *apex* headgear (Fig. 4.1). Several figures, including the priests on the small procession relief and several figures in the north and south friezes, wear the simpler Republican toga, whilst Augustus and his family and friends, including both male and female children, are depicted in the new one,[36] reflecting a desire – both sartorially and politically – to reconcile the old with the new.[37] The new togas are depicted with especially rich drapery, and it seems evident that the Ara Pacis was intended, among other things, to promote the new style of dress that symbolized the renewal of Roman society. The regeneration element is also evident in the copious vegetal ornamentation on all sides of the monument, the figure of Tellus on the back, and in the decision – a first in Roman public art – to depict entire families, including women and children, in what would have come across as natural and familiar poses.[38] It shows that, just as it was anchored in the past, the Ara Pacis was also oriented toward the future, and was intended to represent the dawn of a new Golden Age.[39]

The non-elite perspective is often overlooked in discussions of Augustus' renewal programme, especially those focusing on major public monuments like the Ara Pacis. But the messages contained in it and other similar monuments were intended for ordinary people as well: the depiction of the imperial family on the Ara Pacis, for example, created a visual *exemplum* for the copious legislation enacted by Augustus to regulate family life and promote fertility.[40] Whilst aimed primarily at the elite, their concrete stipulations would have had an effect on some non-elite people as well, and on even wider circles in the general ideological tone they conveyed. Augustus' clothing laws also had implications for wider society: for the man on the street, they would have both incentivized the wearing of the toga at public events, and led to greater visual segregation between those who were not allowed to wear the toga, such as slaves and *peregrini*, and those who were. Some scholars have argued that the development of the enormous new Augustan toga was aimed mainly at indulging the elite in elevating themselves above the masses,[41] but again it is important to remember the corollary of this for non-elite toga-wearers: in the first instance it would have had an 'othering' effect, demarcating the exclusive Augustan elite from those outside it. In this context, Roche's description of the advent of the man's suit in nineteenth-century Europe rings true for the Augustan toga as well: '[I]t was part of a new delineation of public space, it established distances, a code of human and social relations, and was all the more persuasive in that it developed an aesthetic' (1994: 231).

But like many manifestations of elite culture even now,[42] it is likely also to have inspired a more general pride in the dignity and splendour of the Roman state in both elite and non-elite circles.[43] It provided a structure for every man to understand the new world order and his place in it, whilst retaining a reassuring link with the past. Finally, it is not insignificant that the *umbo* toga, if perhaps not in its very largest forms, was nonetheless rapidly adopted by many in the wider population and ended up becoming the most common style on imperial-period gravestones of ordinary people, not just in Italy but across the empire.[44]

The imperial image

The tone set by Augustus continued throughout the first and early second centuries, and some later emperors even emulated his use of clothing laws to create a sense of order and propriety.[45] But in the political programme of the emperors, the toga became above all a means by which to manage public image. Our main sources for this – official iconography and biographical works – both come with their own interpretative problems in terms of the extent to which they reflect the real clothing worn by any given emperor; but they are interesting in their own rights, as they reflect, on the one hand, the image the emperor meant to convey, and on the other, the central role that clothing – and especially the toga – played in narratives surrounding the character and behaviour of imperial personages. In other words, at the very least, the reality they reflect is that of the symbolic power of the toga and the uses to which it could be put. The following seeks to draw out significant developments in these uses over time.

The way emperors and their family members chose to appear in public, particularly in the city of Rome, was a matter of some consideration. We know emperors sometimes changed their dress several times a day according to the occasion, and eventually there were people employed in the imperial household ('*supra veste*'/'*ad vestem*': *CIL* 6.3985; 6.5206) to oversee the different departments of the imperial wardrobe; the latter included the *vestis imperatoris privata* (*CIL* 6.8550), the *vestis publica* or *forensis* (*CIL* 6.5193) and the *vestis sacra* (*CIL* 13.3691). There were, correspondingly, different statue types in which emperors and their family members could be depicted, and these are conveniently listed by Pliny (*HN* 34.18–20) as togate, nude, in military armour, on horseback, in the *paenula* and in the guise of the Luperci.[46] All of these signified different personal qualities: the armoured statue military prowess, for example, and the nude statue heroic virtue. The toga statue portrayed the emperor as citizen and statesman, especially when used with the *adlocutio* gesture traditionally used for addressing an assembly.[47] When paired with *capite velato* it created an impression of the emperor as respectful of the gods.[48] What is often forgotten in discussions of imperial iconography, however, is that coins also represented an important 'picture-language'[49] through which emperors cultivated their image, and unlike statues they provided a means by which they could react relatively spontaneously to current events. Moreover, by virtue of their function, coins would have been viewed by most inhabitants of the empire on a regular basis. For people living outside the larger towns with their public statuary, they would have provided the main source for the image of the emperor.

Very few images of Augustus present him in military dress (such as the Prima Porta statue), and in keeping with his cultural programme and his desire to draw attention away from the monarchical flavour of his new regime, he was mostly represented as a modest and austere citizen in service to the state: the majority of extant statues of him from Italy show him in the toga *capite velato*[50] and much of his coin imagery shows him as a togate magistrate seated on a *sella curulis*.[51] The toga was so important to Augustus' self-image that he wore it even in scenes in which he addresses troops ('*adlocutio*': e.g. *BMC* Augustus 443) or receives barbarian children (e.g. *BMC* Augustus 492). However sceptical we might be about Augustan publicity in view of the political reality behind it, the image of Augustus as civilian and *primus inter pares* is the one that won through in posterity, and in Suetonius' early second-century biography of him he cuts a decidedly virtuous and simple-living figure:

> He deliberately wore normal clothes in the house, that his sister, wife, daughter or granddaughters had hand-made;[52] his togas were neither too tight nor too full, his purple stripe neither too narrow nor too broad, but his shoes were somewhat high-soled, to make him appear taller than he actually was. He always kept a toga outfit (*forensia*) and *calcei* handy in case of sudden and unexpected occasions.
>
> *Aug.* 73

The Julio-Claudian emperors appear largely to have continued the *Herrscherideal* created by Augustus. They are usually described as appearing in the *toga praetexta* at public events (Suet., *Cal.* 17.2; Dio Cass. 48.4.5; 56.31.3), which perpetuated the image of the emperor as elevated magistrate, but ironically also set in motion the process by which the garment gradually became a symbol of monarchy.[53] Triumphal dress was used very sparingly in the first dynasty, at least according to the written sources. Claudius, for example, is said to have eschewed it even when granted by *senatus consultum* for the rededication of the Theatre of Pompey, choosing the *toga praetexta* instead (Dio Cass. 60.6.9). (That said, in reality his perceived deficiencies as a commander figure led him to exploit the conquest of Britain for all it was worth with military busts and startling triumphal imagery.[54]) Julio-Claudian coinage tended to largely maintain the image of the emperor as citizen: frequent motifs included the togate emperor addressing a group of identically-clad citizens or addressing an individual togate citizen from a *sella curulis* (e.g. *BMC* Nero 136–138), in both cases asserting a direct relationship between emperor and *populus*.[55] *Adlocutio* scenes on coins also at this stage still depicted the emperor in a toga rather than military dress (e.g. *BMC* Caligula 33; Nero 124–126, 304; Fig. 5.1), presenting him as 'the representative of a civilian world of toga-clad citizens and interacting on their behalf with the soldiers'.[56]

Not all Julio-Claudian emperors were considered to have behaved in an ideal way, however, and dress plays a central role in the characterization of 'bad' and 'good' emperors in Suetonius' biographies (a pattern continued and amplified in the *Historia Augusta*). Tiberius' somewhat lukewarm attitude to his official role is symbolized in his frequent abandonment of the toga ('*patrius habitus*') for a

Figure 5.1 Reverse of a bronze *sestertius* of Nero from Rome. *BMC* Nero 122. Photo: Werner Forman Archive/Bridgeman Images.

pallium and sandals (*Tib*. 13.1) and Caligula's general depravity in his effeminate tunics and predilection for the *toga picta* (*Calig*. 52).[57] According to Dio, Nero's dress habits also revealed his true character: he is said to have received senators at his house wearing not the toga but the more leisurely *synthesis*, and then only one part of it (63.13), whilst on other occasions he besmirched the honour of the toga by wearing it to compete in chariot races (62.9.2).[58]

Julio-Claudian image management gave rise to a custom that continued into the second century in which imperial heirs were depicted in the toga (*praetexta*).[59] Likewise, in historical narrative from Augustus onward the bestowal of the *toga virilis* marks the beginning of such heirs' lives as public figures and rulers-in-waiting.[60] In the reign of Claudius this led to an éclat when under the influence of his wife Agrippina, the emperor's son and heir apparent, Britannicus, was passed over for the *toga virilis* in favour of his stepson Nero, setting the latter on course to become the next emperor, as Tacitus writes:

> In the consulate of Tiberius Claudius and Servius Cornelius, the *toga virilis* was prematurely bestowed on Nero so that he might be seen to be qualified for political life.... At the games in the Circus, put on to make him popular with the ordinary people, Britannicus rode past in the *toga praetexta* and Nero in triumphal clothing.

> The people could see the one in the dress of a general, the other in the dress of a child, and could thus foresee the respective destinies of the two.
>
> *Ann.* 12.41[61]

The toga apparently also played a central role in the battle for hearts and minds during the civil war that followed the death of Nero: Suetonius tells us that Galba refused to change back into a toga until all his foes were vanquished (*Galba* 11), and Vitellius had to be persuaded by his advisers to change from military gear into a toga when he entered Rome victorious so as not to appear to have been at war with the Roman people (Tac., *Hist.* 2.89). Vitellius' coinage is, in fact, conspicuous in its frequent depiction of him togate and seated on the *sella curulis* (e.g. *RIC* 1.94–97; 134–135), conveying an image of him as civilian magistrate seeing to domestic matters when really his short reign was characterized by military struggle and precarious legitimacy. Also interesting in this context is a coin of Galba that Vespasian released posthumously depicting his rival in an *adlocutio* scene wearing military dress rather than the hitherto customary toga (*BMC* Galba 249); Laurence has suggested it be viewed as Flavian propaganda, deliberately drawing attention to Galba's role as military pretender, and calling to mind the shocking incident recorded by Suetonius in which he once wore a cuirass within the city walls of Rome (*Galba* 19).[62]

In many ways the Julio-Claudians represented the era of 'peak toga' in imperial imagery, both in the role played by the garment and in the number of statues produced; from the late first century onward, additional image types gradually entered the canon that conveyed an altogether different image of the emperor. For example, the Flavians appear largely to have followed the example of the Julio-Claudians in their emphasis on civilian and modest dress in their official imagery (the 'good' emperor Vespasian is described as having been especially modest in his clothing habits: Suet., *Vesp.* 2), but the period also saw the beginning of a series of coins in which the personified senate in a toga is depicted crowning the *princeps* in military dress;[63] this reveals a subtle change in ideology from the emperor as civilian to the emperor as soldier but deriving his legitimacy from civilian authority.[64]

Although often depicted in military dress in official portraiture,[65] in historical narratives, the 'bad' final Flavian emperor Domitian is often described as wearing the flagrantly monarchical *toga purpurea* to public events such as games (Suet., *Dom.* 4.4) and triumphal clothing as general gala dress, for example for senate hearings (Dio Cass. 67.4.3). The (ab)use of these two garments was to recur in later generations (see below), and there is a sense in which the sartorial excesses of 'bad' emperors like Nero and Domitian served to permanently lower the bar

Figure 5.2 Reverse of a gold *aureus* of Trajan from Rome. *BMC* Trajan 378. Photo: Museo Nazionale Romano, Rome/Bridgeman Images.

in terms of modesty, leading to a gradual inflation in the use of the more elaborate toga types, but also making it easier for 'good' emperors to appear humble by eschewing such garments.

With the adoptive emperors we enter a period of both political stability and astute image management on the part of the imperial family. Trajan, for example, whose successful and popular military campaigns saw the empire expand to its greatest extent, was the first to mainly be depicted in statuary in military dress rather than the toga.[66] But although his coins frequently draw attention to his military exploits (e.g. *RIC* 1.98; 524; 685; 2.557), he was equally keen to stress his domestic social policies such as his formalization of the *alimenta* welfare programme for orphans and poor children, commemorated in coins depicting him in a toga handing food and money to togate children (Fig. 5.2). The intention here is to stress Trajan's role as civilian and helper of civilians.[67] The period of the adoptive emperors also saw the beginning of a coin type in which the togate personification of the senate helps the emperor hold the globe of world dominion,[68] asserting an even balance between imperial and senatorial power; in reality senatorial power had diminished, but at this stage it was still important for emperors to be seen to show them due respect. The second century also saw the first instances of what would become an increasingly popular practice in both imperial and private art: the selective use of old-fashioned toga draping styles. Marcus Aurelius, for example, appears on a relief from his lost arch wearing what by then would have been considered an antiquated style with prominent *umbo* whilst the *Genius Senatus* behind him wears the newer *balteus*-style.[69] Olson has suggested that this signified a deliberate association with the ideal emperor Augustus,[70] but it is just as likely that the older toga conveyed a more general aura of authority and continuity, in a similar way to the archaic ceremonial dress used by royal personages today.

In general, however, the further time progressed from the violence and chaos that ended the Republic and put Augustus in charge of the empire, the less taboo depiction in military dress became, and by the second century popularity with the troops and successful management of the role of commander-in-chief was seen as a *sine qua non* of the virtuous emperor. Even emperors less associated with martial ideology like Hadrian, Marcus Aurelius and Antoninus Pius had themselves depicted in military guise.[71] In a series of coins the latter is even portrayed in triumphal costume despite the fact that he never actually celebrated a triumph (*RIC* 1.93; 161; 767a):[72] it seems the *vestis triumphalis* was beginning to be seen as something that could legitimately be worn by emperors in their role as consul.[73] *Adlocutio* scenes on coins – now increasingly labelled '*exercitus*' – also underwent a fundamental change: the emperor now always addressed troops wearing military attire (e.g. *BMC* Hadrian 1689–1690).

Hadrian represents an interesting case in image management: generally well liked, his love of all things Hellenic did, however, meet with some disapproval, causing his biographer in the *Historia Augusta* to claim that he wore Greek dress in private and even sometimes to official banquets; but the same source also says that he generally wore a toga when in Italy, and urged equestrians and senators to follow suit (*Hadr.* 22; see also Dio Cass. 69.16.1). Apart from his introduction of the beard as a nod to Greek style, scholars have also been keen to spot subtle signs of philhellenism in the way Hadrian wore his toga in public statuary: Stone, for example, has argued that the *sinus*- and *umbo*-free plain toga worn in the *capite velato* statue in the Conservatori Museum was intended to make it resemble a *himation*,[74] and Goette sees the images in which the toga is pulled over the back of the right arm in a similar light.[75] But it is possible to overdo it, and a statue purportedly showing Hadrian in a *himation* in the British Museum, traditionally seen as an unreserved profession of his philhellenism, has since been proven to have originally had a different head.[76] We have no evidence that Hadrian ever wore a *himation* in public imagery, and the images we do have invariably show him in perfectly respectable military dress or toga.[77] One of his coins, in fact, celebrates his third consulship by depicting him on the Rostra addressing a throng of citizens; both he and the crowd are identically dressed in togas, conveying a scene of civic unity in keeping with the *mos maiorum* (Fig. 5.3).

Figure 5.3 Reverse of a bronze *sestertius* of Hadrian from Rome. *RIC* II.639–641. Photo: Granger/Bridgeman Images.

The reign of Hadrian marks the beginning of the coverage of court affairs in the *Historia Augusta*, our prime written source for the later emperors until 284 CE. Whilst the work is indubitably unreliable, especially for earlier periods, and its employment of dress imagery to characterize individual emperors borders on caricature, the dress chosen to populate these caricatures is nonetheless revealing of what different toga types symbolized: 'good' emperors are invariably described as showing modesty and accountability by wearing plainer versions of the toga, whilst 'bad' emperors wear 'barbarian' clothes or the purple robes of tyrants.[78] The adoptive emperors tend to be portrayed as figures of virtue, wearing the toga in public and even instructing their troops, when in Italy, to do likewise (e.g. *Hadr.* 22; *Ant. Pius* 12; *Marc. Aur.* 27.1–3), and we have every reason to believe these particular rulers did, in fact, manage their image quite successfully: the impression we get from the *Historia Augusta* and official portraits is corroborated by Cassius Dio, who, for example, describes Marcus Aurelius as wearing the plain *toga virilis* for *salutationes* (albeit in the time before he was emperor), 'rather than the clothes to which his rank entitled him' (71.35.4). And whilst the 'bad' emperor Commodus is described in the *Historia Augusta* as attending games dressed in the outlandish *dalmatica* (*Com.* 8.8) or mourning clothes (*Com.* 16),[79] the fact that this is considered shocking, coupled with that emperor's production of coins showing him in a toga shaking hands with a togate personification of the senate (e.g. Alföldi 1970: pl. 1.8), is testimony to the garment's enduring relevance as a symbol of virtue and legitimate authority. The symbolism of the *toga virilis* in the *Historia Augusta* is also noteworthy: from this period onward, it is especially when military emergencies create the need for an additional commander-in-chief that imperial heirs are suddenly bestowed with it and dispatched to the theatre of war (e.g. *Marc. Aur.* 1.10; *Comm.* 1–2; *Sep. Sev.* 16.8–9; see also Dio Cass. 72.17.2).

During the Severan period the empire was threatened with instability of various kinds, and the image of the emperor acquired a decidedly more military flavour, resulting in a proliferation of statuary with armour and military cloaks.[80] It also, however, saw a significant expansion of the use of the *vestis triumphalis* and its ultimate establishment as regular festive dress of the emperor, signifying his role less as sometime warlord and more as permanent general-cum-consul and defender of empire.[81] Septimius Severus had a particularly fraught relationship with the senate in Rome ('look after the soldiers and damn everyone else!'[82]), and it is no coincidence that he was the first to be depicted in triumphal regalia on the front of a coin.[83] The 'triumphal' relief on his arch in Leptis Magna also portrays him in the *toga picta* during his *adventus* into Rome.[84] An altogether more restrained image emerges of the 'good' emperor Severus Alexander in the *Historia Augusta*, where it is said that he preferred to be seen in plain togas rather than fancy ones (*Alex. Sev.* 4), and when he did use the *vestis triumphalis* it was only when he was required to appear as consul, and then only the publicly-owned set kept in the Temple of Jupiter rather than his own (*Alex. Sev.* 40). The latter indicates, yet again, the gradual elision of the role of consul with that of emperor and commander-in-chief.

The first signs of what was to become an increasing estrangement between the emperor and the city of Rome is also already visible in the Severan period, for example when the North African-born emperor-to-be Septimius Severus is described as having turned up to his first official banquet in Rome dressed in a *pallium* instead of a toga (Marcus Aurelius apparently saved the day by lending him one of his: *Sep. Sev.* 1.6–8), and in the alleged wearing of effeminate eastern clothing in public by Elagabalus (Dio Cass. 80.9.2; SHA *Heliogab.* 15.6). It is nonetheless significant that the latter emperor is also reported to have tried to do the right thing by wearing a *toga praetexta* for official occasions, even, it is said, eschewing the *vestis triumphalis* (Dio Cass. 79.8.3; 79.9.2; SHA *Heliogab.* 15.6).

By the time we get to the succession of short-lived reigns of the mid-third century, in which military might was all-decisive, the subordination of the civilian to the military side of imperial rule was almost complete, and this is also reflected in imperial imagery. Whilst plain tunics and togas were still used as symbols of modesty and virtue for individual figures in the *Historia Augusta* (e.g. *Gall.* 16.4; *Tac.* 10.1[85]), the *toga picta*, and to a lesser extent the *toga praetexta*, were now seen as the principal garments for public occasions (see, e.g., SHA *Gall.* 8.5; *Aurel.* 13.3). Gordian I is said to have been the first to own a *toga picta* privately (SHA *Gord. Tr.* 4.4).[86] Most importantly though, the toga, along with the office of consul that it increasingly symbolized, was now associated exclusively with the city of Rome.[87] In truth, emperors were now spending most of their time away from the imperial capital, fighting rivals and dealing with incursions. Rome, the toga and the civilian power it represented, though still symbolically powerful, became a diminishing factor in the *Realpolitik* of late antiquity.

The image of the emperor in the provinces

The imperial image was able to permeate even the remotest parts of the Roman Empire through coinage, and any town of a reasonable size tended to have at least some official statuary. How effective this was can be seen in the relatively rapid take-up of new toga fashions and hairstyles by ordinary people in the provinces, as seen for example in votive and funerary art.[88] A large number of these images, even when produced in the provinces themselves, were based on officially sanctioned prototypes from Rome itself, but there is some indication that representations of imperial power were sometimes selected and adapted for local use.

In general terms, a fundamental distinction seems to have been made between the relationship of the emperor to Italy on the one hand, and the provinces on the other, seen, for example, in the fact that travelling emperors apparently customarily changed back into a toga when they reached Italian soil (e.g. SHA *Marc. Aur.* 27). Both Tiberius and the ardent traveller Hadrian are reported to have sometimes worn the *pallium* in Greece (Suet., *Tib.* 13; SHA *Hadr.* 22; Dio 60.6.1–2), and there is some indication that emperors occasionally dressed in special clothing to fit local provincial occasions.[89] But in most cases the dress worn by the emperor in the provinces would have been that of military commander, both when he was engaged in actual war and on peacetime visits, to indicate the status of the province as conquered territory.[90] Changing back into the toga upon arrival back in Italy signalled that the emperor was now at home, where the symbolism of subjugation was no longer appropriate.[91]

It would seem that this distinction also manifested itself in official iconography. On the one hand, the toga was quite common in statuary and coin depictions of the emperor and his family in the provinces,[92] and especially in the Greek East this would have contrasted sharply with the dress of the local population.[93] On the other hand, as several scholars have pointed out, military depictions of the emperor are significantly more common in the provinces.[94] The status of a province as imperial or senatorial also played a role here: Dio tells us that already Caesar had stipulated that governors going out to senatorial provinces should not wear military dress or arms of any kind (53.13), and Howgego has argued that the depiction of emperors on provincial coinage in military or non-military dress signified the status of the province as militarized or pacified.[95]

Conclusion

The unique symbolism of the toga and its role in public life meant that it was destined to be used for political ends, and this chapter has shown how it represented a central component in the strong and historically persistent visualism of Roman political discourse. The longevity of this particular function of the toga is also noteworthy in light of claims by some scholars that it was only in the Augustan period that it played a central role in political ideology.[96] What sparse evidence we have for the period before the late Republic shows clearly that the use of different types like the *toga candida* and *toga pulla* often lay at the heart of key political developments, and by the late Republic the garment had become deeply implicated in the ideological battles that culminated in the founding of the Principate. The reign of Augustus was indeed an important milestone in the application of the toga for public relations, but coinage and imperial imagery show that its symbolism continued to be a force to be reckoned with by later emperors, and this continued into the third century and beyond, as will be shown in Chapter 7. Moreover, whilst this chapter has mainly focused on members of the political class in Rome, the messages conveyed by them in legislation, public statuary and coinage were also of relevance to people outside elite circles, even though their responses are not always visible to us. Beyond the borders of Italy, the saturation of provincial cities with specially selected imperial imagery in statues and coins, especially in the form of portraits of the emperor and his family members, played a central role in the communication of Roman power. Local reactions to this were, however, varied, as the next chapter will show.

6

The Toga in the Provinces

The focus of this book until now has been on Rome and, to a lesser extent, Italy, as it was here that the toga originated and developed its core meanings, including the link to Roman citizenship. But Rome was not just an Italian civilization, it was an empire, and the way in which it conquered and integrated large swathes of the Mediterranean basin and beyond is in many ways its most distinctive characteristic, both as a culture and as a subject of historical enquiry. In such a culturally diverse territory, the possibilities for playing out imperial power and negotiating personal identities were virtually as numerous as the empire's individual inhabitants, and the role of the toga in the provinces is a subject that could fill several tomes. The discussion that follows is, therefore, necessarily limited in scope, and aims to illustrate, by means of a small selection of case studies, the distinctive role the toga played in the reception and formulation of identity in provincial societies. The dress of the Roman provinces has not been the subject of a great deal of scholarly enquiry until now, and the toga itself has only been mentioned in the context of either regional dress studies[1] or those focusing on official portraiture when the relevant artworks happen to have been found in a provincial setting.[2] But it is impossible to have a complete picture of the toga without focusing at least some attention on its use in the areas conquered by Rome.

As already discussed in Chapter 1, the Romans had a complex, fluid and in many ways unique attitude to their own ethnicity.[3] In his study of the Roman 'Cultural Revolution', Wallace-Hadrill defined Greek and Roman cultural identities as fundamentally different: whilst 'Hellenic' was a cultural category describing a people 'with a shared language and culture', 'Roman' was a 'juridical category, defined by citizenship, by membership of the populus Romanus, or by relationship to Roman imperium'.[4] Whilst largely true of the inhabitants of the Roman Empire generally, this fundamental distinction becomes particularly important when addressing the provinces. Although the myth of Romulus' Asylum[5] is likely to be just that, the history of Roman civilization is indeed one of expansion, and that more or less from the beginning. By the late Republic at the latest, the Romans were formulating a citizenship system in which those who were conquered could eventually become Romans themselves, whether as freed slaves or as free provincials, as well as a corresponding narrative that finds its most eloquent expression in Claudius' speech on the admission of Gauls to the Senate (Tac., *Ann.* 11.24: see Chapter 1).[6] As implausibly idyllic a picture as it paints,[7] it is of huge importance to our understanding of Roman relations that a version of it was also represented on a large inscription in the very region in question (the so-called 'Lyon Tablet': *CIL* 13.1668): it means not only that the speech must actually have been given in one form or another, but also that it held enough meaning for the people of Gaul to render it worthy of public commemoration.[8] Citizenship, and to a lesser extent inclusion in the Roman political structure, was central not just to Roman ideas about what constituted 'being Roman', but also to the extent to which people in the provinces could hope to be included; and as will be shown below, the toga was a visual symbol of this.

Like the garment that symbolized it, Romanness was something that men could acquire, regardless of their cultural background; and also like the toga, it could be 'put on' or 'taken off', depending on the context, and co-exist with other identities. Moreover, some contemporary Romans appear to have been aware of this: a song that was sung about an earlier Gallic admission into the Senate in Caesar's time went:

> Caesar led the Gauls in triumph, and led them to the Senate
> The Gauls took off their trousers (*bracae*) and put on the *latus clavus*.
>
> Suet., *Iul.* 80.2[9]

Whilst the song may be using sartorial metaphor, it in any case reveals both that clothing and identity were intrinsically linked in the Roman mind, and that the Gauls who 'put on the *latus clavus*' were doing more than simply donning a garment.

Roman archaeologists have, in recent decades, developed an especial interest in the question of how and to what extent Roman culture spread in the provinces, especially in the west.[10] Whilst adherence to Roman laws and some religious obligations were virtually non-negotiable for provincial inhabitants, we have little evidence to suggest the authorities forced imperial culture per se onto conquered peoples. On the other hand, certain structures were imposed from above including, in areas that were not previously fully urbanized, cities; and the few concrete testimonies we have of the way in which Roman authorities expected urban life to be conducted reveal that the toga was indeed required dress for political functionaries, at least in the west, as stipulated, for example, in the *Lex Ursonensis* city charter (*CIL* 2.5439: line 62);[11] moreover, Roman cities in the provinces were home to official portraits of emperors and their family members, as well as local dignitaries, and the toga featured heavily here.[12]

The toga also played a role in the way Roman authors wrote about cultural change in the provinces. In the passage of Seneca's satirical eulogy for Claudius cited in Chapter 4, the emperor is teased for wanting to see 'all Greeks, Gauls, Spaniards and Britons in a toga' (referring to his citizenship policy: *Apoc.* 3), and in an oft-cited passage, Tacitus tells us that his father-in-law Agricola, whilst governor of Britannia, encouraged the pursuit of Roman culture and education amongst the local elite, as a result of which the toga 'became frequently worn' (*Agr.* 21). Strabo uses the term '*togati*' to describe those inhabitants of Spain who had become 'peaceful' and adopted 'the refined culture of the Italians' (e.g. 3.2.15; 3.4.20).[13] It would seem that for these writers, the toga was a symbol of both Roman citizenship and Roman culture. But for actual people in the provinces, it could symbolize a whole range of other things, as will be outlined below.

The first togas to have arrived in any area conquered by Rome will usually have been worn by representatives of the administration, and possibly also high-ranking military officers. Aside from members of the imperial family, such people are likely also to be over-represented in the earliest honorific sculpture in Roman towns (unsurprisingly, these are generally toga statues), especially in the western provinces. However, the story of the toga in the provinces goes beyond what Roman writers and officials thought or did: for people on the ground, being part of the Roman Empire had real implications, presented real opportunities and produced real tensions, and in this chapter we are interested in the ways in which local people used the toga, rather than the view from the imperial core.

The cultural and political diversity of the territories conquered by Rome continued after Roman rule, and every region reacted differently to integration into the imperial system.[14] What has become increasingly clear from various recent studies is that local identities often existed on a different level to membership of a wider Roman, imperial culture, and the two could co-exist in harmony, alongside other aspects of identity like age, gender and wealth status.[15] As will be shown in this chapter, however, there were many ways in which these different identity factors could be combined. Modern dress scholars have shown how the Western suit as worn in non-Western countries, whilst often denoting a link to Western-oriented business or political networks, can sometimes carry quite different meanings depending on the cultural context; in Indonesia, for example, it symbolizes Western notions of masculine authority, but is not used as the dress of political power in the way that it is in, say, many countries of sub-Saharan Africa.[16]

The corollary of the 'globalizing' nature of such objects as the suit or the toga is that their meaning is invariably transformed when they become imbedded in local structures. For Roman dress, longevity of Roman rule may have played a role in the extent to which it was adopted, but local social structures, the means by which regions were annexed by Rome, and how they developed subsequently also played a part, and some of these varied circumstances are evident in the vastly different meanings the toga could take on depending on the region in question.

Our sources for dress in the provinces are limited: textiles survive only in hot, dry climates like Egypt and Syria where togas were rare (see below) or in waterlogged conditions like at Vindolanda,[17] and we do not have a surviving toga from anywhere in the empire. Metal artefacts, which do survive in great numbers, do not tell us anything about garments like the toga that did not contain them. By far the most numerous and informative type of evidence for the dress of local people are the stone monuments that became a popular method of funerary commemoration in many areas and which generally lined the roads out of all major Roman towns.[18] They all performed the same basic function as public statements of the achievements, cultural orientations and aspirations of the people who commissioned them, and provide a means by which it is possible to compare dress behaviour across time and space.[19] As such, they form the basis of the discussion to follow. Clearly, dress chosen for portraits may not always have reflected everyday reality, but this is in many ways a boon rather than a weakness: created by stonemasons as individual artworks and thus relatively expensive, we can be sure that the imagery grave portraits contain was a matter of some consideration by those who commissioned them, and the dress choices they display consciously reflect what people wanted to say about themselves. And whilst they would have been too expensive for the poorest members of society, they were both within the means of and often commissioned by non-elite people as well.

A symbol of citizenship

Roman citizenship could be acquired by people in the provinces in a variety of ways, including as an inhabitant of a city that was granted blanket citizenship rights (this applies especially to *coloniae*), or, depending on the status of the city, as someone who had served a term of office,[20] as a slave who had been manumitted[21] or as an auxiliary soldier (or his wife or child) after 25 years' service.[22] There were certain incentives: whilst the original political rights involved (voting in assemblies, running for public office) were less important to most people in the provinces, the right to legal marriage (*conubium*), legitimate children, relatively favourable tax conditions, and especially freedom from torture and right of appeal against capital punishment[23] were all good reasons to aspire to it. Once granted, citizenship could be inherited by children from parents, and thus, over time, the franchise grew.[24] In the *constitutio Antoniniana* of 212/13 CE,[25] Caracalla granted Roman citizenship to all free inhabitants of the empire who did not yet have it (Cass. Dio 77.9.5; *Dig*. 1.5.17; *P. Giss*. 40 I). Traditionally, it was argued that by this stage there were few people left to whom this applied,[26] but recent studies have suggested citizenship levels might still have been relatively low in 212, and that the impact of the *constitutio* may have been underestimated in previous scholarship,[27] a question not unrelated to toga-wearing in later periods that will be discussed at intervals below. Due to the fact that the toga was a prime symbol of Roman citizenship,[28] it is unsurprising that men depicted wearing it in provincial funerary portraits are usually – when the information is extant (i.e. *tria nomina*) – Roman citizens, although examples like the gravestones of Apana and Quartus below show that it is unwise to see this as a hard-and-fast rule. Regardless of the precise ratio of citizens to non-citizens at any given time, certainly in the earliest phase of Roman rule in any given region the choice of a toga for the portrait would have at least partially stemmed from a desire to display this as yet rare privilege.[29]

An example of an early provincial inhabitant who was keen to show off his citizenship is the legionary veteran Poblicius in Cologne. The 15 m-high grave pillar for him and his family featuring a gallery of portrait statues, now housed in a special atrium in the Römisch-Germanische Museum, was erected sometime between 1 CE and 40 CE. Poblicius, who was originally from Italy, had served in the *legio V Alaudae*, stationed on the Rhine in the early first century CE (Tac., *Ann*. 1.45). He settled down locally and appears, given the size of his grave monument, to have been successful in his post-military life in the oppidum Ubiorum. Both he and another male in the gallery wear the imperial toga with *umbo*, and they are among the first to do so in the region: other images from Cologne dating to this period depict men still wearing the older 'armsling' style,[30] showing that clothing fashions may sometimes have taken a while to penetrate provincial society.[31] Whilst one of the two female figures that probably depicts Poblicius' wife wears the generic Roman women's ensemble of *tunica* and *palla*, the figure representing his daughter is dressed in a toga that Gabelmann has interpreted – surely correctly – as a *toga praetaexta*.[32] Whilst Poblicius' wealth and former role as one of the people who helped conquer, or at least control, the region would also have played a role in the dress he chose to wear, it is especially the girl's toga which suggests that it was specifically the legal status of the family that was the main message here: as outlined in Chapter 4, apart from notable exceptions like the Ara Pacis, in Italy it is in the monuments of freedpeople that we find children depicted in *togae praetextae* (e.g. Fig. 4.3), displaying not only their freeborn status but also that they were the legitimate children of a legally recognized marriage, both of which were rights confined to those who held citizenship. The depiction of children in togas is, however, extremely rare in the northern provinces.[33] Poblicius' imposing monument when first erected will likely have been an awe-inspiring sight in what was still at that time a fledgling Roman frontier town, and the privileged status represented in his *tria nomina* and the togas of his family members would have set them apart from the majority of the population of Cologne in that period.[34]

Cologne presents an interesting case study for the link between the toga and citizenship in the provinces, as it was characterized from its foundation by a population consisting of former members of the Ubii tribe transplanted to the region from the other side of the Rhine, Roman officials and military personnel, and other newcomers from around the empire taking advantage of the town's commercial opportunities.[35] In addition, it acquired full *colonia* status at a relatively early stage – around 50 CE – which would have cleared the path for many of its inhabitants to become Roman citizens. Both of these factors are likely to have contributed to the fact that this city has the highest proportion of men wearing togas in funerary art anywhere in the Roman north-west,[36] and the dress was not confined to wealthy individuals like Poblicius: we eventually also see it on more modest stones for people like slave traders, teachers, sailors and retail merchants.[37] In this cosmopolitan town with its *colonia* status and large number of citizens, the toga appears to have become part of the general cultural landscape to a higher degree than elsewhere in the wider vicinity. Nonetheless, there is some indication that even after Cologne was made a *colonia*, there was added social value to be gained from having oneself portrayed in a toga on one's gravestone: on a stele for a legionary veteran from Spain called M. Valerius Celerinus and his wife Marcia Procula dating to the late first century (Fig. 6.1), the portrait relief is in the style of the *Totenmahl* (funerary banquet) that came from the East but was popular in the northern frontier provinces.[38] Generally in these scenes in the East, as well as most in the West, the man is depicted reclining with a *himation* draped over his hips and left shoulder (with or without his wife standing or sitting nearby).[39] On Celerinus' stone, however, it is very clearly a toga, as an *umbo* is shown protruding over the *balteus*. The fact that Celerinus has taken a formulaic depiction and deliberately added the somewhat incongruous detail of the toga means the latter must have been an important factor in his identity. We can only speculate why, but it is likely to have been either pride in his citizen status or his

Figure 6.1 Grave stele for M. Valerius Celerinus from Cologne. Römisch-Germanisches Museum, Cologne, inv. 86. Rheinisches Bildarchiv Köln.

former membership of the Roman imperial apparatus, or a sense of affinity with Rome itself. Perhaps it was a mixture of all three. The fact that he came from a region in which the toga seems to have been relatively common (see next section) may also have played a role, because whilst Cologne seems to have a large number of toga-wearers, the same cannot be said for the north-west in general.

More broadly, a 2009 study of northern Gaul and the central Rhine area by the author revealed that the proportion of men wearing a toga in funerary portraits was at its highest in the late Republic and early Empire, i.e. soon after conquest and at the time in which the Roman funerary habit began in the region. Over time, the percentage of men depicted in a toga declined, whilst at the same time Roman citizenship spread to larger numbers of people.[40] Although this may partially reflect the over-representation of incomers to the region like Poblicius in the earlier stones, we know that many of the other early toga-wearers in the region were locals.[41] The most likely wider explanation for the gradual decline in the toga in funerary monuments is that the sense of privilege the garment symbolized diminished as ever greater numbers of people obtained citizenship.[42] The fact that the *constitutio Antoniniana* of 212/13 does not seem to have made any difference to the numbers of toga depictions in funerary art in the north-western provinces[43] both supports this idea and suggests that other factors were at play in the choice of the toga for one's lasting image.

Clothed in Romanness?

In terms of what one might prosaically term 'toga density', Spain represents a relatively unusual case as a region that was geographically on the periphery of the empire, but where virtually all men in funerary and honorific monuments who wear civilian dress wear togas.[44] With some very few exceptions,[45] the portrait art of the Spanish provinces gives the impression not just that the toga was widely worn in Spanish cities, but also that it belonged to the identity vocabulary of both wealthy people and those further down the social scale. In her study of the sculptural art of Mulva-Munigua, for example, Hertel (1993) showed that many of the toga depictions belonged to relatively small and modest monuments. Moreover, they were not confined to honorific or portrait art but also appear – unusually for the western provinces – on votive monuments[46] and terracotta figurines.[47]

So how do we account for the apparent wide use of the toga on the Iberian Peninsula? One factor may, of course, be that the region was conquered by Rome at a relatively early date – albeit over a prolonged period.[48] If Livy is to be believed, local people were also producing togas themselves from an early stage: in 205 BCE, two Spanish tribes were required to provide '*saga et togae*' to Roman troops as part of reparations following a revolt (29.3). Spanish cities also benefitted from a relatively generous Roman citizenship policy from an early stage, beginning with cities like Carteia, Corduba and Valentia receiving the *ius Latii* already in the second century BCE and ending with the wholesale bestowal of the *ius Latii* on all cities of Spain by Vespasian in 73/74.[49] Like most of the Roman West, apart from the east coast, the Iberian Peninsula had not had many cities (in the Mediterranean-Roman sense) before Roman conquest,[50] and both Caesar and Augustus founded many new colonies with both Latin and Roman *ius*. But citizenship cannot have been the only reason for displaying the toga. For example, in the statuary art of Munigua, the 'armsling' style of toga played an important role, and that long into the period beyond which it was fashionable; whilst it is possible that, as mentioned above for Cologne, toga fashions took a while to get to the provinces, Hertel has convincingly argued that Muniguan men must have known the new style but used the older one in order to align themselves with Italian Republican ideals of public duty and *prisca gravitas*.[51]

The fact that aspiration to more general Roman cultural norms were at play in the use of the toga on the Iberian Peninsula is also well-illustrated in a gravestone from Galicia dating to the early-mid-first century CE (Fig. 6.2): it was set up – as

Figure 6.2 Grave stele for Apana and family from Prado de Arriba, Crecente, San Pedro de Mera, Lugo, Spain. Photo: Museo Provincial de Lugo.

the inscription states – for Apana, daughter of Ambollus, a member of the local Supertamarici tribe, by her brother Apanus.[52] Four figures are depicted in the portrait, including Apana, another woman and a girl in Roman dress; Apanus behind them is clothed in what is clearly an early imperial toga with pouch-*umbo*. The name forms in the inscription, however, suggest none of the family members were citizens. Aside from the obvious implications of this for the commonly held belief that a toga always denoted citizen status, what is perhaps more important for us is that the lack of citizenship means the presence of Roman dress – including the toga – in Apana's portrait scene must pertain to a more generalized sense of Roman identity in this family. The fact that the stone is relatively modest in size and quality, coupled with its location in a region at one of the farthest reaches of the empire, shows that perceived membership of a wider Roman community was not confined to the elite in larger urban centres. However, the fact that the same family also took pains to mention their tribal membership in the inscription shows, like many examples to follow further below, that local and Roman identities could and did co-exist, apparently without contradiction.

The dress of international businessmen

An interesting further insight into the meaning of the toga in the provinces presents itself in northern Gaul. Here, like in Cologne, a large number of the men in the earliest gravestones wore a toga,[53] and, again, the numbers dropped off as time progressed. In the second and third centuries, the vast majority of men on gravestones in all of the Tres Galliae chose to have themselves depicted in the general regional ensemble of sleeved, ungirt Gallic tunic and hooded Gallic cape,[54] even if they were Roman citizens.[55] Some few toga depictions remained, however, and the details of these men's gravestones allow us to gain an insight into who these people were and what the toga may have meant to them.

The first striking feature is the size of the second/third-century toga-wearers' gravestones: they are the largest and most elaborate funerary monuments in the region,[56] showing that the people commemorated had considerable wealth at their disposal. It is interesting that when women are depicted in the portraits on these stones, they too wear Roman dress, despite the fact that in the wider Gallic milieu this was very rare. This suggests a more general cultural orientation of the family toward Rome. From these facts alone, one might simply conclude that they were the local elite, and that Roman dress was part and parcel of their leadership role in the community. But local magistracies are conspicuously absent from the inscriptions on these monuments where extant, and although they are adorned with various scenes displaying the everyday life of the people commemorated, not one of these relates to public offices or priesthoods.[57] Instead, we see leisure activities like the man out hunting, his wife having her hair done by servants or the family having a meal together,[58] and, more importantly, scenes from the working lives of the family. From the latter it is clear that they were involved in both large-scale landownership, as can be seen in scenes of tenant farmers paying rent, and commercial activities, evident in those that show products being sampled, displayed, packaged and transported.[59] It is also clear from the nomenclature and other details in the inscriptions that the families were local people rather than newcomers to the area.[60] It would seem that these northern Gallic *togati* were men who had benefitted from the economic boom in Gaul in the second/early third century that was based in no small part on international trade in commodities like wool, cloth and wine.[61]

The most famous, and also most informative, example of this group of monuments is the so-called Igel Pillar in the village of Igel near Trier, ancient Augusta Treverorum and the capital of the Treveran *civitas* (Fig. 6.3).[62] Dated to the early–mid third century and commemorating a wealthy local family with the *nomen gentile* Secundinius (or variations thereof), this 23 m-high grave pillar is covered on all sides with relief scenes, most of which relate to the working and domestic life of the family. (These are now heavily eroded, so images are provided here in the form of earlier drawings.) The base shows various stages of textile production and dispatch: a textile workshop (eastern side), textiles being tested for quality and money being paid out (southern side: Fig. 6.4 bottom), textile wares being tied up for transport (western side) and unpacked at their destination (northern side).[63] On the frieze, tenant farmers bring agricultural products to the lord of the estate or his manager (western side), products are brought in on donkeys (northern side), food for the family is prepared in a kitchen/bakehouse (eastern side) and at the front (southern side), the family is shown enjoying a meal while servants bring dishes. The main block shows mythological scenes on the eastern, western and northern sides, and the main family portrait on the southern side, which consists of a man and a boy wearing sleeved Gallic tunics and partly contabulated togas, another man in a tunic and *sagum* and medallion portraits of a woman and two children (Fig. 6.4 top).[64] The grave inscription (*CIL* 13.4206) simply lists the names of the people commemorated, but does not make any mention of occupations, magistracies or priesthoods. For this reason, the Secundinii have been described as 'Aufsteiger' who hadn't quite 'made it' yet in terms of holding positions of political power in the region,[65] but there is no reason to think that this is something to which they necessarily aspired.

Figure 6.3 Igel Pillar in the village of Igel near Trier. *LUPA* 24000–24009. Photo: Berthold Werner/Wikimedia Commons.

It is conspicuous that of all the many everyday life scenes from Gaul, of which those on the Igel Pillar are just one set of examples, not one of them depicts a man in a toga: the toga is restricted to main portraits only. It is not difficult to see why the garment is not worn in leisure scenes of the *paterfamilias* out hunting or driving a cart, or by men engaging in physical labour,[66] but its absence from the office scenes shows either that the men depicted in them were clerks and employees of the family, rather than family members themselves, or that the toga was not used for this kind of everyday work in the family business. Either way, what emerges is that the toga was restricted to specific people and/or contexts, and as such its symbolism must have been all the more distinctive. On the other hand, the Igel portrait shows that it was not simply a 'Bildformel' applied to portraits and never worn in real life: the two men in this image wear their togas over the long-sleeved

Figure 6.4 Scenes from the south face of the Igel Pillar. Top: main portrait. Bottom: cloth inspection. Drawings: L. Dahm in: E. Zahn/Rheinischer *Verein für Denkmalpflege und Landschaftsschutz, Die Igeler Säule in Igel bei Trier* (Rheinische Kunststätten Heft 38), 5th ed., Cologne 1982, pages 8 and 10.

Gallic tunics worn by the vast majority of men in Gaul, and in so doing defy any formulaic image of togate men that might have reached the region from Italy.

So what does the toga mean on these monuments? We know from epigraphic evidence that Gallic merchants like the Secundinii travelled a great deal on business, especially around wider Gaul and the north-west.[67] Together with the elaborateness of these monuments, it would seem that in northern Gaul the toga was the dress of what we might today call international businessmen: rich provincials who had an international outlook and flourished in the economic environment the Roman Empire created. In this context, it is again perhaps helpful to see it as playing a similar role to the modern business suit. As recently shown by Breward, the fact that the Western suit had its origins in the introduction of the vest from the Ottoman Empire into the court dress of King Charles II mixed with the parallel development of military uniforms has had no bearing on its later use: today it is seen as the embodiment of a Westernized but also globalized political and business community.[68] As Mazrui observed in 1970, '[t]he Japanese businessman, the Arab minister, the Indian lawyer, the African civil servant have all found a common denominator in the Western suit'.[69] It seems likely that in northern Gaul, and perhaps many other provincial contexts as well, the toga represented a 'common denominator' that became the appropriate dress for people conducting business with men from other parts of the Roman Empire. Whether or not it also formed part of a more general orientation amongst this group toward Roman imperial culture is unclear, but if it does, the Gallic tunics of the Secundinii show yet again that local and imperial identities were not mutually exclusive categories.

A masculine identity?

Whilst Apana's family in Galicia showed its combined local and Roman identity in Roman dress coupled with mention of tribal membership in the inscription, and the male Secundinii in Igel in their mixed styles of dress, in other parts of the empire it is clear that twin identities were divided along gender lines. In the provinces of Noricum, Pannonia Inferior and Pannonia Superior on the middle Danube, for example, the vast majority of gravestone portraits show women in a striking array of elaborate and locally specific Celtic dress styles,[70] whilst their husbands and other male family members wear either the toga[71] or generic cloak styles[72] that were common to both the Roman and local male wardrobes.[73] The majority of the monuments from this region date to the second and early third centuries CE, when large numbers of local inhabitants would have been enfranchised. In most cases, the inscription has not survived intact with the portrait, but where it does the women in local dress have both peregrine (i.e. filiation-based)[74] and citizen (i.e. with *nomen gentile*)[75] name forms, as do the men wearing both rectangular cloaks and togas (see below). In other words, the togas in these portraits must represent something other than merely legal status. Similarly, although the region did experience a great influx of new inhabitants from other parts of the empire in the form of military personnel in the camps along the Danube as well as Roman officials and migrating civilians,[76] it is difficult to believe that only they are represented in the male figures in what is after all one of the largest bodies of Roman funerary art anywhere in the Roman Empire.

A good example of the gendered dress dynamics of the middle Danube region is a late-first/early-second-century gravestone from Celje (Roman Celeia) in

Slovenia (Fig. 6.5), formerly the southern part of the Roman province of Noricum. The portrait shows a woman wearing the local Norican bonnet, a tunic held with large vertical brooches at the shoulders, a torques with lunula pendant, copious pectoral jewellery, and a short cloak draped around both shoulders.[77] On the right is a man depicted in a tunic and imperial toga with *umbo*,[78] and between the two adults are the head of a boy and the bust of a girl in a plain tunic sporting the typical bobbed hairstyle of girls in this region.[79] The inscription is somewhat intriguing. The first two names given are those of a couple: a man called Quartus and his wife (*'uxor'*) Licovia Ingenua. The monument was, the inscription says, set up by Quartus while he was still alive. Quartus is clearly not a Roman citizen: his name form is '*Quartus Sirae*', the most likely expansion of which would be '*Quartus Sirae filius*' ('son of Sira'), rendering him of peregrine status;[80] the name form of his wife, on the other hand, shows that she did possess citizenship (probably the Latin form as Celeia became a *municipium* with Latin rights under Claudius: *CIL* 3.5143; 5227), so we are looking at a mixed-status marriage. This is underlined by the fact that of the nine further people named in the inscription,

Figure 6.5 Grave stele for Quartus, Licovia and family from Celje. *LUPA* 3616; Pokrajinski Muzej Celje, inv. L 80. Photo: Ortolf Harl.

four derive their *nomen gentile* from Licovia Ingenua: in mixed-status marriages the children took the legal status and *gentilicium* of their mother.

It stands to reason that the adult couple depicted in the portrait are the parents Quartus and Ingenua and that the two children are the 10-year-old daughter Leucimara and 6-year-old son Finitus named immediately after them, whilst the other names are for family members not depicted and perhaps added later to the inscription.[81] As such, it is all the more interesting that it is the *peregrinus* father Quartus who has had himself depicted in a toga, while his citizen wife wears the local dress: here, gender roles have clearly trumped any notion of legal status. Interestingly, there are a good many other grave monuments in the region that also show men with peregrine name forms wearing togas.[82] Regardless of whether they represent knowing usurpation of the insignia of citizenship or sincere attempts to appear Roman, they render it even more unlikely that citizenship, or the lack thereof, was the sole reason for the disparity in dress styles between men and women in the Danube region.

It is not clear what distinguished the toga-wearing from the non-toga-wearing men in these otherwise very similar portrait scenes. Erwin Pochmarski has argued that the rectangular cloak with brooch worn by many of the men is in fact a Roman *sagum*, and that these men were thus connected to the military,[83] but the Romans derived their *sagum* from the Celts in the first place, and it is perfectly conceivable that a similar cloak was traditionally worn in the Danube region by local Celtic men.[84] What is clear, given the gender disparity in dress styles, is that the toga formed a significant part of a repertoire of acceptable male dress in this region in a way that did not apply in the female sphere: those few gravestones that do show women in Roman dress are almost exclusively very late in date.[85] In other words, in the middle Danube provinces from the first to the early third century, Roman identity – at least in clothing – would seem to have been something that men displayed, and not women. Some scholars[86] have seen this is as evidence of a progressive attitude on the part of the men that stood in contrast to a conservative stance of the women displayed in their local – probably tribe-based[87] – dress styles; but as the many examples of similar gendered dress behaviour in more recent colonial settings show, there are a great many other possible explanations, such as that the incoming styles of female dress did not provide adequate means to display status and power as locally defined, or that they did not conform to local ideas of female beauty or decency.[88]

What is clear from comparative evidence is that gender groups do not act in isolation, and that men and women form part of social and familial systems. In such systems, due to the fact that they tend to operate within the private sphere, it often falls to women to continue local cultural traits and identities considered valuable by the entire group, allowing the men – usually acting primarily in the public sphere – to take on the dress of a hegemonic external culture without threatening the cultural identity of the group.[89] Rather than viewing the men and women of the middle Danube provinces as having diverging cultural outlooks, it is more useful to see them as each playing separate but integrated roles in a wider social system in which both local and Roman elements were needed to maintain a desired cultural equilibrium. In this scenario, the toga was closely linked to masculinity and the public role of men in the local provincial society; but it was also representative of the Roman identity of the entire family in the same way as the women's dress signified the whole family's embeddedness in local cultural traditions.

The toga in the East

All of the case studies discussed above were taken from the western Roman provinces, and that with good reason: when we turn to the Greek-speaking eastern provinces we enter a very different cultural landscape. As a region that had already possessed both a written *lingua franca* in Greek and urban centres that corresponded largely to how the Romans defined cities, the eastern Mediterranean experienced fewer of the fundamental social, political and structural changes that were imposed on the west to enable Roman domination. And despite the fact that the regions of the East were annexed by Rome in different stages over several centuries and contained such distinctive cultures as that of Egypt, Palestine and the Nabataean Kingdom, when it comes to the toga, a general rule emerges from the visual evidence: namely, that the garment was neither widely worn, nor commonly used as an identity symbol in this area.[90] For example, in private funerary art only three togas are depicted in the entire catalogue of grave reliefs from the eastern Aegean and Thrace collected by Pfuhl and Möbius (1977), even fewer in Tuchelt's (1979) survey of monuments in Asia Minor, and not a single one is amongst the 577 steles in von Moock's (1998) study of the Attic grave reliefs from the first three centuries CE. They do not appear at all in the many hundreds of painted mummy portraits from Roman Egypt dating to the period from the mid-first to the late fourth century CE.[91] Togas are more common in public honorific statuary, but compared with other dress styles they still represent a minority (see below).[92]

The reason for the paucity of the toga in the eastern provinces is not especially difficult to ascertain: apart from the indeterminate role played by the Romans' more favourable attitude to Greek culture[93] (in comparison with their view of most other cultures with which they came into contact), the fact that the Roman East not only had an actual *lingua franca* in Greek but also a long-standing sartorial one in the *himation* must surely have made a big difference to the region's reception of the toga.[94] As Wueste has pointed out in her survey of late antique statuary, whilst the *himation/pallium* was a symbol of private leisure and scholarly activity in Rome and the west, in the Greek East it was not only the most widely worn garment for men in general: it also played a similar role to the toga as the garment of civic engagement.[95] The social and political life of the Greek East was based on the 500-odd *poleis* that already existed at the advent of Roman rule, and integration into the Roman Empire did not fundamentally change their internal political structures; even the few colonies founded by the Romans very soon also conformed more or less to the structure of the neighbouring urban centres.[96]

As Meyer-Zwiffelhoffer (2003) concluded in his study of the Greek cities under Roman rule, the idea of being a citizen of a Greek *polis* did not change as much as one would think under Roman rule. Roman citizenship, where people had it in addition to their *polis* citizenship, meant some privileges and honours, but it did not change the basic identity of the Greek *polis* citizen, and even elite Greeks who lived abroad to hold imperial offices usually returned to their hometowns.[97] Moreover, the Greek cities, although possessing popular assemblies as well, had been developing their own aristocracies since the Hellenistic period and these showed their status through various euergetic activities; the Hellenistic Greek *poleis* were thus more similar to Rome than the classical democracies had been. The honorific epigraphy relating to this group of people is also telling of the relationship to Rome: although honouring the Roman state and the imperial family, as well as mentioning imperial Roman offices and membership of one of the *ordines*, these usually take a secondary position in the list of virtues and achievements, and a more prominent role is invariably given to the local political offices and public acts, along with statements of local patriotism.[98]

Given the large overlap between the symbolism of the *himation* in the Greek cities and that of the toga in the West, it is easy to see how the latter would have struggled to gain a foothold in the East. Nonetheless, depictions of the toga do exist. Smith has asserted that they signify 'simply and forcefully Roman citizenship' and points out that they decreased in popularity over time (for him, a sign that increasing enfranchisement diluted the status' privileged character in a similar way to the north-western provinces discussed above).[99] But the toga depictions are in fact too small in number to be explained only by possession of citizenship: even if enfranchisement rates may have been lower in the East than in the West, there must certainly have been a much higher proportion of citizens amongst the elite men represented in the statues than those depicted in a toga. As a result, although toga depictions are small in number, the people and situations to which they are linked tell us something about what 'Romanness' may have meant in the eastern provinces. As mentioned at the beginning of this chapter, the few Roman city charters in the West that survive, like, for example, the *Lex Ursonensis* (*CIL* 2.5439) stipulated that the toga had to be worn for public proceedings. It seems unlikely that such a rule applied in the East, where the *himation* was an acceptable alternative. What is clear is that toga-wearers were in a minority even amongst the political elite in the East, and it would seem that those toga depictions we see in the East fall largely into three main categories.

The first consists of people who were directly involved in imperial administration. In a monograph of 1998, Havé-Nikolaus collated all the honorific toga statues from Achaia, Crete and parts of Macedonia, and found that statues depicting men in the *pallium/himation* far outweighed those in a toga in all Greek cities apart from those where Roman administration was centred, i.e. Corinth and Gortyn, where the ratios of *palliati* to *togati* are 10:10 and 3:10 respectively.[100] Corinth, for example, was the seat of the provincial governor, and it is the only place in Greece that has toga statues from the entire timespan of the first two centuries.[101] Leaving aside those that represent the emperor and members of his family, it stands to reason that, given the role of the city in imperial administration, the remaining toga statues predominantly depict either governors or their officials.[102]

The second category of people associated with the toga in portrait art in the eastern provinces are individual people and families with a particularly strong connection to Rome. An example of this is the former Commagenian prince Philopappos: although an influential Athenian citizen, he also had close personal links to the emperor Trajan and held several distinguished positions in Rome, including as suffect consul in 109 CE. He was honoured in a large monument on the Hill of the Muses in Athens that includes one of the very few toga statues to have been found in Athens (probably his grandfather)[103] and a frieze showing him in a chariot wearing a toga – an allusion to his consulship – along with a main portrait of him seated in the intellectual dress of *himation* without tunic.[104] The Roman element of this monument – the toga depictions – was not a norm for Athens at the time, but a result of Philopappos' unusual biography, which meant that Romanness was a key part of his personal identity.[105]

A third category is formed by men who appear from their grave monuments to have held positions that required, or were symbolized by, the toga, but for whom such positions were secondary to other aspects of their identity. The best examples of this come from Palmyra in Syria. This wealthy desert oasis at the western end of the trans-Eurasian caravan routes rose to prominence in the Hellenistic period under Seleucid rule, but it retained a remarkable level of independence both from Rome and the Iranian East until it was finally subdued by Aurelian's troops in 272/3 CE. What remains of the cultural output of the city's predominantly Arab-Aramaean population points to a continued importance of tribal and family identities.[106] The epigraphy of the city – which consists mainly of texts in Greek and the local Aramaean – reflects a mixed identity,[107] as does the dress worn by the local people in the city's abundant and splendid funerary monuments: the majority of men in them wear the generic Greek tunic and *himation*, although a significant number are portrayed in the more ornate, Parthian-style trousers and kaftans that afforded particularly rich means of status display; the women, on the other hand, wear almost exclusively elaborate local/Parthian dress styles.[108] In light of this, it is difficult to contest the predominant scholarly view that Roman influence in the city was both minimal and superficial.[109]

Although extremely limited, the toga does, however, appear in Palmyra. Of the very few honorific statues to have survived from the city, two (of Antonine-Severan date) depict men in a toga;[110] and in private funerary art, one half-figure relief portrait dated to the later second century now in the Liebighaus in Frankfurt depicts a local man (?, son of Nasra) in a toga,[111] and two early–mid third-century sarcophagi show men wearing togas in secondary scenes on the base (Fig. 6.6 depicts the front of sarcophagus A).[112] It is interesting to note that all of these images display an identical drapery style with a small *umbo* protruding over an almost horizontal *balteus*. The lack of variety in draping fashions seen elsewhere in the empire suggests that in Palmyra the toga served as more of a costume than a living garment.[113]

So what explains this minority fashion? On the basis of the honorific statues, Bernard Goldman characterized Roman dress in Palmyra as a matter of 'public, community viewing'.[114] Similarly, Lucinda Dirven has recently argued that the different genres of sculptural art in Palmyra contained very different messages and audiences, and reckons that the once copious honorific statuary art still attested in inscriptions that might have been largely in bronze (and as such susceptible to melting down) was largely Roman/Hellenistic in character, reflecting a greater adherence to the civic ideals of the Greek *polis* than usually assumed.[115] But we must work with the very few honorific pieces we have, and they suggest that civic art in Palmyra contained male figures in both *himation* and toga: the question as to why the toga was chosen for some portraits still stands. Funerary art, on the other hand, with its stylization, stiffness and preponderance of local dress styles, reflects a very different message according to Dirven.[116] Nonetheless, even here we find very few togas, and again there must be a reason for this. Andreas Schmidt-Colinet and Khaled al-As'ad, referring to the sarcophagus bases, saw the depiction of the toga on them as a symbol of pride in Roman citizenship.[117] However, given that we can expect many more men in Palmyra than those few commemorated in the named examples to have been Roman citizens,[118] and that the sarcophagi seem to post-date the *constitutio Antoniniana*, whilst in addition, the man in the Liebighaus relief apparently deliberately eschewed the *tria nomina* for a local filiation-based name form,[119] it seems that something else was at work in the choice of the toga.

In fact, the attributes of the togate figures, where depicted, have one thing in common: they are all related to religious activity. One of the two honorific toga statues has a pedestal depicted at the feet displaying a so-called '*modius*' hat[120] – the cylindrical headwear of Palmyrene priests; the man in the Liebighaus relief holds a libation bowl and wears a laurel wreath on his head (repeated on a pedestal next to his head) of the kind usually worn with the priestly '*modius*' hat; and on the two sarcophagi, the togate men pour libations onto altars next to raised pedestals displaying wreathed '*modius*' hats whilst sacrificial attendants bring further offerings (Fig. 6.6).[121] It seems clear that the toga-wearers of Palmyra had been priests of some form or other.[122] On the other hand, there are a large number of images of priests in Palmyra,[123] but only these very few wear a toga, so it seems likely that the toga related to a specific cult, and one particularly associated with Rome.[124]

Dirven has recently shown that, although Roman influence on religious affairs in Palmyra has traditionally been considered to have been minimal, involvement in the imperial cult held huge prestige and importance in the city.[125] Two statue base inscriptions referring to the imperial cult appear to have originally stood in the Temple of Bel, the city's most important sanctuary, and a further two inscriptions mention a *Caesareum* somewhere in the city,[126] one of which also mentions a statue in the Temple of Bel.[127] Another inscription from the countryside near Palmyra, but which must originally have stood in the city itself, refers to the dedication of two statues of Marcus Aurelius and Lucius Verus by a man who held the position of both high priest of Bel and priest of the imperial cult.[128] As Dirven states, the fact that the imperial cult was so closely related to the veneration of Bel – the principal cult in the city – shows that it must have been held in high regard, and acting as one of its priests is likely to have been a particularly coveted honour.[129] I suggest, therefore, that whilst it was not always the case that priests of the imperial cult in the East wore togas,[130] the handful of men shown wearing a toga in the art of Palmyra might have been priests of the imperial cult.[131]

Figure 6.6 Detail of the base of a sarcophagus from Palmyra showing a sacrificial scene. Palmyra Archaeological Museum, inv. 2677B/8983. Photo: Palmyra Archaeological Museum, Tadmor, Syria/Tarker/Bridgeman Images.

The positioning of the togate men on the sarcophagi is particularly interesting for understanding the role of the toga – and with it the nature of Roman identity such as it existed – in Palmyra. Whilst the lid of sarcophagus B is no longer preserved with its base,[132] the lid of sarcophagus A bears the main portrait of the deceased: here, he reclines on a couch and wears ornate Parthian-style trousers, kaftan and cloak.[133] It would seem that the most important aspect of this man's self-image related to his membership of a local Palmyrene elite that drew its sartorial status symbolism from local and eastern styles of dress. His role as priest of a Roman (imperial?) cult was clearly secondary to this, as it is depicted in much smaller format on the base of the sarcophagus. We can assume a similar constellation for sarcophagus B. The fact that the priestly scene is depicted at all, however, suggests that the role it symbolized was nonetheless of some importance to these individuals.

So what does the toga actually mean in this context? Although the work currently being conducted under the auspices of the Danish *Palmyra Portrait Project*[134] may reveal more toga images, it seems unlikely that enough will be found to challenge the overall impression that the toga was a minority dress style in Palmyra. In their discussion of the sarcophagi, Schmidt-Colinet and al-As'ad claimed that the togas represented citizenship and the adoption of Roman ideals, which, along with the main depiction in Parthian dress, showed a twin cultural identity – local and Roman – in which the Roman element served to 'modernize' the local, Parthian one.[135] But aside from the fact that the archaic form of toga should be enough in itself to render the latter idea questionable, the association of the toga with priesthood suggests that it might have been confined exclusively to a particular cult, of which the imperial cult seems most likely. In other words, rather than showing a general Roman outlook, from its confined context and generic depiction in Palmyra, the toga appears as merely the correct costume for a specific public office. Recent work on religion in Palmyra has shown that being a priest was primarily a symbol of high status, rather than a matter of spiritual orientation.[136] In this context, similarly to the way that Roman magistracies – although mentioned – often took second place in honorific epigraphy in Greek cities, belonging to this prestigious cult in Palmyra might have constituted little more than an additional element in an entire suite of status symbols that were centred primarily on the local social environment.[137]

In summary, then, the toga played a significant but secondary role in the way elites in the Greek East saw themselves and wanted to be seen by others. Again, although Roman citizenship as a legal privilege may have played a role, it is not enough to explain the patterns. As Smith has said, for the Greek urban aristocracy, '[t]heir primary identities were based less on ethnicity and race in a modern sense, than on political and social culture'.[138] In an eastern context, the toga represented a Roman addition to an already existing array of status symbols that did not fundamentally change the nature of that local social environment.

Conclusion: Wearing Rome?

The discussion in this chapter represents a very small selection of places in the Roman Empire in which the toga played specific roles. Many more could have been added to the list, and indeed large parts of the empire are missing from the survey, such as North Africa, where yet another set of dynamics were at play, with individual neighbouring towns sometimes displaying vastly different cultural orientations from one another.[139] As outlined at the beginning of this chapter, Romanness – as formulated by Roman writers and historians – was distinctive in the ancient world as being something that could be acquired and 'put on', just like the toga itself. However, even the few cases discussed here show that, however the Roman authorities and writers saw the role of the toga in the provinces, in reality, once the garment left Italy it took on a life of its own, fitting into local social structures and ideas of what it meant to be Roman. Traditionally, when depicted in the provinces the toga has been seen as a marker of citizenship, and in many cases it will indeed have played a central role, such as for Lucius Poblicius and his family in Cologne. But other examples show that this explanation is too narrow. In places like Spain it belonged to a more general Roman milieu, and was worn both there and in the Danube provinces by men who did not have citizenship. In the Danube provinces, it seems to have been more closely linked to gender roles dictated by the local culture, leading even to cases like the gravestone from Celeia, on which a *peregrinus* man wears a toga while his citizen wife wears the elaborate local dress. In Gaul, the opposite occurred, and men who had Roman citizenship largely eschewed the toga for Gallic dress; here, the toga is confined to a class of wealthy merchants and seems to denote their membership of an international business community. In the East, the toga is rarely seen, and seems to have been worn predominantly by people directly involved in Roman administration or by individual people with a particular link to Rome. In Palmyra, it denoted high status through membership of a prestigious priesthood, probably the imperial cult.

What these examples show is how difficult it is to assign any one cultural meaning – or even a cultural meaning full stop – to the wearing of the toga in the provinces. In recent years, provincial archaeologists have departed from the idea of Roman and local identities as mutually exclusive or even similar in nature. But even widening the approach to encompass a legal definition of 'Roman' linked to citizenship is not enough to encompass the full range of possibilities. The most recent work comparing Roman culture to that of globalization in the modern world probably comes closer to the mark, and it is clear from the examples discussed in this chapter that membership of a wider Roman imperial community could be expressed in the toga, for example of Apana's family in Galicia, or the wealthy businessmen of Gaul. Likewise, these examples show that such an imperial, 'globalized' identity could, like in the modern world, co-exist with local affiliations expressed in tribal ethnonyms and the inclusion of local dress styles alongside the toga. But in the case, for example, of Palmyra, the toga, like many aspects of global culture today like yoga or reggae music, may have become so embedded in the local society that it lost most of its original cultural meaning, and became something that was dictated almost entirely by prevailing local ideas of status and prestige.

7

The Toga in Late Antiquity

This final chapter looks at what happened to the toga in late antiquity, defined broadly as the period from the mid-third century onward, although the origins of some of the developments discussed began somewhat earlier. This period saw the decline in the use of the toga by ordinary citizens and its transformation into an increasingly symbolic garment of civil authority. The chapter also serves as a conclusion of sorts by tracing the main threads of this study of the toga – masculinity, status, politics and the provinces – in the story of what happened next.

The demise of the everyday toga

By the dawn of the third century CE, it is clear that the toga was becoming a less common sight on the streets of Roman cities. The breakdown of toga-wearers in the staunchly Roman city of Carthage by Tertullian (around 200 CE) in *De Pallio* (5.4.1–2)[1] suggests that it was still the garment associated with senators, magistrates, lawyers and rhetoricians in general, as well as government administrators, and the fact that he devoted an entire diatribe to its condemnation means it still must have represented everyday work dress for some people.[2] Nonetheless, the third century saw the beginning of a fundamental shift in Roman society: when, in 212 CE, Caracalla granted Roman citizenship to all free inhabitants of the Roman Empire, he eradicated any last trace of the old status distinction between citizens and non-citizens. From this time onward, those who were not senators, *equites* or imperial officials (*honestiores*) were increasingly lumped together as a generalized underclass (*humiliores*), and the divide between the two both widened and hardened over time as social mobility gradually receded.[3] It was this social mobility that had played such a large role in the use of the toga by the non-elite especially from the late Republic onward – one thinks of the gravestones of freedpeople, the *turba togatorum* greeting patrons of a morning and the donning of the toga by ordinary people in the context of religious festivals, public events and court appearances discussed in Chapter 4.

However, the impulse behind Tertullian's work in itself illustrates one of the reasons why from this time onward people who might once have worn the toga increasingly adopted alternative garments: Christianity. The Greek *pallium* had already established itself in Roman culture as the dress of intellectual endeavour (as the garment itself tells us in *De pall.* 6.2: 'the whole of liberal studies is encompassed by my four corners'), and, as time went on, increasing numbers of people aspired to the ideal of the *mousikos aner*.[4] It is for this reason that the often brutal scenes from classical mythology started to be replaced in funerary art with images that represented introspection and philosophical ideals like *sophrosyne* and *enkrateia*.[5] Now the garment also symbolized the more recent eastern import of Christianity, and this cult provided its followers with a new community of equals just as the remaining vestiges of this aspect of Roman citizenship were dying away.[6] Moreover, whilst the toga had been tied up with outward status concerns, Christianity in this period was concerned with inner purity and true morality, offering an alternative moral framework to the one previously afforded by the figure of the good citizen.[7]

But whilst the *pallium* was symbolically powerful, ultimately it was another item of clothing that finally took hold as the general dress of Roman men in late antiquity: the *paenula*. Originally a Celtic garment,[8] this long, sleeveless hooded cape had established itself as common Roman military fatigue dress on the frontiers by the time of Augustus,[9] as well as being an increasingly popular garment for outdoor use in Rome itself.[10] Ironically, as military dress came to be increasingly characterized by simple cloaks fastened on the right shoulder with a brooch like the *sagum* and especially the *chlamys*, the *paenula* took over from the toga as the main component of civilian dress, especially in Rome, although it never achieved the same symbolic status.[11] For Martianus Capella (3.223) it had even taken over from the toga as the Roman national garment, and Sidonius (*Epist.* 1.5.11) tells us that in his day (fifth century), whilst *honorati* wore the toga, normal citizens got around in the *paenula*. It is the garment worn by the people in the lowest register on the door of Santa Sabina in Rome,[12] as well as by the general Roman populace either side of the Rostra in the forum frieze on the Arch of Constantine (Fig. 2.9). Von Rummel (2007) has discussed in detail these new, 'barbarian' dress elements, including the *paenula* and the general move from draped to more tailored clothing, that gradually came into mainstream Roman culture from the northern and eastern edges of the empire; he has shown that although some of the rhetoric in Rome and Constantinople gives the impression that hordes of foreign ruffians were making their way through the empire and leading people astray,[13] in actual fact the newly popular garments were not 'ethnic' dress but simply new status fashions, and the process by which they were adopted was gradual and reciprocal.[14] The *paenula* itself soon also made its way into Christian liturgical dress, and as a result survives until today – via various intermediate forms – in the habits worn by Catholic monks.

So to what extent did the late third and early fourth centuries see what Marrou once characterized as a 'révolution de costume'?[15] On the one hand, we have evidence like the snapshot of garments available to buy in 301 CE in Diocletian's Price Edict that is instructive for what ordinary people might have been wearing. In it, there is no mention of either toga, *tebenna* or *trabea*, and the cloaks listed are the *birrus* and *paenula* (hooded capes), and the *chlamys*, *sagum* and *fibulatorium* (cloaks fastened with brooches). On the other hand, in the literary evidence the toga is still mentioned until well into the fifth century. For example, Prudentius (348–414) refers to his own *toga virilis* ceremony in his youth (*Cath.*, praef. 812), and passages in Servius (*Ecl.* 4.49) and Augustine (*De civ. D.* 4.11) also attest to the continued practice of *togam virilem sumere* in the early fifth century.[16] There is considerable evidence that, at least in the fourth century, the toga was still the garment associated with lawyers and legal experts (*advocati*), and not just in the imperial capitals[17] but also in Vandal North Africa (Drac., *Rom.* 5). But these sources relate to a learned class, and we must be careful not to attach too much wider significance to Ausonius' (310–395) characterization of the Romans as toga-wearers (*Lud. sept. sap.* 2(prol.).22) or statements like that attributed to the sixth-century Gothic king Theoderic in which he encouraged the Gauls to cast off barbarity and return to the *mores togati* (Cassiod., *Var.* 3.17.1). In keeping with the long-standing Roman trait of looking to the past for *exempla*, in the works of late antique writers the toga became a *topos* for the golden age of virtue and simplicity to which one still very ardently aspired, but which for the majority of the population had long ceased to be an everyday reality.[18]

The imperial image

At the other end of the social scale, the emperor also underwent a fundamental transformation from the third century onward. The main tendency, at least until 400, was an increasingly martial flavour in both his image and his role. The groundwork for this was laid already in the second century with army general-cum-emperor figures like Trajan and Septimius Severus and the growing need for the emperor to appear capable of defending the empire from external threat, as evidenced in the surge of military statues and busts alongside the more traditional toga statues.[19] The upheavals of the mid-third century and the quick succession of rival emperor-generals naturally did nothing to reverse this process, and in truth the emperor increasingly derived his power and legitimacy not from the senate or the people but from the army.[20]

For a time, the *toga praetexta* – which in the second century was the main everyday garment of the emperor[21] – appears to still have played a role, at least according to the *Historia Augusta*: it is mentioned in the lists of gifts and booty owned by third-century emperors like Claudius Gothicus and Aurelian (*Claud. Goth.* 14.10; *Aurel.* 13.3).[22] But by the time of the Tetrarchy (293–313), only elite citizens appear to still have worn it, judging by the stunning, recently discovered reliefs representing an *adventus* from Nicomedia in Turkey (Fig. 3.4). On the same monument the emperors themselves are depicted in fringed purple versions of the more soldierly *chlamys*.[23] The first depiction of a Roman emperor wearing a *chlamys* in the heart of Rome is Constantine speaking on the Rostra in the small frieze on the Arch of Constantine in Rome (Fig. 2.9: central figure), but it became the main dress of emperors from the fourth century onward, and went with them into the Byzantine Empire.[24]

In general, the numbers of new statues of emperors gradually declined over time, but we should not forget that the older statues were still standing, and any new ones were meant as a reaction to, or to complement, the existing ones.[25] Moreover, later emperors did sometimes have themselves depicted in earlier styles of toga, and even recycled older toga statues by replacing the head with a new portrait of them, one example being the figure of Theodosius I or II in the Hadrianic Baths at Aphrodisias.[26] As Smith says, the older styles of depiction were chosen 'because they represented particular roles; and those roles and the costume forms that had been associated with them for several centuries remained valid, legible, and meaningful for late antique society'.[27] In most images of the emperor in a toga from the fourth century onward, however, the garment symbolized his role as consul, and as such, was in fact a *trabea*, the garment to which we now turn.

From toga to *trabea*

In Chapter 4 we saw how triumphal dress, the main feature of which was the *toga picta*, started out as an honour bestowed by the senate on victorious generals – who were usually consuls – for use on the day of their triumph and other special occasions such as when they presided over games. In the Principate these three roles – *triumphator*, consul and master of games – became the prerogative of emperors, and the roles gradually melded together.[28] Likewise, and for the same reason, the triumphal procession gradually merged with the *processus consularis* and the *adventus*.[29] Also tied to this was the fact that from the late second century onward, triumphal dress had become the main festive wear of imperial personages (Chapter 5).[30] At the same time, the consulship did still continue also to be occupied by individuals other than the emperor, and became a particularly important role in the fourth/fifth centuries, when virtually all the other former magistracies fell away (of which more in the next section). The garment that was associated with the late antique consulship was the so-called *trabea*.

As mentioned in Chapter 2, most recent typologies of the toga end with the 'magistrate type' of the early fifth century (Fig. 2.10) or even earlier,[31] but in reality the toga continued much longer in the form of the late antique *trabea*.[32] The term *trabea* had formerly been used to denote the short togas of equestrians with public horses (see Chapter 4), and the precise turn of events that resulted in it being used for the late antique garment of consuls is somewhat unclear, although it may have to do with the encroachment of the *equites* into senatorial positions during the course of the late third and fourth centuries. In terms of its form, the *trabea* still sported the round hem of earlier togas, but was now usually draped over both shoulders, rather than just the left, in thick, flat bands (Fig. 7.1).[33] This latter feature, along with a trailing *sinus* draped over the left forearm, show clearly that it developed out of the 'magistrate type' toga (Fig. 2.10).[34] For the fifth and sixth centuries we have a body of visual evidence in the so-called consular diptychs that shows us how the toga/*trabea* developed in this time period. In his seminal work on these objects, Delbrück created a typology that included a white toga with long, hanging *sinus* worn over a loose tunic still showing wide *clavi* worn by senators,[35] the *toga praetexta* still mentioned in literary sources as the dress of magistrates (although the *trabea* was more common),[36] the simple *trabea* in plain purple worn by the *viri consulares* as normal public[37] dress, the triumphal *trabea* ensemble of purple tunic with gold *clavi*, *colobium* over that in purple and decorated in the same style as the *trabea*, and a red-purple *trabea* with gold decorations, worn by triumphant generals, consuls and suffect consuls for processions and other major public events.[38] The emperor's version of the latter included jewel decoration and was used by him when he addressed the senate.[39]

Figure 7.1 Consular diptych of Magnus(?). Castello Sforzesco, Milan. Photo: Peter Horree/Alamy Stock Photo.

In keeping with the general trend toward increasing ornamentation in late antique dress, it is clear that the decoration of the *trabea* could be very elaborate indeed, as can be seen in Claudian's description of the one worn by Stilicho, which included two scenes merging mythological figures with mythologized events from Stilicho's own life (*Cons. Stil.* 2.339–361).[40] A passage of Ausonius' speech of thanks to the emperor Gratian on receiving the consulship in 379 is also instructive as to the decoration of the late antique *trabea*, as well as its role and meaning:

> Beyond the consulship, have you not also bestowed on me care and diligence that has brought me much happiness? In Illyricum swords are being rattled, but you dispense the robes of civilian office to me in Gaul; whilst in your armour you see to my toga (*toga mea*); you gird yourself for imminent battle,[41] and at the same time see to the decoration of my palm-decorated clothing (*palmata vestis*).... For just as that dress (*habitus*) belongs to the consul in peacetime, it

belongs to the triumphator in victory. Too little, you think, to ask me what kind of *trabea* to send: you arrange to inspect it personally.... 'I have sent you a palmate robe (*palmata*),' you say, 'decorated with an image of my father,[42] the divine Constantius.' What happiness I feel, that such care is taken over my insignia! This is most certainly a robe that is 'decorated' (*vestis picta*), so to speak, and that both with your words and with gold.

Grat. act. 51–54

First, it is clear from this passage that at this stage, the terms *trabea* and toga could be used interchangeably, as can be seen also in other works of Ausonius and those of his contemporary Claudian.[43] Second, the *trabea* described here is not just extremely ornate, it also contains imagery relating to dynastic succession, both of which were key characteristics of the late antique political setting; as Dewar has said in his discussion of this passage, Ausonius' *trabea* 'tells us how far we have come from the days of Augustus'.[44] But remnants of the old toga symbolism also continue to make their presence felt, both here and in other text passages: Ausonius writes of his *trabea* as the 'robes of civilian office' contrasting it with the emperor's own military attire,[45] and he describes it as the dress of both the consul in peacetime and the general in triumph.[46] The peaceful connotation of the toga would have become especially pronounced as the role of the emperor became more military in character, and the connection is made many times by both Claudian and Ausonius (e.g. Auson., *Epig.* 26; Claud. *Cons. Hon.* 4.9; *Cons. Stil.* 2.365–367). It is also still a symbol of masculinity,[47] and Claudian describes it as defiled when it is bestowed on his patron Stilicho's enemy, the eunuch Eutropius (*Eutr.* 1.9–10; 1.224–228).[48] But it is also a symbol of the past, and in the aforementioned episode the figures called on by Claudian to witness the outrage of Eutropius in a toga include the Bruti, the Corvini and Cato (*Eutr.* 1.457–465).[49] It is all of these things that became tied up in the role of consul, and are thus telling of the nature of high office and elite identity in late antiquity.

The toga and the late Roman elite

The *trabea* and the office of consul associated with it were important elements in the world of the elite in the fourth and fifth centuries, but the path to them was a gradual one that is worth tracing in some detail in order to understand how the role of the toga evolved.

A good insight into the development of elite ideology from the mid-second to the fourth century is provided by the imagery of the stone sarcophagi that became popular funerary monuments with the upper classes in this period.[50] Various types were on offer, including ones depicting scenes from mythology, of the *paterfamilias* out hunting, in the midst of battle in military clothing, or reading quietly from a scroll in a *pallium*.[51] They show that, unlike in the late Republic and early Empire with their proliferation of toga statues (see Chapter 3), there were now many ways to symbolize elite status that did not involve the toga and the civic office it represented. It is, in any case, telling that from the mid-third century onward it is only sarcophagi belonging to magistrates that depict the toga. The so-called 'Brothers' sarcophagus' (Fig. 2.8) is a typical example. In it, the same man is depicted four times: in the middle his Roman identity is coupled with his private philosophical leaning by means of a toga with twisted *umbo* and slight shoulder triangle on the right and a *pallium* on the left; on the far left he is shown as a magistrate with an entourage in the contemporary style of contabulated toga;[52] and on the far right he is depicted with his wife in a marriage scene wearing the by then highly antiquated early imperial toga with *umbo*.[53] It is clear that in this monument, and the many like it,[54] the toga fulfilled a variety of iconographic functions; the use of the pouch-*umbo* toga is common in marriage scenes in this period, and it is often contrasted with an up-to-date toga for when the man is depicted as a political figure,[55] indicating that by this stage toga styles constituted an elaborate vocabulary, the current ones signifying the routine public activities of the magistrate, whilst the more old-fashioned styles added an air of tradition to special occasions. It may even reflect a reality in which, for example, the old-fashioned toga was actually worn for weddings.[56] Unfortunately, this vocabulary is not always quite so clear to us: a mid–late third-century sarcophagus in the Palazzo Massimo depicting what appears to be a *processus consularis* also shows men in three different types of toga (pouch-*umbo*, twisted *umbo* and fully contabulated),[57] so other criteria must also have been at play.

It is clear that by the fourth century at the latest the toga was the sole preserve of the elite, but the upper classes were themselves undergoing changes. The earlier senatorial *cursus honorum* disappeared, the quaestorship and praetorship became purely symbolic honours bestowed on young senators and the consulship became a separate entity (although opportunities here were expanded with shorter terms and a greater role for suffect consuls).[58] Moreover, the administrative and military functions senators had fulfilled were gradually transferred to equestrians. At the same time, the consulship was opened up to equestrians as well, blurring once and for all the distinction between the *ordines*, and leading to a new designation for this class: *viri consulares*.[59] When Constantine created his new capital at Constantinople, one consul was appointed at any given time to Rome, and

Figure 7.2 Detail of the south-east face of the pedestal of Theodosius' obelisk, Istanbul. Photo: Jan Butchofsky/Alamy Stock Photo.

another to the new capital, planting the seed for the development of a class of *viri consulares* in Constantinople as well. When the two halves of the empire were divided in the late fourth century, each retained one consular position. Importantly, though, the changes in the nature of imperial rule also led to the emergence of a whole raft of new administrative and military positions filled by a new class of officials who did not owe anything to the traditional ideals bound up in the toga. Thus, we see a gradual division of the elite into an increasingly symbolic class of *viri consulares*, who clung on to the toga, and an increasingly dominant *Beamtentum*, who wore the new symbol of high status, the *chlamys*.

All this is well illustrated in the reliefs on the pedestal of Theodosius' obelisk in Constantinople (392 CE), depicting the emperor's court watching games at the hippodrome from a *kathisma*. On the south-east face (Fig. 7.2) all the male family members in the central gallery wear the *chlamys*, apart from one figure at the bottom right – usually identified as a young emperor-designate – who wears a 'magistrate-style' toga. On all four sides the royal family is shown surrounded by the imperial court, including separate groups of *viri consulares* in 'magistrate-style' togas (south-east/north-east face: see Fig. 7.2: front figures in both side galleries) and officials and soldiers in *chlamydes* (south-west/north-west face). A lower register on the south-east face depicts the general population, wearing –

where decipherable – *paenulae*.⁶⁰ The honorific statuary newly collated in the University of Oxford's *Last Statues of Antiquity* project and database (2009–2012)⁶¹ is also illustrative of the process described above. Wueste has analysed the dress on all of the statues of aristocratic men⁶² dated between 284 and 550, the majority of which date to the fourth century, when the composition of the Roman elite was most in flux. A little over half the figures wear a toga, whilst roughly a fifth wear the *chlamys*, the remainder wearing *pallia* and military gear; all the *chlamys* and *pallium* depictions come from the eastern provinces, showing both that the older Greek cloak and the new power-dress continued to be worn by the eastern elite, and that the *chlamys* was primarily an eastern phenomenon emanating from the new capital in Constantinople.⁶³ The toga-wearers, on the other hand, are roughly equally split across the two halves of the empire, showing that the garment retained currency in both new spheres of power. From the corresponding epigraphy it is clear that the vast majority of the toga-wearers were provincial governors, city prefects, consuls and proconsuls, all of them traditional Roman status positions. This confirms the impression given in the works of contemporary authors like Claudian, who see the toga/*trabea* as virtually synonymous with the consulship and the old traditions it embodied (*Ruf.* 1.249; *Cons. Stil.* 3.85; *Carm. Min.* 41.13–14).⁶⁴ All of this stood in stark contrast to the new offices of the transformed imperial structure, the holders of which are represented in the *chlamys*.⁶⁵

Von Rummel's *Habitus Barbarus* (2007) is by far the most comprehensive and meticulous study of late antique dress and what it tells us about the nature of the elite in this period. He has argued that the traditional scholarly view, in which the honourable togate elite was gradually undermined by *chlamys*-clad barbarian upstarts, has been unduly influenced by the rhetoric of the late antique authors who wrote of the toga as if it were the only legitimate garment of officialdom.⁶⁶ In reality the dress rhetoric reveals the internal conflict within the elite between the traditional, civilian *viri consulares* – the authors of our texts – and the new men in imperial administration who were usually not from Rome, nor necessarily literate, and often started their careers in the military.⁶⁷ The increasing role of the military in late antique government is for von Rummel simply a fact of history that was only considered problematic by the people it threatened: most of the clothing manipulatively described as 'foreign' by late antique authors was, in reality, the normal dress of the late Roman military aristocracy.⁶⁸

The nature of the toga had, however, also fundamentally changed. In itself a sign that rank distinctions were becoming increasingly rigid, the *lex vestiaria* of 382 CE, determining that senators must wear togas for official duties, but could wear *paenulae* at other times (*Cod. Theod.* 14.10.1), shows that normal everyday wear even for the old elite was by this time the *paenula*; as strong as the symbolism of the toga continued to be, it had become a gala costume rather than the workaday dress of statesmen.[69] The most striking manifestation of this change is the fact that all of the elite statues depicting a toga in Wueste's catalogue are cases of reuse.[70] The recycling of older statues, although already sometimes practised in earlier periods,[71] became a widespread and systematic phenomenon in late antiquity that has been the focus of much recent work.[72] One example from Rome is the fourth-century statue of C. Caelius Saturninus *signo* Dogmatius in the Lateran Museum,[73] showing him in an early-second-century toga and the special shoes of the *ordo equester* that had also disappeared by this time. The long honorific inscription (*CIL* 6.1705) details a distinguished career in financial administration ending in acceptance to the senate, illustrating especially well the aforementioned elision of the equestrian and senatorial orders. This and the many other statues like it show the enormous symbolic power in late antiquity of the very toga statues that had been so central to the civic ideal of the earlier Roman elite (Chapter 3). As Wueste has said, 'the appeal was not just the specific garments, but in the archaizing visual effect and perhaps the traditional Roman values it represented',[74] and Bodnaruk has suggested that the continuity they embodied was especially appealing in the face of the profound changes being inflicted on the aristocracy in this period.[75]

As a garment of anyone but the emperor, however, the *trabea*'s days were numbered as the consulship became increasingly obsolete. It is telling that although almost all of the late antique garments found their way into Christian liturgical dress in one form or another, the *trabea* did not.[76] By the sixth century the role of consul had become entirely symbolic, as even their last remaining function as master of games disappeared. The office was terminated in the West in 534 and in the East in 541.

From *trabea* to *loros*

In 1898 Wilpert declared that the final toga went to the grave with the last of the consuls,[77] but this is not entirely true. Whilst the consulship itself ended, consular affirmation still played a role in the titles given to emperors in the East until at least the seventh century,[78] and the *trabea* never stopped being an element of the emperor's clothing repertoire to signal this. Already third-century emperors like Trebonianus Gallus and Probus had had themselves depicted in ornate *trabeae* on their coins,[79] and the practice continued throughout the fourth and fifth centuries in both East and West, as can be seen in countless coins and medallions, such as one dating to 339 depicting the three sons of Constantine, Constantinus II in a *chlamys*, but his two brothers, who were consuls that year, in the *trabea*,[80] as well as consular diptychs like that of Constantius III (421) in which he wears an identical *trabea* to the figures either side of him except that his is ornately decorated.[81] At the turn of the sixth to seventh century, long after the office of consul had been abolished, the emperor Maurice still saw fit to depict himself in a *trabea* on his coins.[82]

And so it is that in the East, the *trabea* gradually transformed into a special imperial vestment of the Byzantine Empire called the *loros* (Fig. 7.3). This gradually became more of a wide band than a cloak, but the resemblance to the late antique *trabea* is clear: like it, the *loros* was customarily draped over both shoulders and then vertically down the front of the body, and also like the *trabea* it retained the ancient toga feature of being draped over the left forearm. It was the special dress of Byzantine emperors for civil ceremonies, and was worn throughout the Middle Ages.[83] Thus, just like the Roman Empire itself, the toga never actually disappeared: it just transformed into something else.

Figure 7.3 Detail of a miniature showing Nicephorus III, Bibliothèque Nationale de France Manuscript Coislin 79 folio 2 bis verso (John Chrysostom, *Homilies*). Photo: History and Art Collection/Alamy Stock Photo.

Epilogue

The toga is still with us. Like the kimono and the kilt, for most people, at least in Western countries, it is a term that immediately conjures up a particular style of garment and a specific time and place. But to a far greater extent than with those two examples, there exists a general misunderstanding of what it was: it tends to be seen as the draped dress of all people in Roman antiquity rather than a specific garment of Rome. This is the sense in which it appears in settings like the 'toga parties' that are an enduring feature of student life on university campuses, and it comes in no small part from the tendency in Western films set in Rome to side-line the copious evidence we have for what the Romans wore in favour of fantastical costumes that conform to the idea of Rome that directors and producers wish to convey.[1] The tendency to generalize ancient dress goes back even further, however: from the Renaissance onward an increasing interest in classical antiquity meant that ancient remains in Greece and Rome came into the sphere of interest of European aristocrats and intellectuals, and ancient artworks gradually made their way from Mediterranean soil into the houses and gardens of the European nobility, forming a template for their ideas about the appearance of ancient people. The links between ancient writers and intellectual developments such as the Enlightenment led to a whole array of portraits of European poets and thinkers in the eighteenth and nineteenth centuries in draped attire, a style that was meant to evoke a general idea of classical learning, rather than recreate specific ancient dress codes.[2]

There were, however, in this period also more specific evocations of Roman dress, and these are illustrative of the ideological landscape of the seventeenth to nineteenth centuries: European monarchs, for example, sometimes had themselves depicted in the cuirass and cloak of Roman army generals to assert an ancient pedigree for the idea of the right of conquest and absolutist power,[3] while at the other end of the ideological spectrum the toga statue was employed by key figures of modern Republicanism to visualize their adherence to ancient Roman political theory and democratic statecraft. An example of this is George Washington, whose ideas for a new American constitution were modelled closely on those of Republican Rome.[4] Whilst today the most commonly illustrated statue of him is the one by Greenhough in the National Museum of American History depicting him as a Greek god, he was also sometimes portrayed in statue form wearing a toga (such as in the Massachusetts State House, Boston), and it is especially this form of depiction that made its way into mass culture in the nineteenth century in the form of ornamental figurines[5] and even stove decorations.[6]

However, of all the political leaders of the modern period, none modelled their ideas and appearance more explicitly on Roman models than Napoleon Bonaparte. Napoleon saw himself as the heir to the Roman emperors and used Augustus' *de iure* restoration of the Republic and *de facto* monarchy as the role model for his own constitution, which he peppered with Roman terms and offices (e.g. consuls, tribunate, even *senatus-consulte*). In language that would have swelled the heart of an ancient Roman like Cato, Napoleon often said that he preferred the utilitarian genius of the Romans (in the form of military know-how and the engineering of public infrastructure) over the philosophy and art of the Greeks, and when Canova carved a statue of him as an ancient god he is said to have disliked it for being too nude and too Greek.[7] As such, it is perhaps not

Figure E.1 Statue of Napoleon Bonaparte by Jérôme Maglioli in the Place-du-Maréchal-Foch, Ajaccio, Corsica. Photo: John Elk III/Alamy Stock Photo.

Figure E.2 Musée de la Romanité, Nîmes, France. Photo: Anthony Maurin for ObjectifGard.

surprising that one of his most famous statues – the one that stands in Place Foch in his hometown of Ajaccio in Corsica – portrays him as '*premier consul*' in a perfectly rendered Augustan-style *umbo*-toga (Fig. E.1).

The accurate portrayal of the toga in the statue of Napoleon is, however, unusual, and today it is especially the term itself that has survived in the general imagination, rather than any detailed knowledge of its form. But this does not mean it has lost its power to embody Romanness for a modern audience: 2018 saw the opening of a new museum near the Roman amphitheatre in Nîmes designed by Elizabeth de Portzamparc, the central building of which is swathed in waves of white tiles meant to convey the drapery folds of a toga (Fig. E.2). The name of this new institution – Musée de la Romanité – taken together with the symbolism of its architecture are striking proof of the continued connection of the toga to all things Roman in the modern mind.

Glossary

Dress terms

angustus clavus the narrow purple stripes that ran vertically from shoulder to hem on the *tunica* of a man of equestrian status

balteus the top, straight edge of the toga that in most draping styles was worn diagonally across the chest

birrus a sleeveless hooded cape that became increasingly popular in the later Empire

calcei the closed boots worn with the toga that came in various styles denoting rank status

caligae the hobnailed boots worn by Roman soldiers

capite velato the covering of the back of the head with the edge of the toga for ritual activities

chlaina a light Greek cloak usually draped around the body but sometimes also fastened at the right shoulder with a brooch

chlamys a Greek cloak usually fastened at the right shoulder with a brooch

clavus, clavi see *angustus clavus/latus clavus*

dalmatica a long tunic for men and women with long, drooping sleeves

exomis a short, belted tunic for men that left one shoulder free; originated in Greece but became the dress commonly worn in the Roman Empire for hard labour and by the god Vulcan

himation the most common form of Greek cloak consisting of a large piece of rectangular cloth draped around the body; the Romans called it a *pallium*

lacinia the two wedge-shaped corners of the toga usually seen hanging between the ankles in toga depictions

laena a special type of toga worn by some priests that was roughly circular in shape and folded in the middle to create a double-layered appearance

latus clavus the broad purple stripes that ran vertically from shoulder to hem on the *tunica* of a man of senatorial status

paenula a sleeveless hooded cape probably derived from the Celts

palla the female *pallium*

pallium see *himation*

sagum a rectangular cloak fastened with a brooch on the right shoulder; the main military cloak for most of Roman history but originally derived from the Celts

sinus the semi-circular extra portion of cloth added to the straight edge of the toga in the early imperial period rendering it almost oval in shape, but appearing as a second, short layer when draped as the entire garment was folded double along the *balteus*

stola the pinafore-like garment worn over the Roman woman's *tunica* that symbolized respectable married status

synthesis the garment ensemble worn by Roman men for banquets probably consisting of a colour-coordinated tunic and cloak

tebenna the semi-circular cloak of the Etruscans out of which the toga evolved; also the Greek word for the toga

toga candida the bleached white toga worn to signal candidature for political office

toga picta the purple toga decorated with imagery in gold thread worn with the *tunica palmata* by victorious generals at triumphal celebrations

toga praetexta the plain white toga with purple border worn by freeborn children and priests/magistrates

toga pulla the dark-coloured toga of mourning

toga pura see *toga virilis*

toga purpurea the fully purple toga associated with the early Roman kings but later worn by certain magistrates and, eventually, emperors

toga virilis the plain, everyday toga of the Roman man, usually the off-white colour of undyed sheep's wool

trabea the short toga worn by equestrians who had a publicly funded horse for the *transvectio equitum* parade; in late antiquity it elided with the *toga picta* and became the dress of Roman consuls

tunica palmata the purple tunic decorated with palm leaves in gold thread worn with the *toga picta* by victorious generals at triumphal celebrations

umbo the pouch-like fold of cloth pulled out over the *balteus* in the toga drapery styles of the first and second centuries CE; in drapery styles of the late second century onward it was increasingly stretched to the shoulder in a triangular, then rectangular, shape

Notes

Chapter 1

1. Alternative dates have been put forward based on chronologies given by other writers such as Polybius and Plutarch, but the exact date is irrelevant here.
2. E.g. Caes., *BGall.* 1.41–43; Tac. *Ann.* 3.44.1; 45.2; *Hist.* 4.54.2; 59.2.
3. Unless otherwise stated, all translations are my own.
4. E.g. Terrenato 1998; Keay/Terrenato 2001; Stek 2013.
5. See Dench 2005 for the role of Italy in the Roman imagination and Lavan 2016b: 157–160 for Italy's privileged status in the empire.
6. Various terms can be found in Latin literature relating to appearance: *vestis* or *amictus* are used for actual clothing, *cultus* for personal adornment, style of dress and grooming, while *habitus* is used for all of the above but with the addition of comportment and state-of-being. *Habitus* is more commonly used than other words, reflecting the Roman attitude that appearance and character were inseparable.
7. See also App, *Mith.* 1.2 for an abbreviated account of this.
8. See also Maecenas' lost work *De Culto Suo*.
9. Edmondson 2008: 29. See also Starbatty 2010.
10. E.g. *Digest* 34.2.23, which distinguishes between the dress of the *paterfamilias* – togas, tunics and *palliola* (cloaks); the *materfamilias* – *stolae, pallia*, tunics, undergarments, head coverings and belts; children (*puerilia*) – *togae praetextae, chlamydes* and *pallia*; and of slaves – tunics and mantles.
11. Edmondson 2008: 22; Rothfus 2010: 431.
12. See also Isid., *Etym.* 19.23.6: 'different peoples (*gentes*) can be distinguished in their dress (*habitus*) just as in their speech (*lingua*)'.
13. For clothing in the *Aeneid*, see Bender 1994.
14. See below Chapter 2 and Coarelli 2011: 165–167, figs 148–149; D'Ambra 1998: 14 fig. 4.
15. Ennius frg. 1.61 in Fest., pp. 394.6–9 L.
16. See below Chapter 4.
17. See also the inscription of Philip of Macedon in Larisa: *IG* 9.2.517.
18. For an extended discussion of these myths and their role in the Roman self-image see Dench 2005: 17–25.
19. See also Cic., *Balb.* 31 for a lengthy self-congratulatory description of Roman generosity with citizenship.

20 Although see his *De Republica* for a critical stance on the inclusive nature of Roman citizenship. See also Juv. 8.272–275, where he writes that aristocratic families were obsessed with their family trees, but if they looked at them too closely they would find ignoble characters in them.
21 Verified, at least in essence, in the Lyon tablet: *CIL* 13.1668. See also Vell. Pat. 1.14. But see also recent, more sceptical views of Roman citizenship and the ecumenical ideal such as Lavan 2016b and Ando 2016.
22 See most recently Wallace-Hadrill 2008.
23 Most famously embodied in Verg., *Aen.* 6.847–853.
24 Dench 2005: 63–69.
25 E.g. Pausch 2003: 24–27; Zanker 2010: 162–166. See below Chapter 2.
26 See also Dench 2005: 195–217.
27 Dench 2005: 113.
28 Dench 2005: esp. 28.
29 Dench 2005: esp. chapter 5, section 2.
30 See, e.g., Dio 50.5.2–3; 50.25.5; 50.26.5; Plut., *Ant.* 55.1.
31 Ferris 2000; von Rummel 2007; Chauvot 2016.
32 See Woolf 1998 for the idea that the Gauls, through their elites, were incorporated into the Roman community through the adoption of shared values such as *humanitas* and Dench 2005: 32; Lavan 2016b and Ando 2016 for criticism of this and other works that stress the integrational nature of Roman identity at the expense of its capacity for chauvinism.
33 *RRC* 301/1; 372; 413/1; 419/2.
34 Possibly for the sake of historical plausibility: Bender 1994.
35 Potthoff 1992: 67–70; Varro, *Ling.* 3.132; 5.114.
36 While his cloak is draped in an archaic style that calls to mind the Greek *himation*, the diagonal upward curve at the bottom, and the fact that it is worn *capite velato*, show that it was meant to suggest a toga.
37 For other examples see von Rummel 2007: 84 n.11.
38 See also Martial 6.48.1; Juv. 1.96.
39 Caes., *BGall.* 8.24.3; 8.52.1–2; Cic., *Phil.* 8.27; Pompon. 2.59; Pliny, *HN* 3.112; Suet., *Gram.* 3.6; Mart. 3.1; Dio Cass. 48.12.5. See also Brennan 2008 for the alleged naming of Carthage Alexandria Commodiana Togata by Commodus (SHA *Commodus* 17.7–8), and his suggestion that '*togatus*' was a term of subjugation.
40 E.g. Arminius in Tacitus: 'one thing the Germans could never condone, that they had seen the rods, the axes, and the toga between the Elbe and the Rhine' (*Ann.* 1.59.4).
41 See Bonfante Warren 1973: 586.
42 E.g. Micali 1835; Marquardt 1886; Johnstone 1903.
43 See also, e.g., Blümner 1911.
44 See also Wilpert 1898; Albizzati 1922.

45 E.g. Müller 1888; Anderson 1891; Courby 1919.
46 E.g. Bonfante Warren 1966; 1970; 1971; Bonfante 1978; 1975/2003.
47 E.g. Wegner 1939; 1956; Wegner/Bracker/Real 1979; Wegner/Daltrop/Hausmann 1966; Wiggers/Wegner 1971. See also Bergmann 1977; Niemeyer 1968; Gercke 1968.
48 E.g. Frenz 1977; Kockel 1993.
49 E.g. Boschung 1987.
50 E.g. Koch/Sichtermann 1982; Amedick 1991; Huskinson 1996.
51 Chausson/Inglebert 2003; Cleland/Harlow/Llewellyn-Jones 2005; Köb/Riedel 2005; Edmondson/Keith 2008.
52 George 2008.
53 Sebesta 2005; Dolansky 2008.
54 Davies 2005.
55 Vout 1996: 213.
56 George 2008 is in many ways an exception and will be looked at in greater detail in Chapter 4.

Chapter 2

1 Potthoff 1992: 199.
2 Dion. Hal., *Ant. Rom.* 3.61; Quint., *Inst.* 11.3.139; Ath. 5.213; App., BC *iv.* 5.11; Isid., *Etym.* 19.24.3. Wilson's earlier idea that the toga, like other 'primitive' garments (kilt, *himation*), was originally rectangular (1924: 17) is no longer taken seriously.
3 Amelung 1903: 44; Goette 1990: 2–3; Zanker 1989; 2010. See also Wallace-Hadrill 2008: 43.
4 Pausch 2003: 24, my translation.
5 E.g. Goette 1990: 2–3.
6 See, e.g., Hdt 1.94. It is worth noting in view of the passage quoted above that Dionysius believed the Etruscans to have been indigenous, rather than hailing from Lydia (*Ant. Rom.* 1.30).
7 Courby 1919: 348.
8 Richardson 1953.
9 Pallottino 1952.
10 Hafner 1969.
11 E.g. Bonfante Warren 1966; Bonfante 1975/2003; 1978.
12 See also Bücheler's early linguistic work (1884); Bieber 1934/1967: 37; Heurgon 1961: 218–222; Stone 1994: 38 n.2. Wrede's review of Goette 1990 also expressed scepticism of his Greece theory (1995: 548).
13 See also the sixth-century 'Apollo of Veii' in the Villa Giulia (Bonfante 1978: 19).
14 For these textiles and their reconstruction see Stauffer 2013.

15 Bonfante 2003: 49.
16 Bonfante 2003: 50; 193 fig. 113.
17 Bonfante 2003: 50; 200 fig. 143.
18 Bonfante 1978: 25–26; see Bonfante Warren 1973 for an overview of all Etruscan survivals in Roman dress.
19 von Haase 2013.
20 The Verucchio finds have caused some scholars who had proposed Greek origins for the toga to rethink their views: see von Haase 2013; Goette 2012; 2013.
21 E.g. Chantraine 1968–1980: 1113.
22 See, e.g., Polybius 10.4.8; 26.10.6.
23 Some initially promising fragments of a rounded Roman cloak from southern Egypt that seem to be of northern Mediterranean origin have since been interpreted by Granger-Taylor 2008 as a hooded cape, not a toga.
24 Bonfante 2003: 49.
25 See, e.g., Goethert 1937 and examples of round-edged cloaks in Etruscan wall paintings of the fifth century: Tomb of the Triclinium, Tarquinia (Pallottino 1952: 78); Tomb of Francesca Giustiniani, Tarquinia (Pallottino 1952: 87); and third century: Tomb of the Shields, Tarquinia (Pallottino 1952: 105). In the latter, the musicians already wear recognizable white togas without tunics underneath.
26 E.g. the sixth-century BCE figurines in Richardson 1953; Bonfante 2003: 50; 192, figs 110–112.
27 See, e.g., the third-century BCE bronze figurines from Carsoli in Richardson/Richardson 1966: 264.
28 See Ovid, *Fasti* 6.570–71 for an oblique mention of a figure of king Servius wearing a toga.
29 This explanation seems more likely than that of Rothfus (2010: 432 n.19), that the *f.t.* was so-called because the *socii* were rendering a service *to the Romans*, i.e. *togati*. See also Baronowski 1984.
30 Wrede 1995: 548. Cf. Mommsen 1887: 222, who supposed that serving in the Roman army qualified *socii* to wear the toga.
31 Coarelli 2011: 165–167 figs 148–149.
32 Ennius frg. 1.61 in Fest., p. 394.6–9 L.
33 See also Asc., *Scaur.* 29.
34 D'Ambra 1998: 14 fig. 4.
35 Cic., *Phil.* 2.44; Tert., *De pallio* 5.2 (for *calcei*); Quint., *Inst.* 11.3.138; Cicero, *Cat.* 2.22 (for appropriate length and colour of tunic). Cf. Greek cloaks like the *himation*, which were usually worn with sandals (*crepidae, soleae*).
36 Bonfante 2003: 182 fig. 84.
37 Non. 867–868L=540–541M; Afranius, *Frat.* 182; Serv., *Aen.* 1.282.
38 See below Chapter 3.

39 See also Livy 22.54, in which during Hannibal's invasion of Italy (218–216 BCE) the inhabitants of Venusia give the Roman troops togas and tunics.
40 See also Frontin., *Str.* 4.26.
41 See, e.g., the statue of the 'Arringatore': Fig. 2.5.
42 Dubourdieu 1986.
43 New colonies: Servius, *Aen.* 5.755; *sacra Ambarvalia*: Livy 5.46.2; Val. Max. 1.1.11; App., *Pun.* 48; *Mith.* 45; Temple of Janus: Livy 8.9.9; 10.7.3; warfare: Val. Max. 1.1.11; Verg., *Aen.* 7.601–615; Livy 10.7.3; Lucan, *Phars.* 1.596. See also Festus 251L; Serv., *Aen.* 7.612; Isid., *Etym.* 19.24.7; *CIL* 11.1420.
44 See Fröhlich 1991.
45 Dench 2005: 76.
46 E.g. Stone 1994: 13; Bonfante 2003.
47 Goette 1990: Aa22.
48 Linen was available but used mainly for undergarments as it does not dye well, although Pliny does say that some togas were made of poppy-stem fibre (*HN* 8.195). Silk was not unknown in the late Republic and Empire (Prop. 1.22; Ovid, *Am.* 2.298), but it was very rare before late antiquity and its effeminate associations meant it would not have been appropriate for togas (see, e.g., Pliny, *HN* 11.76–78).
49 Cross-breeding: Varro, *Rust.* 2.2.4; Columella, *Rust.* 7.2.5; wool sourcing: Pliny, *HN* 8.190; Varro, *Rust.* 2.2.18.
50 Mart. 8.28.1–8: 'Gown, welcome gift of an eloquent friend, tell me, of what flock would you like to be the fame and pride? Did the Apulian grass of Ledean Phalanthus flourish for you, where Galaesus saturates the tilth with Calabrian waters? Or did Baetis, Tartessian nourisher of the Iberian fold, wash you too on the back of a Hesperian ewe? Or did your wool number many-cleft Timavus, whom faithful Cyllarus drank with starry mouth?' (trans. Shackleton Bailey 1993).
51 See Quint., *Inst.* 12.10.47 where he says that the toga of the orator should not be shaggy (*hirta*), but also not silky smooth (*serica*), implying, like Pliny, that the tendency in his day was away from a long nap to a short one, achieving an ever smoother toga. For another '*hirta*' toga see Cato's dress in Luc., *Phar.* 2.386.
52 Light togas: Mart. 2.85.4; Juv. 2.97; heavy togas: Mart. 2.44; Suet., *Aug.* 82.
53 See, e.g., Plaut., *Epid.* 229–235; Ovid, *Am.* 3.169–192 and recent research on Roman dyeing techniques, e.g. Martelli 2014.
54 The white colour appears to have been a key feature of the toga from an early stage, as we see it already worn by the Roman figures in the François tomb paintings at Vulci (Coarelli 2011: 165–167 figs 148–149) and the Esquiline tomb paintings (D'Ambra 1998: 14 fig. 4).
55 See also his melancholy later memory of how 'bright' (*nitida*) this toga had been when it was new (9.49).
56 See, e.g., Pliny, *HN* 9.137.

57 Wilson 1924: 71: she suggested it was sewn together from two parts and was sure that she could see the requisite seams on some statues, but I have not been able to identify these.
58 Granger-Taylor 1982; 2007.
59 Stauffer 2013.
60 Harlow 2018: 134.
61 Granger-Taylor 1982; 2007; cf. Goette 1990: 5.
62 E.g. *CIL* 6.964; 6.5206; 6.8554; 6.9979–80; 6.37724.
63 E.g. *ILS* 8393–4 (the '*laudatio Turiae*'); 8402–03.
64 See Larsson Lovén 2007.
65 E.g. the early-first-century CE grave inscriptions in the *columbarium* of the Statilii Tauri mention four weavers, eight spinners, two dyers and four fullers among their slaves: *CIL* 6.6213–6640.
66 Dross-Krüpe 2017: 40.
67 E.g. *CIL* 6.9489: *lanarius*; 2.5812; 4.3529: *fullones*; 2.5519: *infector*; 6.9813: *plumarius*; 13.7737: *textor*; 11.862: *negotiator lanarius*; 3.5824: *negotiator artis purpurariae*; *ILS* 7290a: *lanarii pectinarii*.
68 See Jones 1960; Dross-Krüpe 2011; 2017: 41–42.
69 Jones 1960: 184, although he surmises that the initial processes of carding and spinning continued to be domestic-based, or at least a cottage industry. See also Wild 1970; Vicari 2001 for textile production and trade in the western empire.
70 See Jones 1960 for a detailed list of the – mainly epigraphic – evidence for dyers and fullers in different parts of the empire, and for the textile industry in general: Rogers/Jørgensen/Rast-Eicher 2001; Gleba/Pásztókai-Szeőke 2013; Flohr 2013.
71 E.g. *CIL* 4.3130; 6.3680; 6.4476; 6.8556; 6.33920; 11.868; 13.4564; 14.3958; *ILS* 7568–75 (Rome); 6668 (Bononia); 6688 (Aquileia); P. Oxy. 2230 (Oxyrhynchus). For *vestiarii tenuarii* (sellers of fine garments), see Liu 2009 and 80 n.101 for a list of inscriptions.
72 Holleran 2012: 83–84. Vicus Tuscus: Martial 11.27.11; *CIL* 6.9848; 6.9976; 6.33923; 6.37826; 14.2433; Horrea Agrippiana: *CIL* 6.9972; 14.3958; Horrea Volusianis: *CIL* 6.9973.
73 Plaut., *Aul.* 512; Juv. 7.221; *Dig.* 14.3.5.4. See also the cloth and clothing sellers in the frescoes in the House of Julia Felix in Pompeii: Baldassarre 1991: 253 figs 117–118.
74 E.g. *CIL* 5.5925; 6.33906; *ILS* 7576; 7578–79. See Liu 2009 for the guilds of the various clothes-trading professions.
75 E.g. Mart. 2.44.1–4; 3.36; 9.100; Juv. 1.119.
76 E.g. Mart. 3.36; 7.10.11; 12.36.
77 E.g. Mart. 7.86; 9.49; 10.73.
78 Holleran 2012: 54; 229; Plaut., *Epid.* 455; Petron., *Sat.* 12–15; Juv. 3.147–53; Amm. Marc. 15.12.2.

79 *Centonarii/sartores*: CIL 14.4573; 14.4364.
80 *Sarcinator/-trix*: CIL 5.7568; 6.3051; 6.6348; 6.4029; 6.4030–31; Pliny, *HN* 8.191; Juv. 3.254; Cato, *Agr.* 2.3.
81 In the copious textile remains from Mons Claudianus in Egypt, for example, a third of all clothing showed signs of repair and patching (Mannering 2000).
82 See, e.g., the curse tablets in McKie (forthcoming): tablet ID 52–53; 60; 65; 71–75; 84; 110; 122–124; 134; 139; 153; 180; 193; 196; 200; 263.
83 The following is based chiefly on this work, but the reader is advised to consult it directly for finer art-historical details, stylistic features and workshop chronologies.
84 Goette's type Aa (1990: 20–24) and Wilson's first form (1924: 17–42).
85 Granger-Taylor 1982; N. Goldman 1994: 228.
86 Hor., *Epist.* 1.19.13, in which he describes Cato's deliberately archaic dress style.
87 D'Ambra 1998: 14 fig. 4.
88 Kuttner 2004: 317.
89 See Vermaseren 1957; for a debate about the date see Zadoks-Jitta 1932: 61–63 and Goethert 1931: 21–25.
90 Goette 1990: 20–21.
91 Goette's type Ab (1990: 24–27), Wilson's second form (1924: 43–60) and Hafner's 'Manteltoga' (1969: 40–42).
92 Goethert 1937; Goette 1990: 24.
93 E.g. examples in Hafner 1969: 40–42 and third-century BCE figurines from Carsoli in Richardson/Richardson 1966: 264.
94 Cf. Wrede 1995: 543–546, who not especially plausibly sees the 'armsling' as an ancient Italian style, rather than a result of Hellenization, and a way to better display the ornate togas of triumphant generals, through which it gained traction as a status symbol, whilst the diagonal drape was better for showing off the right *clavus* of the tunic (the width of which signalled senatorial or equestrian status).
95 E.g. Kleiner/Kleiner 1980–1981: 133; Filges 2000.
96 Rothfus 2010: 426.
97 Richardson/Richardson 1966: 266; Wrede 1995. Davies (2018: 143) has argued that although superficially similar, the 'armsling' drapery of Greek statues like 'Aeschines' and their Roman counterparts show markedly different gesticulation and body language, the raised arms resting on hips or clutching at the cloak of the former showing self-assurance, whilst the arms straight down the sides of the latter signalled humility and restraint. For more on the variations and origins of the 'armsling' style see Filges 2000.
98 See below Chapter 3.
99 Richardson/Richardson (1966) were probably right to suggest that Quintilian was making a mistake because he was aware of old 'armsling' statues but not of the even older style which left the right arm free.

100 See below Chapter 4.
101 Olson 2014a: 442.
102 Although see Bieber 1959, where she wrongly identifies some togas as *pallia*.
103 Goette's type B (1990: 29–54); Wilson's third/fourth form (1924: 61–73).
104 Goette 1990: 4; Granger-Taylor 1982.
105 See below Chapter 5.
106 Zanker 2010: 124 fig. 100b; 159 fig. 124.
107 Stone 1994; Goette 1990: 29–40.
108 Goette's type Ca (1990: 54–57); Wilson's fifth form (1924: 73–75).
109 Goette 1990: pl. 32.1–2.
110 E.g. on the Arch of Titus: Goette 1990: pl. 32.1–2 and Trajan's Column: pl. 32.4.
111 See Tert., *De pall.* 5 for the skill and tools needed to create this. Tertullian calls the *balteus* an *umbo*, so by this time the terms have elided. Stone and Wilson suggested that to keep the bands in place they must have involved concealed stitches (Wilson 1924: 79; Stone 1994: 25; 34).
112 Goette's type Cb (1990: 57–62); Wilson's sixth form (1924: 76–79).
113 Goette 1990: pl. 34.1. NB Goette classes this toga as the previous style Ca.
114 See, e.g., the *Concordia Augustorum* relief on the Arch of Septimius Severus (Stone 1994: 24 fig. 1.15).
115 Pochmarski 2006; Rothe 2012: 155–157; 156 figs 9–10; 204 fig. 52.
116 Goette's type D (1990: 59–62); Wilson's seventh form (1924: 79–84). This is Stone's final toga type (1994). See also Hula 1895; Ross 1911.
117 Goette 1990: pl. 40.1; Stone 1994: 25; 33 fig. 1.17a.
118 E.g. the Mucianus monument from the Via Salaria: Goette 1990: 61–62; pl. 43.1. In this portrait the woman even wears a contabulated *palla*.
119 See also Stone 1994: 34.
120 Goette 1990: 71ff.
121 Borg/Witschel 2001: 107.
122 Fejfer 2008: 192.
123 Goette's type E (1990: 62–63).
124 Goette 1990: pl. 46.1–2.
125 E.g. Wilson 1924; Stone 1994.
126 See Delbrück 1929.
127 Olson 2017b: 4.
128 E.g. Davis 1992; Entwhistle 2000.
129 E.g. Davis 1992: 17; Entwhistle 2000: 43. A notable exception is König 1973: 49.
130 See also Ovid, *Am.* 3.149 where he says how difficult it is to keep up with changing hairstyles.
131 See, e.g., the different toga drapery styles in grave reliefs in Italy and the provinces in Chapters 4 and 6 below. Cf. Rothfus, who argued that changes in *both* size *and*

style were elite phenomena, and that poorer Romans had little to gain by following them (2010: 427).
132 See, e.g., Larsson Lovén 2013. Although see Plaut., *Epid.* 222–235 for a fictionalized discussion of women's clothing fads. As we don't have much in the way of visual evidence for women for Plautus' time, and his plays were set in Athens, it is difficult to know how much importance to ascribe to passages like this.
133 E.g. Stone 1994; Vout 1996. See Chapter 4.
134 See Chapter 4 below.
135 Stone 1994: fig. 1.11; Goette 1990: 42.
136 Stone 1994: 24 fig. 1.12.
137 E.g. Goette 1990: pl. 25.1; 138 Bb 153 pl. 25.6; 38.1–2; Stone 1994: fig. 1.14.
138 Wilson 1924: figs 61A–61B.
139 Goette 1990: pl. 29.
140 Goette 1990: pl. 27.5–6.

Chapter 3

1 For women's dress in general see Scholz 1992; Olson 2008b; for the *stola* see Olson 2006; 2008b: 27–33.
2 E.g. Goette 1990: 6; Dixon 2014.
3 As well as priests and magistrates: see below Chapter 4. For the *toga praetexta* of children in general, see Gabelmann 1985; Sebesta 2005.
4 Festus 282L; 283L=245M; Pers. 5.30; Val. Max. 8.1; Juv. 2.170; Macrob., *Sat.* 1.6.17.
5 See also Festus 282–284L=245M.
6 A passage in Livy (42.34.4) also suggests marriage as a girl's transition to adulthood when a man lists how many of his sons have assumed the *toga virilis* and how many of his daughters are married.
7 Gabelmann 1985: 520.
8 Olson 2008a: 140–142; George 2001: 184. For Roman girlhood in general, see Caldwell 2015.
9 George 2001. Possibly of the same date is a similar depiction in the Palazzo Conservatori: Fittschen/Zanker 1983: 39 no. 42.
10 Olson 2008a: fig. 6.5.
11 E.g. a Claudian freed family relief in the Ince Blundell Collection, Liverpool (Mander 2013: 116 fig. 103) and a grave relief for a one-year-old girl dating to 100 CE (Mander 2013: 154 fig. 131).
12 As claimed by Gercke (1968: 199).
13 Olson 2008a: fig. 6.2.

14 Olson 2008a: fig. 6.3. Scholars who see it as a toga: Gabelmann 1985: 524; George 2001: 189 n.25; in contrast, Stone (1994: 20 and n.39) sees it as a *palla*. See also Davies 2005: 128.
15 Goette 1990: 5.
16 E.g. McGinn 1998: 171.
17 Nonius 653L; Porph., *schol. Hor. Sat.* 1.2.63; Ps.-Acro, *schol. Hor. Sat.* 1.2.63.
18 Olson 2006: 196: 'it is not a tangible piece of clothing that is indicated by the adjective, but a moral system'; Heskel 1994; Dixon 2014: 298–304.
19 See above Chapter 2.
20 Ps.-Acro, *schol. Hor. Sat.* 1.2.63. The corresponding Horace passage (1.2.61–63) says: 'to destroy a good reputation, to squander a family's fortunes, is always terrible. What difference does it make if you misbehave with a *matrona* or a *togata*?'
21 See Macr., *Sat.* 1.6.13; *ILLRP* 977; *CIL* 10.6009 and discussion of this evidence in Olson 2008b: 28–30.
22 For more on the *stola* and the term *stolata* see Olson 2008b: 27–33.
23 The lack of gender distinction between children in Roman portraiture was already remarked on by Fittschen (1992: 301–305), and more recently Edmondson has argued that for pre-pubescent Roman children, 'their incipient Romanness, their membership in the *gens togata*, was much more crucial than whether they were male or female' (2008: 26).
24 For this see Gleason 1990; Harrill 2002. For anthropological context see Cornwall/Lindisfarne 1994: esp. 12.
25 Olson 2017b: 6.
26 See below Chapter 4.
27 Gleason 1999: 67.
28 McDonnell 2006: 12–104.
29 McDonnell 2006: 341. Cicero used the term *consul togatus* (e.g. Cic., *Cat.* 3.23) to lay claim to the victories of a military man, but in the political sphere, esp. his overthrow of the Catilinarian conspiracy (McDonnell 2006: 349, also Nicolet 1960).
30 McDonnell 2006: 385–389. Cf. more recently Olson, who has argued that there was very little change in Roman ideas of masculinity between the second century BCE and the second century CE: 2017b: esp. 169.
31 See further McDonnell 2006: 173: 'In ancient Rome, however, patriarchy, although unusually strong and enduring, was not the only hegemonic masculinity. It was precisely because of the peculiarly strong and enduring nature of Roman patriarchal power that an alternative form of manhood was not only fashioned, but institutionalized. The institution was the *res publica*.' See also p. 180: 'public *virtus* was a counterbalance to private powerlessness'.
32 Livy 3.26.7–10; Nonius 653L; Quint., *Inst.* 11.3.137; SHA *Hadr.* 22.2; Tert., *De pall.* 5; Dio Cass. frag. 39.7; *Cod. Theod.* 14.10.1.

33 E.g. Cic., *Rep.* 5; Lactant., *Epit.* 33.4–5; Livy 34.2.1–4. See McDonnell 2006: 11 for the idea that having females interfere in politics was a characteristic of monarchical rule, esp. eastern varieties, in contrast to which the Roman Republic defined itself.
34 Amedick 1991: main portraits: no. 169, pl. 40.6; no. 259, pl. 109.4; no. 240, pl. 113.5; men in banquet scenes wear the *synthesis* (no. 68, pl. 1.2; no. 208, pl. 7.4; no. 113, pl. 9.4; no. 271, pl. 10.3; no. 174, pl. 11.1), and those travelling the *paenula* (no. 254, pl. 41.1) or the *sagum* (no. 298, pl. 41.2; no. 128, pl. 43.2). See also Galinier 2012; Birk 2013 for similar observations.
35 See, e.g., Mart. 7.51, where an acquaintance is described as 'steeped in the law and skilled in the various practices of the toga'.
36 Starbatty 2010.
37 E.g. Stone 1994; Vout 1996; Pausch 2003: 34.
38 See below Chapter 4.
39 See also Pers. 5.14 for the phrase *'verba togae'* to mean an urbane way of speaking.
40 See also Mart. 3.4; 4.66; 8.48; 10.47; Juv. 3.171–172; 11.203; Pliny, *Ep.* 5.6.45. For country vs city life in satire in general, see Braund 1989.
41 I.e. clothing native to Gaul and Germany. Presumably he had considered it more practical for the colder climate.
42 See also *Verr.* 4.24; 5.13; 5.16; 5.52.
43 E.g. Cic., *Cat.* 2.10.22 (describing Catiline's friends); Stat., *Silv.* 5.2.58 (a governor rules justly wearing his toga); Plut., *Cato Mai.* 23 (Cato's views on Greek culture).
44 See evidence collated in Mommsen 1969 vol. I: 418 and Heskel 1994: 143 n.6.
45 E.g. in defence of Rabirius, citing earlier precedents of Roman statesmen in Greek dress: *Rab. Post.* 25–27. Scipio Africanus was said to have worn *pallium* and sandals in Sicily (Livy 29.19.12; Val. Max. 3.6.1) and Tiberius did the same in Rhodes (Suet., *Tib.* 13). See also Heskel 1994: 136.
46 Zanker 2010. Except Sulla, although see a coin depicting him in an equestrian statue wearing a toga in the British Museum (Zanker 2010: 37 fig. 30b).
47 E.g. Cic., *Orat.* 3.168; *Pis.* 72; Ovid, *Met.* 15.745; *Rem. Am.* 152; Vell. Pat. 1.12.3; 2.29.3; 2.125.5; Val. Max. 3.2.19; Juv. 10.8; Luc., *Phars.* 1.129; 5.382; 9.199; Quint., *Inst.* 2.16.7; SHA *Marc. Aur.* 27.3; Auson., *Epig.* 26.
48 See also below Chapter 5.
49 E.g. Galleria Lapidaria, inv. 9261 (Vatican) and numerous examples in Amedick 1991.
50 Cf. Pausch 2003: 34, who sees the Republican toga as a symbol of political status and that of the Principate as purely religious in character.
51 Coarelli 1968.
52 For this see Huet 2012: 51–52.
53 Huet 2012. See below Chapter 5.
54 For the covering of the head at Rome in general, see Fantham 2008. For uncovering as a mark of respect, see Chapter 4, n.103.

55 Scheid 1995; Huet 2012.
56 Trajan's Column scenes 53; 86; 91; Marcus Aurelius' Column scenes 13; 30; 93.
57 See Scheid 1995.
58 See Amedick 1991; Reinsberg 2006.
59 Reinsberg 2006: 170.
60 For the significance of the body language of such scenes, see Davies 2018: 233–258.
61 *Maximen und Reflektionen* (1824) no. 293.
62 See Pliny, *HN* 34.34 for 2000 being looted by the Romans from the Volsinii 264 BCE.
63 See, e.g., Sehlmeyer 1999; Kuttner 2004.
64 See Sehlmeyer 1999: 48–52; 68–74 for the idea that the earliest honorific statues in Rome were equestrian ones in the mid-fourth century and that the statues of earlier kings that Pliny mentions actually dated slightly later to a time in which the story of Brutus the tyrant-slayer became canonical (i.e. third century).
65 See, e.g., Val. Max. 3.1.1; Cic., *Cons.* frg. 2.33–46 S.=frg. 10.33–46C.; *Cat.* 3.19.
66 For more on this as well as a comprehensive account of the evolution of early statuary in Rome, see Sehlmeyer 1999.
67 For this see Sehlmeyer 1999: 272–273.
68 McDonnell 2006: 195–205.
69 Note that the figures in early equestrian statues often wore togas: e.g. Camillus and Maenius (338 BCE) and Q. Marcius Tremulus (306 BCE) (Pliny, *HN* 34.23; Livy 9.43.22), underlining the more universal use of the garment in earlier times.
70 See Chapter 5 below.
71 Granger Taylor (1982) has argued that this is not, in fact, a border at all, but simply the reinforced closing border that would have been the last bit woven (the opposite of '*praetexta*'), but this argumentation is difficult to follow, and in any case does not preclude that closing border from being in a different colour.
72 Prayon 1999.
73 Fittschen 1970; 2008.
74 See Dohrn 1968: esp. 9–10. See also Fittschen 1970; Granger-Taylor 1982 for discussion of the stripes across the toga as either fold lines or Hellenistic-style decoration.
75 Cf. Fittschen 1970; 2008. Prayon's 1999 argument, namely that the man is not Roman but Etruscan and that his face is not an individual portrait but that of a general persona, must surely be rejected on the grounds of the depicted attributes and clothing markers, as well as the details of the inscription.
76 Davies 2018: 12–17.
77 See, e.g., Livy 34.7; Hor., *Sat.* 1.5.34–36 and the statue of M. Holconius Rufus in Naples: Fittschen 1970: pl. 76.2.
78 E.g. Kleiner/Kleiner 1980–1981.
79 Sehlmeyer places its development as early as the third century BCE: 1999: 110–131.

80 Kuttner 2004: 297.
81 Kleiner/Kleiner 1980–1981 is still the most comprehensive collection of these objects, although it is important to note their warning that many of their 'Republican' pieces are in fact likely to be imperial copies (126).
82 See Sehlmeyer 1999: 270–271 for the idea that he did this because his ancestors were not represented there.
83 According to Suetonius he even reinstated a statue of Pompey: Suet., *Aug.* 31.5.
84 Edmondson 2006: 274. See also Dupont 1992: 172; Sehlmeyer 1999: 11. For Rhodes see Dio Chrys., *Or.* 31, a speech dedicated entirely to honorific statues and the practical implications of having too many in one city, and Pliny, *HN* 34.36–37 for the large numbers of statues in Rome and other cities.
85 See Gehn 2012: esp. 11–12. For the demographics of honorific statuary in Rome in general see Lahusen 1983.
86 For the many issues surrounding this statue's provenance and meaning, see Marlowe 2013: 71–75.
87 See, e.g., Cic., *Verr.* 2.2.150. For an excellent discussion of this, see Kuttner 2004: esp. 301.
88 For this see Alföldy 1984 (esp. 15); Gleason 1999; Sehlmeyer 1999 (esp. 45–48).
89 E.g. the statue of C. Fundilius Doctus from near the Temple of Diana at Nemi: Davies 2010: 71 fig. 11.
90 The standard gesture for the toga statue from the first century CE onward was the left arm raised just enough to hold the folds of the toga and the right arm raised slightly at the elbow, corresponding largely to how Quintilian suggested an orator should stand at the start of a speech: Davies 2018: 129; 134; Quint., *Inst.* 11.3.159. See also Davies 2010 for the link between oratorical ideals and togate statuary.
91 For the differing roles of the body and head in Roman statues and the resultant 'appendage aesthetic' see most recently Stewart 2003: 42–59. See below Chapter 7 for the implications of this for the recycling of older statues in later periods.
92 Hollander 1994: 112.
93 Davies 2005; 2018. She compares toga statues to those of women and 'barbarians' in Roman art, which both tend to show arms drawn in fiddling with drapery and holding it in place. In practice it is likely that only the most accomplished of toga wearers would have been able to get away with not using their arms to hold the toga in place for any length of time.
94 A good example of this is the relaxed and open stance of the young Nero in a toga in a statue now in the Louvre in Paris (inv. MR 337): Giroire/Roger 2007: 80–81.
95 Christ 1997: 28.
96 Davies 2018: 138–145.
97 See Gleason 1999: 69.

98　Hollander 1978: 184.
99　For all of the above see Tarlo 1996: 23–93. There were minority British views that concurred with the Indian view: see, e.g., the late-nineteenth-century social critic Edward Carpenter: 'The truth is that one might almost as well be in one's coffin as in the stiff layers of buckram-like clothing commonly worn nowadays. No genial influence from air or sky can pierce this dead hide, no effluence from within escape ... No wonder the Arabian has the advantage over us. Who could be inspired under all this weight of tailordom?' (Carpenter 1887: 92–93).
100　Rothe 2009: 31–34; Rothe (in prep.).
101　Tarlo 1996: 170–171; 190; Banerjee/Miller 2003: 51; 68–71; 237; 249.
102　See above Chapter 2 for the peculiarity of the expression here that the toga was 'cut', when everything else we know about it suggests it was woven to shape.
103　Most editions see this as '*tunicam*', but Spalding read '*togam*', which makes a great deal more sense as the hem of the tunic would not have been visible under the toga.
104　Starbatty 2010. See Richlin 1997 for the link between rhetoric and masculinity in general.
105　Davies 2018: 31–32. For Cicero, e.g., only the appearance of a woman should aspire to *pulchritudo* ('loveliness'); that of a man should be characterized, first and foremost, by *dignitas* (*Off.* 1.130). In *Off.* 1.122 he lends advice to his son on how to behave in public life, revolving largely around restraint, dignity and seriousness of attitude.
106　Davies 2018: 34–56. See also the example of the sari, for which, as Banerjee and Miller write, the wearer is 'engaged in a constant battle to make a five-metre piece of rectangular cloth obedient to her will' (2003: 70). It is interesting that in the case of the sari it is female virtue that is embodied in this control, whilst at Rome it was an element of male virtue. In both cases, however, the physical control of the garment symbolizes inner self-control.
107　Williams 2010.
108　Davies 2005: 121: 'What makes the garment *virilis* is not so much the toga itself as how it is worn, and the behaviour of the wearer.' See also Amiotti 1981: 139. Tert., *De pall.* 5 provides us with a parody of this when he describes a togate man who is in control neither of his toga nor his life.
109　See also Juvenal's delight at escaping the toga (*effugiatque togam*) in 11.203–204.
110　E.g. Stone 1994; Vout 1996.
111　Whilst the suit itself might not require skill to put on and wear, the tie certainly does.
112　See also Banerjee/Miller 2003: 68–76.
113　Olson 2014b; see also Davies 2018: 53–55. A further example is Maecenas and Seneca's invective against his behaviour in *Epist.* 114.4–8: Graver 1998. For references to loosely draped (*laxae*) togas, see Tib. 1.6.40, 2.3.78.

114 See, e.g., Ovid, *Am.* 1.505–524; Sen., *Epist.* 114.4–8; 114.21–22; 122.7; Gellius, *NA* 11.2; Tac., *Dial.* 26.1.
115 See also Macrob., *Sat.* 3.13.4.
116 Starbatty 2010.
117 See also Gabelmann 1985: 537 for the connection between the toga and the learning of proper deportment.
118 Bonfante 2003: 15. Although see the Verucchio cloak that was worn by a high-ranking person in that early community (Fig. 2.2).
119 Livy 1.8; Diod. Sic. 5.40; Pliny, *HN* 8.195; 9.136–137; Florus, *Epit.* 1.1.5.
120 E.g. Goette 1990: 2–3; Bonfante 2003. Cf. Fittschen 2008, who argues that although there are borders on Etruscan cloaks, none of these can be identified as *togae praetextae*, and as such the *toga praetexta* cannot have come from the Etruscans. However, the rounded cloaks worn by the Romans in the François tomb paintings have a purple border and as such are almost certainly *togae praetextae*: Coarelli 2011: 165–167 figs 148–149.
121 See also Pliny, *HN* 33.10.
122 Gabelmann 1985: 508; 504 figs 1–2. See this work more generally for the *toga praetexta* of children.
123 Also depicted on a coin minted by an ancestor in 61 BCE: *RRC* I (1974): 443 no. 419.
124 Bonfante 2003: 15; 189 figs 102–3.
125 See also the Republican-era paintings in Delos: Bulard 1926: 46; 82–82; 141–142; pls VII.2; XIX.
126 See Wilson 1924: 54; Goette 1990: 5; Stone 1994: 13–15 for the shifting of the border to the *sinus*, but cf. Wrede (1995: 545–546) who argues that this is where the border had always been placed and Fittschen 1970, who maintains the border was always on the lower edge. Linderski (2002: 359–360) thinks that there were two types.
127 E.g. Goette 1990: 5.
128 We know this from copious textile evidence, e.g. from Egypt: Bender Jørgensen 2011.
129 Stauffer 2013.
130 Granger Taylor 1982; Sebesta 2005: 116, pointing out that only in this light a passage in Quintilian (*Inst.* 5.10.71) makes sense: 'I cannot expect a *toga praetexta* when I see the beginning (*exordium*) is grey/brown (*pullum*).'
131 See also numerous examples in Fröhlich 1991.
132 See below Chapter 4. For more detailed discussion of the sacred nature of the *toga praetexta* see Sebesta 2005; Dolansky 2008: esp. 54.
133 Festus says something very similar: 282L; 283L=245M.
134 Cicero is not so forgiving of Mark Antony when he chides him for having been already bankrupt whilst he was still in the *toga praetexta* (*Phil.* 2.44: see beginning of this chapter).

135 See below Chapter 4.
136 Huskinson 1996: 22 no. 1.23; pl. 2.1; 22 no. 1.24; pl. 4.1; 22 no. 1.31; pl. 3.1; Gabelmann 1984: 165 no. 74. See also Isid., *Etym.* 19.24.16.
137 Huskinson 1996: 22 no. 1.23; pl. 2.1.
138 The influence of actors should, according to Quintilian, be limited, lest the boy learn the more effeminate and lower-class habits of acting, like mimicry and melodrama.
139 Banerjee/Miller 2003: 65–79.
140 McDonnell 2006: 179.
141 For fathers and oratorical education, see Gunderson 2003.
142 See the *album decurionum* from Canusium dated to 223 CE, a list of decurions proper and then twenty-five names of *praetextati*, obviously decurions *in spe*: Garnsey 1974: 243ff.
143 This is made clear in the final passage in Macrobius' discussion of the *toga praetexta*: *Sat.* 1.6.17.
144 E.g. Mander 2013: 41 fig. 25; 150 fig. 129; and the young poet Q. Sulpicius Maximus: 151 fig. 130.
145 So-called because it was made from natural, undyed wool. See Cic., *Att.* 131.5; Catull. 68.15; Pliny, *HN* 8.194.
146 Mothers: Apul., *Apol.* 87.10–11; Prop. 4.1.131–132; brothers: Ovid, *Trist.* 4.10.27–28; Apul., *Apol.* 73.9; 87.10–11; cousins: Cic., *Att.* 5.20.9; 6.1.12; uncles: Cic., *Att.* 5.20.9; 6.1.12; Apul., *Apol.* 98.5; friends: App., *B Civ.* 4.5.30; important friends of the family/patrons: Pliny, *Epist.* 1.9.1–3; 10.116; Tert., *De idol.* 16.1–3.
147 This was apparently woven on an archaic loom and thought to bring good luck: Festus 342L=274M s.v. *rectae* and 364L=289M s.v. *regillis tunicis*. See also Dolansky 2008: 50 but cf. Fraschetti 1997: 65 who says he must have worn it to bed the night before like brides. See Pliny, *HN* 8.74 for the idea that newly initiated young men ('*tirones*') kept wearing the *tunica recta* for a time.
148 Marquardt (1886: 125–6) suggested that on this occasion the boy was also entered into the list of citizens in the *tabularium*. See also Amiotti 1981: 137; Dio Cass. 56.29.5.
149 Ovid, *Fasti* 3.787–788; Pliny, *Ep.* 10.116; Apul., *Apol.* 87.10–11; Stat., *Silv.* 5.3.116–120; *CIL* 10.688.
150 Rawson 2003: 323; Harlow/Laurence 2002: 67–69. For more detail on the ceremony in general, see Dolansky 2008. For the close link between political and religious duty contained in it see Amiotti 1981.
151 Augustus: 18 October (*ILS* 108); Tiberius: 24 April (*Inscr. Ital.* 13.2.448); Galba: 1 January (*Inscr. Ital.* 56.29.5); Severus Alexander: 26 June (*CIL* 6.2799). See also Cic., *Att.* 6.1.12.
152 Cf. Suet., *Claud.* 43, where the emperor is said to have decided to bestow the *toga virilis* on Britannicus when he was tall enough, even though he was still emotionally immature.

153 See Dolansky 2008 (esp. 49) and Grilli 1997 for the copious passages in Cicero on the *toga virilis* ceremony.
154 See Apul., *Apol.* 70.7 and a long list of sources in Dolansky 2006: Appendix 2.
155 Although, as this passage states, without the accompanying ceremony. Known ages of other famous people: Cicero: 16 (*Brut.* 88); Augustus: 16 (Suet., *Aug.* 8); Vergil: 15 (Suet., *Verg.* 6); Agrippa Postumus: 15 (Dio 54.28–29); Tiberius: 14 (Suet., *Tib.* 5; Dio 55.22); Persius: 16 (Persius 5.30); Nero: 14 (Suet., *Nero* 16); Caracalla: 13 (Spart., *Serv.* 16).
156 See La Follette 1994.
157 See below Chapter 5.
158 Inheritance: Dio Cass. 61.34.1–2; Suet., *Aug.* 66.4; Cic., *Orat.* 1.180; assets: Gaius, *Inst.* 1.145; Ulp. 11.28; wills: *Dig.* 28.1.5; 28.6.2; Gaius, *Inst.* 2.113.
159 *Convivia*: Nic. Dam., *Augustus* 8.18; 13.28–30; Apul., *Apol.* 98.6; Petron., *Sat.* 85–87; marriage: SHA *Marc. Aur.* 1.4; sexual freedom: Cic., *Fam.* 189.2; Plut., *Mor.* 37c–e/*De aud.* 1; Apul., *Apol.* 98.5–7; Prop. 3.15.3–4: 'when for me the modesty of the *praetexta* was lifted away, and freedom to know the path of love was given to me'.
160 Prop. 4.1.131–134; Ovid, *Trist.* 4.10.27–30; Catull. 68.15–17; Persius 5.30–37.
161 One of life's joys: Sen., *Epist.* 1.4; 4.2; Val. Max. 7.1.1; '*toga libera*': Ovid, *Fasti* 3.771; *Trist.* 4.10.28; Prop. 4.1.132.
162 McDonnell 2006: 10.
163 Cf. Cicero's scathing sartorial characterization of Mark Antony's scandalous behaviour on receiving the *toga virilis* in *Phil.* 2.44 (see the beginning of this chapter).
164 So McDonnell (2006: 177).
165 See also Amiotti 1981.
166 For the relationship between biological and cultural maturity see also Christ 1997: esp. 25.
167 E.g. Apul., *Apol.* 98.5–7; Cic., *Att.* 201.6; *Cael.* 5.11; Sen., *Controv.* 2.6.4; Tac., *Ann.* 13.2; *Dig.* 4.4.11.5. See Hor., *Sat.* 1.2.16–17 for young men who have 'just put on the *toga virilis* under rigid fathers' falling under the dangerous influence of unscrupulous older men.
168 Trans. Morton Braund 2004.
169 For the pitfalls of this liminal period see also Fear 2005.
170 Tac., *Dial.* 34.1–7; Cic., *Cael.* 4.9; 5.11; *Brut.* 303; 306; Fronto, *Epist.* 1.10.1 (Naber, p. 180).
171 For this training see also Richlin 1997.
172 For the *tirocinium militiae* see Livy 22.57.9; Vell. Pat. 2.29.5.
173 Christ 1997: 29. See the discussion of the body language of toga statues above.
174 Richardson/Richardson 1966.

175 For a similar view and a more detailed discussion of the specific body language conveyed in the 'armsling' toga, see Davies 2018: 138–145.

Chapter 4

1. Seneca (*Clem.* 1.24) tells us that the Senate once debated having a system of clothing but decided it was too dangerous as slaves would see how numerous they were. Several centuries later, the deeply unreliable SHA *Sev. Alex.* 27 alleges that the jurists Ulpian and Paul convinced the emperor not to introduce official dress for different ranks, including slaves, for similar reasons.
2. Reinhold 1971: 282; Edmondson 2008: 32; Olson 2006; 188–189.
3. See Duncan-Jones 2016.
4. Rothfus 2010: 431.
5. E.g. Goette 1990; Stone 1994; Vout 1996; Edmondson 2008; Rothfus 2010; Olson 2017b.
6. See also Diod. Sic. 31.25.2.
7. Dench 2005: 113.
8. See, e.g., Suet., *Nero* 57 for praetextate statues of Nero in the forum.
9. See Chapter 3 for the *toga praetexta* of Roman children.
10. E.g. Pliny, *HN* 9.137; Hor., *Sat.* 1.5.34–36; Val. Max. 9.12.7; Livy 2.54; 7.1; 8.9.5; SHA *Alex. Sev.* 40.8; Cic., *Sest.* 144; *Verr.* 2.5.36.
11. See Fröhlich 1991 and Flower 2017 for numerous other examples.
12. See also Plut., *Pomp.* 24.6.
13. See also Livy, *Per.* 74, and another episode in Plut., *Sulla* 9, where Sulla's men strip two praetors of their *togae praetextae* (περιπορφύροι) as an act of political aggression.
14. For a fictional example see Trimalchio in Petron., *Sat.* 30. Abramenko (1993: 83) warns against seeing all *seviri Augustales* as freedmen – in the beginning the cult was also popular with *ingenui*.
15. See Goette 2012 for the link between the *laena*, the *chlaina* and depictions of Greek priests.
16. Replicated later in Serv., *Aen.* 4.262.
17. Whence Bonfante (2003: 50–51) suggested it came from the sometime 'back-to-front' draping of the Etruscan *tebenna*.
18. Others include a statue from Merida in Spain (Edmondson 2008: Fig. 1.5), a statue with the head of Antoninus Pius in the Ny Carlsberg Glyptotek in Copenhagen (Poulsen 1940 vol. 2: 96, no. 78; pl. CXXV) and those in Goette 1990: 7–8. For the wearing of the *laena* over the *toga praetexta* see also Serv., *Aen.* 4.262.
19. Suetonius frg. 167 also says explicitly that it was worn to sacrifice, and Serv., *Aen.* 7.612 mentions it along with the *lituus* in connection with augurs.

20 It is somewhat perplexing, in this context, that the *laena* is also associated in later satirical works with keeping warm and people of low social status (e.g. Mart. 14.138; Juv. 5.131).
21 See above Chapter 2.
22 Fröhlich 1991; Flower 2017. See also Stone 1994: 39 n.6; Bonfante Warren 1973: 596–597 for figures wearing round mantles tied around their waists for physical activity common in Etruscan art.
23 For the manufacture and symbolism of purple in antiquity see Reinhold 1970 and more recently the *Purpureae Vestes* volumes: Alfaro/Wild/Costa 2004; Karali/Alfaro 2008; Alfaro/Brun/Borgard/Pierobon Benoit 2011; Alfaro/Tellenbach/Ortiz 2014; Ortiz/Alfaro/Turell/Martínez 2016.
24 Dion. Hal., *Ant. Rom.* 3.61; 6.95; Festus 209M; Plut., *Rom.* 25; Pliny, *HN* 9.136 (Romulus). For a more detailed discussion of the origins see Bonfante Warren 1970; Gabelmann 1985: 498.
25 For a detailed discussion of this with a survey of the evidence see Gabelmann 1977: 329.
26 E.g. SHA *Alex. Sev.* 40.6; porphyry statues in Goette 1990: 45–49 and pl. 18, although Stone (1994: 39 n.12) is right to point out that there is no mention of an emperor in a *toga purpurea* outside the *SHA*.
27 For a possible earlier date for aediles being allowed to wear it, see Dion. Hal., *Ant. Rom.* 6.95.4.
28 Although see discussion of the Vel Saties tomb painting below; Goette thinks an Augustan coin from Spain (*BMC RE* I 69f. no. 397–402, pl. 8.20; 9.1–3) depicts a *toga picta*, but even if true, it shows very little detail of the garment's ornamentation (1990: 6).
29 App., *Pun.* 66; Festus 228L; Livy 27.4.8; 31.11.11. Although usually translated as 'embroidered', the word used for this decoration, which is only specified by Appian, is ἐνυφαίνω in Greek, which means 'to weave in'. Decorations in textiles were usually woven into the fabric on the loom: embroidery, which involves adding thread to an existing fabric, was only commonly practised from late antiquity onward (see Dross-Krüpe/Paetz gen. Schieck 2014).
30 See previous note for details on how this decoration would have been applied.
31 Allowed for triumph: Polyb. 6.53.7; App., *Pun.* 66; Livy 30.15.11–12; Festus 228L; allowed for games: Livy 5.41; Vell. Pat. 2.40.4.
32 E.g. Versnel 1970; Bonfante Warren 1970; Bonfante 1978: 26.
33 E.g. Lesky 1998.
34 E.g. Frazer 1890: 175ff.; Wissowa 1912: 126–128; Ross Taylor 1931: 44; Alföldi 1970: 146; Scheid 1986.
35 Beard 2007: 233.
36 Bonfante 1978: 22–23.

37 Although Lesky's (1998) somewhat fanciful reconstruction of the form as a rectangle with parts cut out takes this stylized depiction too literally to be plausible.
38 E.g. Bieber 1928: 68 pl. 34.1–2.
39 E.g. Bieber 1961: 27 fig. 96.
40 E.g. Agamemnon in the Tomba dell'Orco II and Nestor, King of Argos in the François Tomb (Lesky 1998: figs 4–5).
41 See Hom., *Od.* 3.125, where Helen decorates a cloak with battle scenes.
42 See the visual evidence compiled in Schäfer 1989.
43 For the regal origins of the *toga purpurea* see above n.24; for the *toga picta*, see Livy 30.15.11–12; Dion. Hal., *Ant. Rom.* 3.61.1; 4.74; Florus 1.5.6.
44 Dion. Hal., *Ant. Rom.* 2.34; 2.54; 3.22; 3.31; 3.41; 3.54; 3.59; 4.27; Plut., *Rom.* 25; Livy 1.38.3.
45 Lesky 1998: 180.
46 See also later Serv., *Eclog.* 10.27: *Iovis insignia*.
47 See Bonfante Warren 1970: 61 and n.73.
48 This was already suggested by Deubner in 1934 and discussed more fully in Versnel 1970: 84–93.
49 A further two passages have been used to disprove the scenario described above: in Livy 10.7.10 a triumphant general is described as 'dressed in the costume of Jupiter O.M.' (*iovis optimi maximi ornatu decoratus*) and so attired descending the Capitol to the Temple of Jupiter, meaning he was dressed this way *before* he got to the temple; but this does not preclude the dress being brought to him from the temple before the ceremony began. Writing about Pompey's funeral, Lucan (*Pharsalia* 9.177–178) describes the *toga picta* as 'the dress which Jupiter thrice beheld', referring to Pompey's three triumphs. Again, all this shows is that entering the temple in triumphal robes was part of the ceremony, and still makes sense if Jupiter himself was dressed in something similar.
50 For such practicalities see also Beard 2007: 230.
51 Versnel 1970: 87.
52 For a summary of these and other sartorial status markers and their significance see Edmondson 2008.
53 E.g. Potthoff 1992: 203.
54 Wilson 1924: 38–39. She also saw the lines that decorate the surface of the toga worn by the 'Arringatore' as striped decoration, arguing that Metellus is in fact wearing a *trabea*.
55 πάρυφος, which directly translates as 'woven along/beside', suggests much more plausibly a border than stripes. See also Gabelmann 1985: 498.
56 See also 7.188, where he describes the *trabea* as 'the augur's red and purple toga' and 11.334, where he likens it to the curule chair as a symbol of authority amongst the Romans.

57 This has caused some to argue it wasn't a form of toga at all (e.g. Bonfante Warren 1970: 60 n.70; Palmer 1998), but there is no reason why the toga could not be fastened in place using a brooch, perhaps as a relic of archaic practice, and it is in any case not a strong enough reason to discount other, more concrete evidence (such as Dion. Hal., *Ant. Rom.* 6.13.4) that explicitly describes it as 'a type of toga'. (For more on this including the idea that Dionysius based this characterization on the late antique *trabea*, which was definitely a toga, see Olson 2017b: 115f.)
58 E.g. Pliny, *HN* 8.195; Vergil (*Aen.* 7.187) and Ovid (*Fasti* 2.503; 6.796) describe it as the dress of Romulus. Cf. Artem., *Oneir.* 2.3, who says it was Greek in origin. See also Isid., *Etym.* 19.24.8, who describes it as a kind of toga made out of scarlet and purple fabric and the festive dress of Roman kings.
59 See also a coin of Octavian depicting Sulla on horseback in what appears to be a *trabea*: Zanker 2010: 37 fig. 30b.
60 Gabelmann 1977. See also Wrede 1988: 399–400.
61 See Nicolet 1966; Wiseman 1970; Alföldy 1981.
62 Val. Max. 2.2.9; Tac., *Ann.* 3.2; Suet., *Dom.* 14.3; Stat., *Silv.* 5.2.18; Pers. 3.29.
63 For the *trabea* and horseriding see Bonfante Warren 1973: 592; for the iconography of the *transvectio* see Veyne 1960.
64 E.g. the tomb of T. Flavius Verus in the Lateran Museum (Veyne 1960: pl. 7).
65 E.g. the 13-year-old Lollianus (Reinsberg 2006: 206–207 no. 47; pl. 112.4) and the 15-year-old Lucianus (Borg 2013: 192 fig. 121).
66 Scholars who have expressed scepticism: Fittschen 1970: 179; Goette 1990: 2; Pausch 2003: 24; Rothfus 2010: 442 n.42.
67 Mustakallio 2010: fig. 13.
68 Sinn 1987: no. 522.
69 Goette 1990: 57; Ca34; *CIL* 6.22972; Kleiner 1987: 195–196 no. 68. Wrede (1995: 549) has suggested Eutyches was freed posthumously; cf. an inscription in the Ashmolean Museum, Oxford (ANChandler 3.90), which commemorates a boy with the *tria nomina* of a citizen but who is described as a *verna*, although here the boy may have been manumitted before he died: Kohl 2018: 248–250 and fig. 5.
70 See already Mommsen 1888 (III.3): 222.
71 Rothfus 2010: 432 n.19.
72 Wrede 1995: 548. Cf. Mommsen in *Staatsrecht* (1887: 222), where he supposed that serving in the Roman army qualified *socii* to wear the toga. In the *Staatsrecht* Mommsen grappled more generally with the problem of the toga and citizenship, and cited the fact that the so-called *fabulae togatae* were generally set in Latium as proof that the toga was not confined to Rome (1887: 222 n.4); however, the earliest use of the term is from the first century BCE (Cic., *Sest.* 118; Varro, *Ling.* 5.25). For the *formula togatorum* in general, see Baronowski 1984.
73 For detailed discussion see Mommsen 1887: 218–222; Sherwin-White 1973 (esp. 98).

74 See Gardner 1986.
75 There must have been some leeway, though, because when members of an Alpine tribe assumed citizenship as a show of allegiance to Rome, they were granted the status retrospectively (*CIL* 5.5050).
76 See also Bradley 1994: 95–99, who argued that the free non-elite would have been indistinguishable from slaves in their dress.
77 Here he is quoting Verg., *Aen.* 1.282 (see Chapter 1).
78 Pausch 2003: 28f.; Zanker 2010: 162–166.
79 Pausch 2003: 32.
80 See the Romans in *togae praetextae* in the François tomb paintings at Vulci: Coarelli 2011: 165–167 figs 148–149 and Chapter 2 above.
81 See the scene of the aftermath of a battle in the Esquiline tomb frescoes: the Samnites wear short skirts and greaves whilst Romans like Q. Fabius wear the white toga (Capitoline Museums, Palazzo dei Conservatori: D'Ambra 1998: 14 fig. 4).
82 See above Chapters 1 and 2. Pausch's (2003) claim that the absence of the toga in the plays of Plautus is evidence it was barely worn in the middle Republic must be rejected on the grounds that the plays were set in Athens, not Rome.
83 See, e.g., Plut., *Cat. Min.* 6.3 for Cato and the countless mentions of the toga in the works of Cicero.
84 See the freedman portraits collated in Kleiner 1976 and Val. Max. 2.7.9, albeit not contemporary, for soldiers in the Servile Wars.
85 See most recently Hackworth Petersen 2003: 244–245; 233 figs 5–7.
86 Zimmer 1982: 227 no. 193.
87 E.g. the cushion seller and cloth seller scenes in the Uffizi in Florence and a further textile-buying scene from the Via Triumphalis in Rome (Zimmer 1982: 124–127 nos 38–40), the knife shop of Atimetus on a gravestone from Ostia (Zimmer 1982: 180–182 no. 114) and perhaps some people in Tomb of the Baker (Hackworth Petersen 2003: 233 figs 5–7). For differing views as to who is represented in these scenes, see Kampen 1981: 97–98; George 2006: 24–25; Olson 2014a: 433.
88 As such, Appian's claim (*B Civ.* 2.17.120) that in the late Republic, 'apart from the senators, free citizens and slaves wear the same dress' must be an exaggeration designed to lend colour to the account of ethnic and social mixing of the era that is the subject of the passage.
89 See above Chapter 3.
90 See, e.g., Zanker 1983b.
91 Maiuri 1953: 139–148; Baldassarre 1991: 252–257 figs 113–124.
92 E.g. most recently Hartnett 2017: 91.
93 Hartnett 2017: 91.
94 Naples Archaeological Museum, inv. 9067. Baldassarre 1991: 255 fig. 121.
95 Naples Archaeological Museum, inv. 9057; Baldassarre 1991: 252 fig. 113.

96 Naples Archaeological Museum, inv. 9071; Maiuri 1953: fig. p. 144.
97 E.g. MacMahon 2005: 74–75. See also Clarke 2003: 259–261.
98 Laurence (2012: 76) has suggested the context is games that the man has donated, which is plausible given the mention of such a practice in *CIL* 4.1186; 4.7989a.
99 Baldassarre 1991: 252–257 figs 114–115; 117–118; 124. For the significance of this see the final section of this chapter.
100 Baldassarre 1991: 253–257 figs 117; 119; 122.
101 Hollander 1994: 112.
102 In *Met.* 10.33, Apuleius describes lawyers as '*togati vulturii*'.
103 Two rather mysterious passages suggest that differences in status could also be expressed in toga gestures: Pliny (*HN* 28.60) tells us that Roman men were supposed to uncover their heads in the presence of magistrates, and in Sallust's *Histories* (5.20), Sulla uncovers his head as an honour to Pompey. As Fantham (2008: 160) has pointed out, the odd thing about this is that it implies that men usually had their heads covered in public, which is not borne out by pictorial or other evidence.
104 E.g. Stone 1994; Vout 1996: 210.
105 Rothfus 2010: 427.
106 See the excavated Campanian houses discussed in Fröhlich 1991, esp. the discussion of demographics in 28–31.
107 See discussion in Fröhlich 1991: 189–210 with relevant literature.
108 See Fröhlich 1991: pl. 2.1; 3.1; 5.1–2; 6.1; 7.1; 8.3; 9.1; 10.2; 24.1; 25.1; 26.2; 28.1–2; 31.2; 42.4; 48.1. Some scholars have tried to use the finer details of the dress worn by these deities (e.g. borders, *clavi*) to deduce the status of the house owner (e.g. Thomas 1963; Gabelmann 1977: 340 n.87), but Fröhlich has identified no meaningful connection (1991: 31).
109 The extent to which this applies to Rome is, of course, questionable, but as Brennan has said, Tertullian's work suggests that 'Carthage had long passed the point of simple assimilation to Rome in dress and hence basic status. The city ... was now an animating force ... for the inspiration not just of the Roman province but of the privileged class of toga-clad citizens, even those of Italy' (2008: 259).
110 E.g. Treggiari 1969; Kleiner 1976.
111 Hackworth Petersen 2003; 2006; 2009.
112 For example, the toga was sometimes bestowed on freedmen at their manumission: Polyb. 30.18; App., *Mith.* 2. For Roman freedpeople and social mobility in general, see Treggiari 1969; Quiroga 1995; MacLean 2018.
113 E.g. Cato, *Agr.* praef.; Suet., *Aug.* 2.3; 4.2; *Vit.* 2.1; *Otho* 1.1; *Vesp.* 1.2–4; Dio Cass. 46.4–5; 7.4; Cic., *Off.* 1.150–151.
114 In the Augustan period this anxiety was addressed by several laws restricting and regulating the manumission of slaves, such as the *lex Fufia Caninia* (2 BCE), the *lex Aelia Sentia* (4 CE) and the *lex Iunia* (17 BC).

115 Hackworth Petersen 2003: 238. Already Veyne (1961) argued it might be more helpful to see Trimalchio as a person using the limited status symbols at his disposal to express his standing in perfectly legitimate terms.
116 Kleiner 1976: 142.
117 Some of these depictions are busts or half-lengths but *contra* Olson (2014a), who thinks they could be wearing *pallia*, I agree with Kleiner (1976: 143–144) that they must be togas because we have no *pallia* in the full-length depictions that do exist, and it stands to reason that people who had once been slaves would choose the toga over the less prestigious *pallium*.
118 Davies 2010: 71 fig. 11; now in Ny Carlsberg Glyptotek, Copenhagen. This was found near the statue of his aristocratic patroness Fundilia C.F. Rufa: see Fejfer 2008: 302.
119 Kleiner 1976: 187.
120 Davies 2018: 145.
121 Giuliani 1986: 160; Hertel 1993 (esp. 51–56). It is true that the gravestones of freedpeople also favour the veristic facial portrait style of the late Republic.
122 Zanker 1983b: 257; Goette 1990: 24.
123 Rothfus 2010.
124 E.g. Kleiner 1976: no. 34; 88; Frenz 1977: 164f. F 4; 165 F 5; 181ff. K 2. See Davies 2018: 139 for the suggestion that the popularity of the 'armsling' style with freedmen had to do with the fact that its restriction of movement precluded its use by orators, and as such was by definition a garment more appropriate to the sub-elite.
125 E.g. Kleiner 1976: 236 no. 71; 242–244 nos 82–84.
126 See above Chapter 3.
127 We do not have the paintwork to prove the togas on these reliefs had purple borders, but as with other togate children in statuary and relief art, we must assume a *toga praetexta*, as it was the only kind of toga associated with children. In 'freedmen art' the accompanying *bulla* further underlines this.
128 See also reliefs in the Museo delle Terme (75–50 BCE: Kleiner 1976: 243 no. 83) and the Tomb of the Vettii (Mander 2013: 104 fig. 89; 161 no. 11).
129 See also Mander 2013: 92.
130 Mander 2013: 74 fig. 55.
131 Laird 2015: 19–21 and fig. 3.
132 Tac., *Dial.* 6: the patron is accompanied by a *comitatus togatorum*; Juvenal refers to the clients outside the patron's house as the *turba togata*: *Sat.* 1.95–96.
133 The discussion to follow owes a great deal to this influential book chapter, as well as to Salles 2003.
134 For the political circumstances in which Martial was writing about the *sportula* see Salanitro 1992.
135 See also 2.44.1–4, where he lists some expensive things he needs to buy: 'a slave, a brand-new toga and three or four pounds of silver plate'.

136 The status pressure to be surrounded by togate clients could also be a burden on patrons: according to Martial some men got into debt hiring people to look like a huge group of clients (2.74), whilst another was surrounded by *togati* and slave boys but had to sell his ring to pay for dinner (2.57).
137 Juvenal tells a similar story in 3.126–130.
138 See above Chapter 2.
139 This is a play on words: in his original effusive description of the new garment he described it as 'challenging fresh snow (*primae nives*)', i.e. as white as snow, whilst now it is 'snowy' in the sense that it is so threadbare it no longer keeps him warm.
140 For *vestiplici* see, e.g., *CIL* 6.7301; 6.9901. For the details of toga maintenance see Tert., *De pall.* 5. Granger-Taylor 1987 has pointed to what look like fold lines on some toga statues and argued that they showed the garment was freshly pressed and as such was a symbol of high status.
141 There might even have been an element of toga inflation over time: Varro reports Cato saying that when he was a boy he only had one toga, implying that by his time elite men usually had several (Non. 155L).
142 Banerjee/Miller 2003: 74.
143 Davies 2018: esp. 32–33.
144 See above Chapter 3.
145 E.g. Hor., *Sat.* 1.3.13–15; Mart. 4.19.1; 6.11.7; Juv. 9.29–31. Olson 2017b: 94: 'Thus, poverty had a color in ancient Rome – *pullus*.'
146 The gradations in quality could also apply to the dye used for the border: Pliny tells us that the first person in Rome to wear Tyrian *dibapha* on his *toga praetexta* was P. Lentulus Spinther in the mid-first century BCE and that it caused a scandal (*HN* 9.137).
147 Already mentioned by the playwright Titinius in the second century BCE (*Com.* 138 in Non. 860L), but also Arn., *Adv. nat.* 2.67; Juv. 3.149; Cic., *Pis.* 23.55.
148 Mart. 4.66; 9.100; 10.74; 11.24.11; 12.70. See also the '*breves togae*' in 10.15; 11.56; 12.36.
149 Stewart 2008: 120 fig. 27.
150 Ryberg 1967: 71–76.
151 Birk 2013: 30 fig. 14.
152 See, most famously, Petronius' description of Trimalchio's funerary depiction in *Sat.* 71, but also, e.g., Mart. 5.23.
153 For a detailed discussion of this see Edwards 1993. See also Seneca, *Ep.* 5.3, where he advises to wear a toga that is 'neither too flashy nor too shabby'.
154 See also 12.70, where he describes an aging moralist wearing a *togula*, and Juvenal 7.145, where he tells us that in his day 'eloquence in rags is a rare phenomenon', suggesting that in the good old days learned men did not need to dress well. For Martial's and Juvenal's attitudes to social mobility in general see Malnati 1988.

155 Although Kampen's 1981 study of images of working women from Ostia already laid some groundwork for this.
156 E.g. Zimmer 1982: 117–118 no. 29; 135–136 no. 51; 143–144 no. 62; 167–168 no. 91; 191–192 no. 129.
157 See also a stonemason and his wife: Zimmer 1982: 157–158 no. 80 and a butcher and his wife: Zimmer 1982: 94–95 no. 2.
158 Zimmer 1982: 66.
159 The latter, when represented in Roman art at all, are usually signified by a loincloth or skimpy *exomis*: see Zimmer 1982: 66 with examples; Amedick 1991: 131 no. 61, pl. 46.1 (fisherman); 155 no. 204, pl. 50.1 (sailor); 161–162 no. 251, pl. 110.4; 157 no. 221, pl. 114.3 (labourers carrying sacks of grain and flour).
160 Zimmer 1982: 6.
161 Zimmer 1982: 7.
162 See, e.g., the Tomb of Eurysaces (Hackworth Petersen 2003: 249: 'Whatever reaction Eurysaces' monument might have provoked, it was one that probably centered primarily on his professional identity rather than a presumed freedman identity').
163 See, e.g., a grave stele from Ravenna for P. Longidienus – a freeborn shipbuilder – that shows him in the toga in the portrait but in a tunic in the work scene below. The inscription says *P. Longidienus P. f. / ad onus / properat*: 'P. Longidienus, son of Publius, busy at work' (Hackworth Petersen 2009: 206 fig. 15).
164 *Dial.* 7 but also Plaut., *Poen.* 1121; Prop. 4.2.37; Cic., *Leg. agr.* 2.94; Appian, *B Civ.* 2.17.120; Hor., *Epist.* 1.7.65: common people as '*tunicatus popellus*'; Pliny, *Ep.* 7.17.9 (*sordidi*); Artem., *Onirocriticon* 2.8: working people do not wear 'white clothes' (i.e. togas). Quintilian refers to the lower orders as '*pullatus*' – in dark clothing (*Inst.* 2.12.10); see also Kühnert 1991.
165 Zimmer 1982: 54; 66. It is clear from the work of Kampen (1981) that the tunic was the sign not just of working men, but women as well; but as the discussion here is focused on the presence or absence of the toga, it is the men who are the focus. For craftspeople in the Roman Empire in general, see Wilson/Flohr 2016.
166 E.g. Kampen 1981: 135; Joshel 1992: 60–61.
167 E.g. Joshel 1992: 162; 167; George 2006.
168 Zanker 1992: 353; Joshel 1992: 92–122.

Chapter 5

1 E.g. *RRC* 301/1; 372; 413/1; 419/2; 351/1.
2 There exist several versions of this story: the head-wrapping also occurs in App., *B Civ.* 1.2.26, whereas in Vell. Pat. 2.3 and Val. Max. 3.17 the toga is wound around the

left arm. In Plutarch it is the other senators who wrap their togas around their forearms. Presumably the purpose was to use the toga as improvised armour.
3   She does not know at this stage that he is not, in fact, dead.
4   For the etymology see Isid., *Etym.* 19.24.6. Several passages in Plautus suggest the *toga candida* might originally, or additionally, have been worn for weddings and festivities: see Plaut., *Rud.* 1.5.12; *Cas.* 2.8.10.
5   For more on the *toga candida*, see Deniaux 2003.
6   For a similar discussion see *Coriol.* 14.1–2, although here he says bribery did not come into it.
7   Heskel 1994: 141. Herzog-Hauser 1937 suggested it was grey/black, but it seems more likely, given that it is also the adjective used to describe poor people's clothes, that it was made from the (cheaper) wool of dark-coloured, i.e. brown-black, sheep.
8   Olson 2017b: 101.
9   Festus 236M; Sid. Apoll., *Epist.* 1.7.9; Cic., *Vat.* 30–32; Dio Cass. 54.35.5; *ILS* 139–140.
10 *Toga pulla*: Cic., *Fam.* 1.2; *Clu.* 18; *Planc.* 21; App., *B Civ.* 2.24; Dio Cass. 38.16; Val. Max. 6.5.2; *sordida*: Sen., *Contr.* 10.1.17; Quint., *Inst.* 6.1.33; Cic., *Orat.* 2.195; *Att.* 3.15.5; *Lig.* 33; *Mur.* 86; *Scaur.* 49; *Rosc. Am.* 147; Diod. Sic. 36.15. In 66 BCE Licinius Macer changed back into his clean white toga at his trial too quickly, assuming he had been acquitted (Plut., *Cic.* 9). See also Heskel 1994.
11 E.g. Appius Claudius, who refused to don mourning clothes when he was on trial in 470 BCE: Livy 2.61; Dion. Hal., *Ant. Rom.* 9.54.3; Suet., *Tib.* 2.4. See also Val. Max. 6.6.4.
12 See also Dyck 2001.
13 Sen., *De ira* 1.16.5; figuratively: Petron., *Sat.* 58.12. Whether '*perversa*' meant it was worn upside down or inside out is not clear (upside down: Linderski 2002: 363; inside out: Olson 2017b: 102).
14 See also Cic., *Sest.* 33: 'Is it not normal practice to spontaneously (*sponte*) change one's clothes (*vestem mutare*) when friends are in danger?'
15 See also a slightly different practice attributed to Julius Caesar, that when entertaining guests in the provinces he always gave two banquets, one for wearers of the *pallium* and the *sagum* (i.e. *peregrini* and soldiers), and the other for *togati* (i.e. citizens and distinguished people in the province): Suet., *Iul.* 48.
16 According to a comment of Asconius he found justification for this dress in the statues of Romulus and Tatius on the Capitol and Camillus on the Rostra, all depicted in togas without tunics underneath (*Scaur.* 46 p. 29 C).
17 E.g. the *lex Metilia de fullonibus* (217 BCE): Pliny, *HN* 35.197. For this and the fraught politics of the *toga candida* in general, see Baltrusch 1989: 50–52.
18 See Dyck 2001 for clothing as a key component in Cicero's 'rhetorical toolkit' (119).
19 See above Chapter 3.
20 See also Cic., *Cluent.* 111.

21 For this see esp. Nicolet 1960; McDonnell 2006: 349f.
22 See, e.g., Cic., *Pis.* 30.73: *sed quia pacis est insigne et otii toga, contra autem arma tumultus atque belli.*
23 See, e.g., Quint., *Inst.* 11.1.24; Plut., *Comp. Dem. Cic.* 2.1–2.
24 E.g. *RRC* 301/1; 372; 413/1; 419/2; 351/1.
25 Bender 1994: 151; Zanker 2010: 3. According to Rothfus (2010: 447–448), there was also a religious dimension to this: it is Jupiter who proclaims the Romans the *gens togata*, and in doing so 'the toga is emphasized as the symbol of the Romans in their role as a victorious people especially dear to the gods'.
26 See above Chapter 2.
27 E.g. Goette 1990: 102; Zanker 1990: 162; Rothfus 2010: 444. Olson has recently argued the opposite (2017b: 58 n.59): that the new style may actually have evolved first amongst the masses; but we do not have any evidence for this, and it must surely be rejected in view of the expense of the new toga and the consistently top-down way in which fashion worked in pre-modern societies.
28 Stone 1994: 17 with n.34.
29 Hafner 1969: 40–41; Gabelmann 1985: 525. See also Goette 1990: 25; Rothfus 2010: 444.
30 Goette 1990: 8; 102; Rothfus 2010: 444–445.
31 Richardson/Richardson 1966: 261; Christ 1997: 26.
32 Suet., *Aug.* 29; Wrede 1995: 546; Zanker 2010: 125–127.
33 See, e.g., the Via Labicana statue, figures on the Ara Pacis and the figure of Augustus on the Altar of the Lares Augusti (Zanker 2010: 124 fig. 100b; 125 fig. 101; 128 fig. 104).
34 Zanker 2010: 127.
35 As Stewart has recently re-emphasized (2008: 112–116), this was allegedly set up by the senate *for* Augustus, not by Augustus himself (*RGDA* 12), but even if Augustus was not directly involved, it deliberately visualizes his ideology.
36 See, e.g., Zanker 2010: 124 fig. 100b.
37 Hertel 1993: 54.
38 Kleiner 1978: 753–757; 772. Kleiner points out that this presents a striking contrast to corresponding Greek art like the Panathenaic procession frieze on the Parthenon, where the sexes are strictly segregated and the figures are grave and stiff.
39 For this see Castriota 1995: 124–169.
40 E.g. laws promoting marriage, incentivizing the having of many children and making adultery a public, rather than private, crime (see, e.g., Dio Cass. 54.16.1; Suet., *Aug.* 34; Paul., *Sent.* 2.26.1–8; 10–12; 14–17; Livy, *Per.* 59).
41 E.g. Hafner 1969: 41; Gabelmann 1985: 525; Goette 1990: 37; and esp. Rothfus 2010 (e.g. 425–426; 448–449).
42 One need think only of popular attitudes to the British royal family today.
43 For this see Hertel 1993: 53.
44 See below Chapter 6.

45 E.g. Claudius (Dio Cass. 60.7.4); Hadrian (SHA *Hadr.* 22.2).
46 No examples of the final two have as yet been found.
47 See Alföldi 1970: 127–128 for the idea that this also corresponded to Hellenistic enlightenment values, in which rulers tried to appear the same as their subjects. For such images, one must assume they were intended to represent the *toga praetexta* of Roman magistrates.
48 For representation types in general, see Niemeyer 1968; Alföldi 1970; Goette 1990; Mittag 2009.
49 Toynbee 1956.
50 E.g. the Via Labicana statue (Zanker 2010: 128 fig. 104). This statue type is usually seen as denoting the emperor as *pontifex maximus*, but Niemeyer has argued it had more to do with Augustus' promotion of the cult of the *Genius Augusti*, which affected how *genii familiares* were depicted as well (Niemeyer 1968: 43–44).
51 E.g. MuM auction 38 (1968) no. 334; Giard 1976: no. 1366. See also similar imagery on the Boscoreale cup: Zanker 2010: 228 fig. 180b.
52 See also *Aug.* 64, which most implausibly alleges he had his daughter and granddaughters learn how to spin and weave. It is interesting that it is not claimed that it was Livia who taught them, as would have been customary; but the passage is testimony to the enduring connection between textile work and female virtue, and the female members of Augustus' family were indeed expected to act as role models in his policy to promote simple family values (with mixed success, as the example of his daughter Julia shows).
53 Alföldi 1970: 136. See below Chapter 7.
54 See, e.g., the bust in the National Museum, Naples, countless coin depictions of his triumph (e.g. *RIC* 1.33) and the relief of him as hero vanquishing the personified Britannia in the Sebasteion at Aphrodisias: Stewart 2008: 151 fig. 36.
55 Laurence 2012: 75–76.
56 Laurence 2012: 77. See also Wallace-Hadrill 1982 for the idea of the '*civilis princeps*'.
57 See also Dio Cass. 59.26.10. Caligula is also, on the other hand, said to have handed out togas as gifts to senators and equestrians: Suet., *Calig.* 17.2.
58 See Davies 2018: 49–50 for expectations surrounding the body language of imperial figures.
59 E.g. Nero: Giroire/Roger 2007: 80–81 no. 23; *BMC* Vespasian 45–46; 338; 430; 443; 455.
60 Tac., *Ann.* 4.4; Vell. Pat. 2.99.2; Suet., *Tib.* 7; *Cal.* 10; 15.2; *Galba* 4.3; *Vesp.* 2.2; SHA *Marc. Aur.* 1.10; *Comm.* 1–2; *Sep. Sev.* 16.8–9.
61 For this incident see also Dio Cass. 61.34.1. Cf. Suet., *Claud.* 43, where earlier Claudius intended to bestow the *toga virilis* on Britannicus and 'thus give the Roman people a genuine Caesar'.

62 Laurence 2012: 77.
63 E.g. Mattingly 1923: 359 no. 260a; pl. 59.3; 1930: 48; 113.
64 See Laurence 2012.
65 See, e.g., equestrian statues in the Roman Forum and at Misenum (Camodeca 2000; Bergemann 1990: P31).
66 E.g. statues in Ostia (Calza 1964: 59–60 n.89) and his forum (Packer 1997) and busts like the one in the Museo Chiaramonti (Vatican, inv. 2269).
67 Laurence 2012: 75.
68 E.g. Alföldi 1970: pl. 3.2–3.
69 Stewart 2008: 120 fig. 27.
70 Olson 2017b: 36.
71 E.g. statue of Antoninus Pius in Museo Chiaramonti (Vatican); busts of Hadrian in Naples (National Archaeological Museum, inv. 6067); Marcus Aurelius in the Louvre (Giroire/Roger 2007: 58–59 no. 7); and Antoninus Pius (Glyptothek Munich, inv. 337; Museo del Prado, inv. E-123).
72 It must be a *toga picta* as he is driving a *quadriga*. For the significance of this see Mittag 2009: 449–452; 462.
73 For these depictions see Mittag 2009: 50–52. For the future trajectory of this development see below Chapter 7.
74 Stone 1994: 24 fig. 1.13; see also Giuliano 1981: 251–252.
75 Goette 1990: 49–50; examples on pl. 21.2–6.
76 See most recently Opper 2008: 69–70; Fejfer 2008: 395; Vout 2010.
77 A *himation* statue in the Istanbul Archaeological Museum has been mooted as Hadrian, but it is far from certain: Inan/Alföldi-Rosenbaum 1966: 71–71; pl. 23.
78 See already Alföldi 1935: 10 and more recently, also for dress in the *Historia Augusta* more generally, Molinier-Arbo 2003; Harlow 2005.
79 See also Hdn. 1.16.
80 E.g. busts in Eskenazi Museum of Art, inv. 75.33.1, Glyptothek, Munich, inv. E145 (Septimius Severus), Museo Arch. Naz. Naples, inv. 6033 (Caracalla) and the Capitoline Museums (Severus Alexander).
81 For a detailed discussion of triumphal dress and the emperors, see Mittag 2009.
82 These are reported to have been his dying words to his sons: Dio Cass. 77.15.2.
83 Mittag 2009: 454 fig. 6.
84 Mittag 2009: 458 fig. 7. Also interesting on this monument is the Concordia scene, in which Septimius Severus and Geta both wear the new form of semi-contabulated toga whilst Caracalla wears the older one.
85 See also an anecdote in the *Historia Augusta*, in which a writer of some wit views an image in Rome portraying the emperor in five different outfits – toga, military cloak, armour, *pallium* and hunting dress – to which he says 'I do not recognise the old man in the armour, I do not recognise the man in the military cloak' and so on, 'but I

do recognize the man in the toga' (*Tac.* 16.2–3). In reality, it seems, he only ever wore a toga, at least in Rome.
86 Alföldi has expressed doubt that this is true (1970: 147) because the *Historia Augusta* already implies it was unusual for Severus Alexander to use the *toga picta* kept in the Temple of Jupiter (40.8) and because we know of special staff already in the time of Claudius employed to take care of the 'regia vestis' (*ILS* 1758).
87 This is explicitly stated in SHA *Gall.* 16.4; see also *Aurel.* 13.3, where a *toga praetexta* and *toga picta* are among the items granted for his new role as consul.
88 See Chapter 6.
89 E.g. Nero, who wore the *chlamys* and Olympic crown in Greece (Suet., *Nero* 25.1) and Hadrian, who wore local dress when presiding over the Dionysia in Athens (Dio 69.16.1).
90 The original meaning of the term *provincia*, of course, being the designated area of a military operation: see Richardson 2008: 8; 80; 115.
91 For more on this see Harlow 2005: 145.
92 E.g. *RPC* 1.2362 (Pergamon); 1.2451; 1.2457 (Magnesia), 1.2654; 1.3627; 1.4842 (Tralles, Caesarea in Cappadocia and Caesarea Paneas).
93 Laurence (2012: 73–74) suggests this asserted the emperor as 'a citizen and as a Roman superior to non-Romans'. See also a coin depicting Judaea personified, Hadrian in a toga sacrificing over an altar and two togate children symbolizing the founding of Jerusalem as a *colonia* that would produce Roman citizens (*BMC* Hadrian 1757).
94 E.g. Harlow 2005: 145; Karanastasi 2013.
95 Howgego 2005: 10–11.
96 Pausch 2003: 28f.; Zanker 2010: 162–166.

Chapter 6

1 E.g. Wild 1985; Roche-Bernard 1993; B. Goldman 1994; Rothe 2009; 2012; Audley-Miller 2012; Carroll 2013a; 2013b; Heyn 2017.
2 E.g. Zanker 1983a; 1989; Goette 1990; Havé-Nikolaus 1998; Wueste 2017.
3 See also Rothe 2017.
4 Wallace-Hadrill 2008: 41.
5 See Chapter 1 above.
6 See also Cic., *Balb.* 31; Vell. Pat. 1.14. Dench sees this as part of a wider tendency in the late Republic and early Empire to retrospectively paint Roman history as one of continuous generosity and inclusion with regard to conquered peoples (2005: 118), whilst the issues that emerged in the Social War prove otherwise (125).
7 See esp. recent work on the realities of the citizenship system and the divisiveness of imperial ideology, e.g. by Lavan (2016b) and Ando (2016).

8 See also the inscription of Philip of Macedon in Larisa: *IG* 9.2.517.
9 Pausch 2003: 36 quite implausibly thinks this means they only acquired the tunic. The reason the tunic is mentioned is that it held the marker of senatorial status – the *latus clavus* – but it was always worn with a toga.
10 See, e.g., Brandt/Slofstra 1983; Millett 1992; Freeman 1993; Hanson 1994; Mattingly 1997; Woolf 1998; Webster 2001; Hingley 2005; Pitts 2007; Versluys 2014; Pitts/Versluys 2015.
11 See also Livy 34.7.2–3: local municipal aristocracy allowed to wear senatorial insignia; P.Oxy 471 no. 7 (columns iv–v, lines 100–107): a local Egyptian man is executed for not 'wearing white' to theatre, which may mean the toga.
12 See Zimmer 1992 for reconstructions of statue programmes in some western cities in the second century and their role in propagating a specific '*Prinzipatsideologie*'.
13 See also Statius, *Silv.* 1.4.11 for '*urbes togatae*'.
14 See Rothe 2014.
15 See, e.g., Revell 2009; 2013; Pitts/Versluys 2015.
16 See, e.g., Nordholt 1997; Maynard 2004: esp. 43–46.
17 There are also no togas in the few places in which textiles survived due to localized chemical circumstances, such as at Les Martres-de-Veyre (Breniquet/Bèche-Wittmann/Bouilloc/Gaumat 2017).
18 See, e.g., Hesberg/Zanker 1987; Zanker 1992; Hope 2001; Carroll 2015.
19 I have argued elsewhere that the setting up of a Roman-style grave monument was not, in itself, necessarily a statement of alignment with Roman culture, but merely, like radio and film in British India, a convenient new means to express a wide range of possible messages (Rothe 2009: 80).
20 See the *Lex Irnitana*: González/Crawford 1986. Inhabitants of *municipia* often held the lesser Latin citizenship.
21 Pliny, *Ep.* 10.104.
22 See the stipulations in military diplomas: Roxan 1978; 1985; 1994; Roxan/Holder 2003; Holder 2006.
23 See, e.g., Acts 25.10–11; Plut., *Pomp.* 24.6–8.
24 For citizenship in general, see Sherwin-White 1973; Gardner 1993.
25 The precise date is a matter of some speculation (see Wolff 1976; Barnes 2012) but need not concern us here.
26 Sherwin-White 1973: 264–274; Spagnuolo Vigorita 1993.
27 See, e.g., Buraselis 2007; Ando 2012; and especially radical new calculations by Lavan (2016a), who sees enfranchisement levels at around only 15–33 per cent in the provinces in 212 CE.
28 See above Chapter 4.
29 For citizenship and its advertisement on gravestones in the provinces, see Meyer 1990; Hope 2001: esp. 13.
30 Rothe 2009: 160 nos U1; U3–4.

31 Hair and beard styles were able to travel faster because they were depicted on coins. News of clothing styles would have been obtainable only from official artworks and visitors. See below for the continuing popularity of the 'armsling' style in Munigua in Spain.
32 Gabelmann 1985: 531–535. NB this constitutes a rethink of my 2009 interpretation of this dress (161) as a *palla*: the hemline is indeed round, while that of the mother's cloak is straight.
33 Mander 2013: 89–94.
34 For this monument in general, see Precht 1975; Andrikopolou-Strack 1986: 9–24; 80f.; 162 MG1.
35 For the ethnic mix of people in early Cologne see Tac., *Hist.* 4.65. For Roman Cologne in general see Eck 2004; Fischer/Trier 2013.
36 Rothe 2009: 63–65; 116 Table 17a.
37 See, e.g., Rothe 2009: 160 no. U3 (pl. 30); 162 no. U11; 164–165 no. U25 (pl. 35); RGM Cologne, inv. Stein 161.
38 For *Totenmahl* scenes in general, see Stewart 2009; for the NW provinces see Noelke 1998; 2000.
39 See, e.g., Rothe 2009: pls 26 no. M14; 33 no. U9; Danube provinces: *LUPA* 2919; 3032; 3055–3056; 3190.
40 Rothe 2009: 49–53; 59–60; 63–65; 108–111 tables 5; 7; 9.
41 E.g. Rothe 2009: 151 no. M11; 156 nos M20; M22; 160 no. U3; 161–162 no. U9; 170 no. U51.
42 See, e.g., Schlippschuh 1974: 162 for the decreasing significance of Roman citizenship among the provincial population during the course of the first two centuries AD.
43 See Rothe 2009: 108 table 5; 110 table 7; 111 table 9.
44 Hertel 1993; Edmondson/Nogales Basarrate/Trillmich 2001. The toga (presumably *praetexta*) is also worn by children in Spain, including a girl in a figurine in Munigua (Blech 1993: 144 no. 47; pl. 63, c–d). According to Plutarch (*Sertorius* 14), Sertorius introduced the *toga praetexta* and *bulla* for elite Iberian children in the first century BCE.
45 See Schlüter 1998: 46–52, albeit without quantification.
46 E.g. Hertel 1993: cat. 1–4.
47 Blech 1993.
48 Richardson 1986; Keay 1988: 25–46; Curchin 1991.
49 Pliny, *HN* 3.30; Hertel 1993: 57–58.
50 Although like in other Celtic regions there were large nucleated settlements: see Cardozo 1996; Millett 2001; Do Carmo Ribeiro/Sousa Melo 2012.
51 Hertel 1993: 47–58.
52 Mander 2013: 93.
53 E.g. Treveran area: Rothe 2009: nos T2; T4–7; T20–21; Auxerre: *LUPA* 25872; Sens: *LUPA* 26020.

54 E.g. *civitas Treverorum*: Rothe 2009: 121–128 nos T12; T16; T23; T26; T28; T30–31; T34; T37–40; T45; 130 no. T59; 133–137 nos T68; T73; T77–78; T82–83; T85; T87–88; *civitas Mediomatricorum*: Freigang 1997: 419–434 nos Med. 153–154; 157–158; 161; 164; 167–174; 179–199; 208–210; Dijon: *LUPA* 25093; 25101; 25122; 25124–25125; Autun: *LUPA* 25104; 25628; 25630; 25779–25780; 25782; 25786; 25791; 25807; 25818; Savigny-lès-Beaune: *LUPA* 25131–25132; Saulieu: *LUPA* 25137; 25146–25147; 25151; 25155; Alligny-en-Morvan: *LUPA* 25647–25648; Sens: *LUPA* 25820; 25836; 25910–25911; 25913; 25932–25937; 25940; Auxerre: *LUPA* 25858.

55 Freigang 1997: 305–307; 387–399; Wolff 1995: 337. For the Treveran area Raepsaet-Charlier (2001: 349ff.) has shown that the vast majority (72 per cent) of people mentioned in inscriptions possessed Roman citizenship. Many of these would originally have been attached to funerary portraits, which show a small number of togas, suggesting many of the men in Gallic dress must have been citizens. Concrete examples of men with Roman citizenship wearing the Gallic ensemble include Freigang 1997: nos. Med. 167; 173; 189; 192; 198.

56 E.g. Rothe 2009: nos T11; T41; T47–51; T56–58; T60; T62. Some of these are fragmentary, but it is easy to extrapolate portrait dimensions from the fragments that remain, and in all cases they were life-sized or larger.

57 Cf. Bertrang (1954: 38) and Freigang (1997: 309) who interpret all Gallic toga-wearers as Roman functionaries.

58 See, e.g., Rothe 2009: pls 3; 7 no. T43; 10–11; 17 no. T117.3; 19 nos T127; T128.1.

59 See, e.g., Rothe 2009: pls 9 no. T47.4; 12; 17 nos T117.1–2; 20 nos 145 and 148; 23 no. T172.

60 E.g. the onomastic evidence of the Treveran epigraphy summarized by Raepsaet-Charlier 2001: 397. Also Schlippschuh 1974: 131; 146; 155; 182ff.; Heinen 1985: 176–177; Freigang 1997: 308; Goethert 2002: 94f. It is also important to note that there is no evidence for significant numbers of outsiders in the region for the period in question.

61 For gravestones depicting these trades, see Rothe 2009: nos T33; T62; T160; T172; M41 (textiles); T90, T102; T104; T116; T149–150; T166–167; T175; T184 (wine). For wine merchants in the Treveran area and northern provinces, see Schlippschuh 1974: 26–36. For trade in the NW see Wierschowski 1991. For the Gallic textile industry see Wild 1970; 1985; Drinkwater 2001.

62 For this region and its inhabitants in general, see Wightman 1970; Heinen 1985.

63 Mehl's (1997) interpretation is that local tenant farmers were the main textile producers, and as such the operation run by the Secundinii was something akin to a closely coordinated cottage industry.

64 For all of the above and for the Igeler Säule in general, see Mehl 1997.

65 E.g. Mehl 1997: 80.

66 See Chapter 3 for the unsuitability of the toga to physical work.

67 Schlippschuh 1974; Krier 1981; Kneissl 1983; Wierschowski 1991; 1995.

68 Breward 2016: esp. 39–43.
69 Mazrui 1970: 22.
70 For a detailed typology see Rothe 2012: 178–221.
71 E.g. *LUPA* 38; 46; 304; 349; 448; 450; 593; 630; 693; 740; 760; 831; 837–838; 840–842; 857; 874; 876; 878–881; 1067; 1152; 1165; 1202–1206; 1229; 1238–1239; 1248; 1268; 1273; 1319; 1328; 1332–1335; 1340–1341; 1350; 1358; 1365; 1402; 1424–1425; 1446; 1452–1453; 1465; 1486–1487; 1489–1490; 1499; 1623; 1676; 1757; 2139; 2254; 2856; 2859; 2977; 3036; 3181; 3196; 3273; 3616; 3626; 3663; 3784; 3863; 4129; 4305; 4628–4629; 4918; 9083; 9784; 12765; 13333.
72 E.g. *LUPA* 31; 40; 53; 60; 65; 301; 307; 479; 492; 495; 585; 682; 685; 734–735; 776; 802; 834; 869; 872; 1127; 1159; 1260; 1267; 1291; 1403; 1414–1415; 1438; 1455; 1460; 1624; 1626; 1884; 2697; 2779; 2838; 2851; 2853; 2973; 3059; 3119; 3136; 3213–3214; 3267; 3269; 3413; 3439; 3613; 3627; 3736; 3814; 3816; 3827; 3878; 3945; 3952; 3974; 3985; 4041; 4128; 4255; 4382; 4700; 5252; 6154; 8511; 9209; 10176; 12766; 12802; 13137; 16736.
73 Rothe 2012; 2013.
74 E.g. *LUPA* 630; 760; 1465.
75 E.g. *LUPA* 1425; 1446; 1623; 3616; 4305; 13333.
76 See, e.g., Mócsy 1959; 1974; Solin 1983; Rothe 2014.
77 For this dress style see Rothe 2012: 178–204.
78 Cf. the description in *LUPA*, which sees it as a *sagum*; however, the pronounced *umbo* leaves no room for doubt that a toga is depicted here.
79 Rothe 2012: 193; 174 fig. 22; 186 figs 34–35.
80 The alternative is '*Quartus Sirae (servus)*' ('slave of Sira'), but this is less likely. Moreover, '*filius/a*' is commonly omitted in inscriptions of this kind. (J. Edmondson – *pers. comm.*). For the legal complexities surrounding unions between slaves and citizens see Edmondson 2016.
81 These display a mix of (adult) ages, name forms and genders, and one can only speculate that they represent the later-deceased children of Quartus and Ingenua and their spouses.
82 E.g. *LUPA* 632; 693; 740; 1248; 1333; 1402; 2856; 3616.
83 Pochmarski 2004.
84 Rothe 2012: 158–165. As so often, it would help if we had the surviving paintwork, because local textiles may have featured different colours or more elaborate weaving patterns like tartan (see the iron-age textiles from the area in Grömer 2010).
85 E.g. *LUPA* 59; 348; 482; 484; 491; 495; 583; 626; 643; 647; 663; 681; 691; 694; 746; 772; 839; 877; 885–886; 1223; 1355; 1371; 1379; 2733; 2742; 2757–2758; 2787; 2852; 2910; 2974; 3036; 3038; 3042; 4600; 4613; 13257.
86 E.g. Jantsch 1934; Noll 1963: 160; Garbsch 1965; Facsády 2007.

87   Rothe 2012.
88   See, e.g., Durham 1999 (esp. 393) for Herero women in southern Africa and Tarlo 1996 (esp. 46) for India.
89   E.g. Nadig 1986 for the Otomi of Mexico and James 1996 for the Sotho of southern Africa.
90   It should be noted that there is some evidence that the *toga virilis* ceremony did play a role in some places in the eastern provinces, such as Bithynia (Pliny, *Ep.* 10.116), Laodicaea (Cic., *Att.* 5.20.9) and Galatia (see Harrill 2002). See also Dolansky 2008: 52; Mander 2013: 89–94.
91   Borg 1996; Parlasca/Seemann 1999; most of the draped cloaks worn by men in these predominately bust-style depictions are white, and as such could conceivably portray togas, but only one displays a draping style that is distinctively toga-like (Seipel 1998: 148–149 no. 44), although even this could be a *himation*. All of the full-length figures of men in these cloaks show a straight hem.
92   Smith 1998: 63–70.
93   See Smith 1998: 63 for the idea that this was especially so in the second century and had an effect on public statuary.
94   As Smith has said (1998: 66), the *himation* 'attached its wearers automatically to five centuries of shared civic values'.
95   Wueste 2017: 190. But see also von Moock 1998: 58–59, where he argues that the few steles from Attica showing men in the *himation* draped diagonally rather than 'armsling'-style were influenced by the iconography of philosophers at Rome and show a pride in belonging to the 'birthplace' of such intellectual activity. Cf. also Bieber 1934 (1967): 42–44, who interpreted this as the *himation* being influenced by Roman styles.
96   Meyer-Zwiffelhoffer 2003. There is also some indication that rates of citizenship were lower in the eastern provinces than in the West: Goldhill 2001.
97   Meyer-Zwiffelhoffer 2003; see also Veyne 1999. But cf. Ziegler 1995 and Mitchell 1993, who claims to be able to identify a certain new 'compensatory culture' (e.g. myths, geneaologies, euergetism) developing in the Greek cities to offset loss of freedom.
98   Meyer-Zwiffelhoffer 2003: 384–386.
99   Smith 1998: 65. He also suggests that Greek nobles' Roman identity could be asserted in other ways.
100 Havé-Nikolaus 1998: 27. The number of toga statues in Eleusis is also high, but likely due to the interest of Roman emperors in the mysteries (34f.). Havé-Nikolaus also discovered that toga frequency tended to correlate directly with levels of interest of any given emperor in Greece, although it is not clear whether this was a result of greater numbers of imperial portraits, or of flattery on the part of local elites in light of new privileges.

101 Havé-Nikolaus 1998: 28.
102 Havé-Nikolaus 1998: 24. For other examples see the magistrate in a toga statue from the *bouleuterion* in Apollonia, Illyria (Balty 1993: pl. 16.4) and one from the basilica on Thera (Fittschen/Zanker 2011: no. 51).
103 Smith 1998: 72.
104 Smith 1998: 70–73 with fig. 3.
105 Other examples of people in this category include Herodes Atticus in Athens (see Smith 1998: 75–78) and the imperial freedman Zoilus in Aphrodisias (Smith 1993).
106 See, e.g., Yon 2002: 57–97. In the inscriptions of the Palymrene elite mentions of important positions in the city are curiously rare, whilst family genealogies and the like are much more common (Yon 2002: 99).
107 Exemplified in the bilingual Greek–Aramaic Tax Law of 137 CE: see Matthews 1984. Greek and Aramaic dominate the public epigraphy, whilst private and sacred inscriptions tend to be in the local language: Gawlikowski 1970. For the few private Latin inscriptions see Millar 2006: 231–236.
108 B. Goldman 1994; Heyn 2017.
109 E.g. Millar 1993: 319–336; B. Goldman 1994; Schmidt-Colinet 2004; Heyn 2017.
110 Colledge 1976: figs 127–128 (*togati*); 121–122; 125 (*palliati*).
111 Böhme/Schottroff 1979.
112 Schmidt-Colinet/al-As'ad 2007; Schmidt-Colinet 2009. Further, smaller toga-wearers are shown in niches sacrificing on the sides of the lid of sarcophagus A: Schmidt-Colinet/al-As'ad 2007: pl. 88.5; 89.1–2.
113 Cf. Schmidt-Colinet/al-As'ad 2007: 272 n.4, who suggest that the newer fashions simply took a while to get to Palmyra; but if that were the case we would still see some variety in toga drapery.
114 B. Goldman 1994: 167. Goldman claimed there is only one honorific toga statue from Palmyra when in fact there are two.
115 Dirven forthcoming a/b. See also Andrade 2012.
116 It should be noted, however, that private funerary sculpture was relatively 'public' in nature as well, as the tower tombs and *hypogea* were accessible from the outside and regularly visited during festivals and commemorations: Dirven forthcoming a: 121; b.
117 Schmidt-Colinet/al-As'ad 2007: 275; 2009: 225.
118 Especially amongst the elite: see, e.g., early second-century Pergamum, where thirty-two of the thirty-six members of the imperial choir had Roman citizenship: Price 1984: 90.
119 For the existence of the *tria nomina* in Palmyrene funerary epigraphy see Millar 2006: 231–236.
120 See Raja 2018 for the argument that the customary modern term '*modius*' for these hats is misleading.

121 See Kaizer 2002: 179–180 for the significance of the scenes. Veyne (2001: 34) has suggested the depiction might additionally symbolize tenants bringing tribute.
122 Whether current or former priests (see Raja 2017a), the overall significance of the depiction remains the same. The laurel wreaths in the artworks listed here call to mind the στέφανοι commonly associated with imperial priests in statuary art in Asia Minor, which include busts of the emperor. These come in a variety of styles, from thick, textile diadems to high, intricately carved crowns, some of them consisting of or including a vegetal wreath (e.g. Inan/Alföldi-Rosenbaum 1966: 109 no. 111; 124 no. 143; 128 no. 151; 137 no. 169; 139 no. 174; 148 no. 190; 164 no. 216; 165 no. 219; 171 no. 228; 177 no. 239; 179 no. 241; 185 no. 251; 204 no. 282). But, as is emerging for the Asia Minor examples as well (Inan/Alföldi-Rosenbaum 1966: 31–32), the bust wreaths depicted in funerary art in Palmyra are more generally associated with priests, including those wearing *himatia* and local cloaks, so they are unlikely to have been confined to a particular cult.
123 The proportion of men with priestly attributes is, in fact, particularly high in Palmyra at approx. 20 per cent of depictions: Raja 2017c: 116.
124 It should be noted that although in the western empire a priestly depiction would usually include the figure with toga pulled up over the head, depictions of the toga *capite velato* are extremely rare in the East, and all the known instances are portraits of emperors or their family members (Havé-Nikolaus 1998: 59–60).
125 Dirven 2011. See also Kaizer 2002: 239; 2016; Yon 2002: 122–123.
126 See Kaizer 2001: 150; Yon 2002: 122 n.192 for suggestions as to its location.
127 Hillers/Cussini 1996: no. 2769; Michalowski 1960: 208 no. 2; full texts and discussions can be found in Kaizer 2002: 148–151; Yon 2002: 122–123; Dirven 2011.
128 Bowersock 1976.
129 In addition, both Colledge (1976: 50–52) and Yon (2002: 99–105) have argued that the Roman authorities funded the Temple of Bel, further underlining the close relationship between Bel and Roman government.
130 *Himatia*: Inan/Alföldi-Rosenbaum 1966: 109 no. 111; 128 no. 151; 185 no. 251; but see also Antinous as an imperial priest wearing a toga in Cyrene (Louvre, inv. MA1781). Dio Chrysostom's description of an imperial priest during a procession gives his dress merely as 'στέφανος καὶ πορφύρα': although it is likely that a *toga purpurea* is meant, this is by no means certain.
131 The fact that Astarte is depicted on the side of sarcophagus A (Schmidt-Colinet/al-As'ad 2007: pl. 86.3–4) does not detract from this: as the patron of caravaneers, she held significance for the Palmyrene elite alongside other cults. Ariadne, Dionysus and Victoria also appear in various places on this sarcophagus.
132 See Schmidt-Colinet/al-As'ad 2007: 278 n.30 for a possible match.
133 Schmidt-Colinet/al-As'ad 2007: pl. 84.1.

134 http://projects.au.dk/palmyraportrait/
135 Cf. Schmidt-Colinet/al-As'ad 2007: 276; Schmidt-Colinet 2009: 225.
136 E.g. Kaizer 2002; Raja 2017a–c.
137 See also Dirven forthcoming a and b for a rejection of the idea that the different artistic styles and dress choices in Palmyrene art were necessarily 'ethnic' in character.
138 Smith 1998: 61.
139 See, e.g., Fejfer 2008: 196 for the correlation of toga-wearing with Latin epigraphy and *himation*-wearing with Greek epigraphy in Africa Proconsularis; for the widespread use of the toga in Carthage: Apuleius, *Flor.* 20.10; Tertullian, *De Pallio* and a more general discussion in Brennan 2008; for dress in the funerary art of Ghirza (Tripolitana): Audley-Miller 2012; for the toga depictions in the theatre at Sabratha: Caputo 1959: 19–23.

Chapter 7

1 See above Chapter 4 and McKechnie 1992.
2 Tertullian rails against the toga in *De Pallio*, but in *De idololatria* 18.3 he says it is acceptable for Christian boys to wear the *toga praetexta* as a sign of respectable descent, but that they shouldn't attend sacrifices associated with *togam virilem sumere*.
3 Jones 1973: 17–18: 523–562.
4 Marrou 1964. See early sarcophagus depictions of teachers (Amedick 1991: 65; 140 no. 1152; 139 no. 107; 149 no. 171) and doctors (135 no. 81).
5 Ewald 2003: 570.
6 See, e.g., Vössing 2012; Urbano 2014.
7 For this see Neri 2004; Upson-Saia 2011; Bartholeyns 2012 and early Christian treatises on appearance, such as Jer., *Ep.* 22.32; John Chrys., *Homilies on Second Thessalonians* 3.3. For von Rummel (2007: 85 n.18), *De Pallio* is not an anti-Roman tract but an appeal to the simple life idealized in Paul's letters and the gospel, and perhaps even contemporaneous iconography of Jesus himself.
8 Rothe 2012: 166–171.
9 See, e.g., soldier gravestones on the Rhine frontier: *LUPA* 7079; 7081; 8258; 13777; 15518; 15520; 15522.
10 Pliny, *HN* 8.190; Martial 2.57; 5.26; 14.130; 14.145; Kolb 1973.
11 Kolb 1974.
12 Delbrück 1929: 34 fig. 13.
13 See also legislation like *Cod. Theod.* 14.10.2–4 forbidding the wearing of various dress elements in the city of Rome: *tzangae* (special type of shoe), trousers (*bracae*),

furs (*pelles*) and long hair (*maiores crines*). Von Rummel (2007: 158–165) argues that none of these were really considered barbarian by the time this was written, but rather too military in flavour for a peaceful urban setting.

14 Von Rummel 2007: 377.
15 Marrou 1977: 15–20. Cf. for a view of the process as more gradual: Mathieu 1992; Baratte 2004.
16 See also for the fourth century a gold-glass image of a young boy in a toga and *bulla* in the Archaeological Museum in Bologna (Ducati 1929: 233–235), and Ausonius, *Epist.* 22.85–93, in which his grandfather recalls the *toga praetexta* he wore as a schoolboy.
17 E.g. Amm. Marc. 15.7.3; *CIL* 6.32031; 8.1297; 10.1201; Sid. Apoll., *Epist.* 2.13; Lydus, *Mag.* 3.8; *Cod. Theod.* 6.2.26; 7.8.10; 12.1.152; Auson., *Com. prof. Burd.* 5.1.1–2. For this see Delmaire 2003.
18 See von Rummel's excellent overview of late antique dress in 2007: 87–96.
19 See above Chapter 5.
20 For all this see already Alföldi 1935: 43, but also 1970: 126; 161–167.
21 See above Chapter 5.
22 See also the fourth-century emperor Julian, who tried to reinstate the old ways by getting pagan priests to wear the *toga praetexta* (Julian, *Frag. epist.* 1.332–335).
23 Ağtürk 2018: 413 figs 3–4.
24 See, e.g., the mosaics of Justinian and his court in San Vitale in Ravenna: Barber 1990.
25 Smith 2007: 204.
26 Smith 1999: 163 fig. 2. See also the statues of Diocletian in the Villa Pamphilij, Rome (Niemeyer 1968: no. 22, pl. 7.2), Maximinianus Herculeus in Syracuse (no. 21, pl. 8.1) and Maxentius in Ostia (no. 27, pl. 8.2).
27 Smith 2007: 205. See also Niemeyer 1968: 47.
28 See also a commemorative coin of 263 depicting the personified senate wearing a decorated toga/triumphal toga/*trabea* (Alföldi 1970: pl. 9.12).
29 For this elision see Alföldi 1970: 151; MacCormack 1981: 33–50; Latham 2016: 197–207.
30 A tangential development of this period is the *vestis alba triumphalis* of the Severan tondo: see Mittag 2009.
31 E.g. Goette 1990; Stone 1994.
32 A view already put forward by Wilson (1924) and Delbrück (1929). For the evolution of the toga into the *trabea*, see Baratte 2004: 121–127.
33 This is in keeping with a gradual shift in clothing aesthetic, from the second century onward, away from asymmetry toward a more symmetrical appearance: see also the increasingly symmetrical draping of the female *palla* in evidence, e.g. in the third-century Brescia medallion in the British Museum (Howells 2015: pl. 1).

34 Already Wilpert (1898) identified the *trabea* as a single garment rather than the two originally identified by Meyer (1879).
35 Delbrück 1929: 51–52. E.g. the marriage of Moses mosaic in Santa Maria Maggiore: Delbrück 1929: 48 fig. 17. See also the early-fourth-century villa mosaics at Piazza Armerina in Sicily, where all the main figures wear *dalmaticae* and *paenulae*, except the master of games, who wears a traditional-looking plain white toga over an old-fashioned tunic with purple *clavi* (Carandini/Ricci/de Vos 1982: 336 fig. 204).
36 E.g. Auson., *Grat. act.* 18; Prudent., *Perist.* 10.142–143; Venantius Fortunatus, *Vita S. Martini* 2.452. Delbrück 1929: 52.
37 *CIL* 10.1709; Sid. Apoll., *Epist.* 9.16.22; Delbrück 1929: 52–53.
38 Delbrück 1929: 53–54. On these diptychs in general, see most recently Cameron 1998; 2013.
39 Claudian, *Pan. Prob.* 206; *Cons. Stil.* 2.331–334; 2.339–340; 3.89; 3.198. The jewels are probably what is represented by small knobs in many coin images, especially those commemorating quinquennial consulships, e.g. Burgess 1988: pl. 26.12; 27.5–6; 28.2.
40 Dewar (2008) and others have raised doubts that this garment ever actually existed, but Cameron (1970) believed it did. Either way, the symbolism of it remains valid.
41 The emperor was in Illyricum dealing with the aftermath of the Battle of Adrianople.
42 He was actually the father of his wife Constantia.
43 E.g. Auson., *Epist.* 22.92; *Grat. act.* 11; Claudian, *B. Gild.* 1.60–61; *Hon. Cons.* 6.372; *Eutr.* 1.9–10; 1.301–302; 1.463–464; 2.58–59.
44 Dewar 2008: 219.
45 For the toga as a symbol of peace and civic duty, see Chapter 3.
46 For these twin uses of triumphal dress see Chapter 4.
47 See Chapter 3.
48 For Claudian and Eutropius see Long 1996.
49 See also a coin of Valentinian III (425–455), on which he is depicted in a toga/*trabea* helping a personification of *res publica* to her feet: *RIC* 10.2038–45.
50 Although placed in tombs rather than public places or open cemeteries, there is a tendency from the late second century onward for these to become more elaborate and, however limited the audience (see Borg 2013: 213–240 for a discussion of this), were obviously meant to portray a certain image of the deceased and his family.
51 See Borg 2013: 164–197.
52 See Borg 2013: 186–191 for a discussion of what exactly this entourage represents and scepticism that it is anything as precise as the *processus consularis*.
53 For the significance of this for questions of fashion, see Chapter 2.
54 See, e.g., Borg 2013: 186–191 with figs 116–118; 124–125.
55 E.g. a relief from Rome in the Vatican: Goette 1990: 62; pl. 43.3–5.
56 Cf. the survival of the morning suit for weddings in Britain: Breward 2016: 50.

57 Birk 2013: 71 fig. 32.
58 See Matthews 1975: 12–18.
59 For these shifts in rank, see most recently Bodnaruk 2017.
60 For all of the above see Rebenich 1991: 447–476; pl. 51–52. It is worth noting that, as ever, we may be missing further gradations of rank – for example in colour/decoration of toga – by not having the original paintwork.
61 http://laststatues.classics.ox.ac.uk/; Smith/Ward-Perkins 2016.
62 I.e. excluding athletes, emperors and members of the imperial family.
63 Wueste 2017: 192.
64 See also Dewar 2008: 220.
65 Gehn 2012: 228–229; Wueste 2017: 182.
66 E.g. Prudent., *C. Symm.* 2.699; Claud., *Eutr.* 1.301; 1.463; 2.58–59; *Cons. Stil.* 1.329–330; 2.366–370; 3.85 Sid. Apoll., *Epist.* 1.5.11; Paulinus of Nola, *Epist.* 45.2; Oros. 5.18.15; Macr., *Sat.* 6.5.15.
67 Von Rummel 2007: 378–381; 405.
68 Von Rummel 2007: 382; 386–390.
69 For dress in legal texts in late antiquity see Delmaire 2004; Arce 2005.
70 Wueste 2017: 189.
71 See Dio Chrys., *Or.* 31.8–9; Fejfer 2008: 215–217.
72 See Lenaghan 2016; Wueste 2017; Bodnaruk 2017. See also the fourth-century sculptor's workshop near Rome containing still headless toga statues: Brown 1971: 21.
73 *LSA* 1266 with further literature.
74 Wueste 2017: 189.
75 Bodnaruk 2017.
76 Wilpert 1898: 13.
77 Wilpert 1898: 13.
78 Stein 1968: 248–253.
79 E.g. Alföldi 1970: 153 fig. 3.5; pl. 10.2.
80 Alföldi 1970: 151 fig. 2. See also trabeate depictions of Theodosius II (Albizzati 1922: 74 fig. 8), Valentinian III (75 figs 10–11) and Leo I (76 fig. 12).
81 Delbrück 1933: pl. 108.
82 Albizzati 1922: 76 fig. 13.
83 Schramm 1954.

Epilogue

1 See Wyke 1997; Verdone 2003: esp. 44–46.
2 See, e.g., Tischbein's portrait of Goethe or the statue of Thomas Babington Macaulay at Trinity College, Cambridge.

3 See Wrede 2000.
4 For the Founding Fathers and classical thought in general, see Richard 1994; for Washington's personal interest in Roman history, see Cunliffe 1959: 154–159.
5 E.g. Heritage Auctions, Dallas: lot no. 33388.
6 E.g. 1stDibs.com Auctions, lot nos LU879111781751; LU837712573471.
7 Huet 1999.

Bibliography

Abramenko, A. (1993), *Die munizipale Mittelschicht im kaiserzeitlichen Italien. Zu einem neuen Verständnis von Sevirat und Augustalität*, Frankfurt: Lang.
Ağtürk, T. Ş. (2018), 'A New Tetrarchic Relief from Nicomedia: Embracing Emperors', *AJA* 122 (3): 411-426.
Albizzati, C. (1922), 'L'Ultima Toga', *Rivista Italiana di Numismatica* 35: 69-92.
Alfaro, C., J. P. Wild and B. Costa, eds (2004), *Purpureae vestes I: textiles y tintes del Mediterráneo en época romana*, Valencia: Valencia University Press.
Alfaro, C., M. Tellenbach and J. Ortiz, eds (2014), *Purpureae Vestes IV: Production and Trade of Textiles and Dyes in the Roman Empire and Neighbouring Regions*, Valencia: Valencia University Press.
Alfaro, C., J.-P. Brun, P. Borgard and R. Pierobon Benoit, eds (2011), *Purpureae vestes III: textiles y tintes en la ciudad antigua*, Valencia: Valencia University Press.
Alföldi, A. (1935), 'Insignien und Tracht der römischen Kaiser', *MDAI(R)* 50: 1-171.
Alföldi, A. (1970), *Die monarchische Repräsentation im römischen Kaiserreiche*, Darmstadt: Wissenschaftliche Buchgesellschaft.
Alföldy, G. (1981), 'Die Stellung der Ritter in der Führungsschicht des Imperium Romanum', *Chiron* 11: 169-215.
Alföldy, G. (1984), *Römische Statuen in Venetia et Histria. Epigraphische Quellen*, Heidelberg: Winter.
Altmann, W. (1905), *Die römischen Grabaltäre der Kaiserzeit*, Berlin: Weidmann.
Amedick, R. (1991), *Die Sarkophage mit Darstellungen aus dem Menschenleben 1.4: Vita privata*, Berlin: Mann.
Amelung, W. (1903), *Die Gewandung der alten Griechen und Römer*, Leipzig: Koehler.
Amiotti, G. (1981), 'Religione e politica nell'iniziazione romana. L'assunzione della toga virile', *Contributi dell'Istituto di Storia Antica* 7: 131-140.
Anderson, W. C. F. (1891), 'Toga', in W. Smith, W. Wayte and G. E. Marindin (eds), *A Dictionary of Greek and Roman Antiquities*, London: Murray, 1845-1850.
Ando, C. (2012), *Imperial Rome AD 193 to 284: The Critical Century*, Edinburgh: University of Edinburgh Press.
Ando, C. (2016), 'Making Romans: Citizens, Subjects and Subjectivity in Republican Empire', in M. Lavan, R. Payne and J. Weisweiler (eds), *Cosmopolitanism and Empire: Universal Rulers, Local Elites and Cultural Integration in the Ancient Near East and Mediterranean*, Oxford: Oxford University Press, 169-185.
Andrade, N. J. (2012), 'Inscribing the Citizen: Soados and the Civic Context of Palmyra', *MAARAV* 19 (1-2): 65-90.

Andrikopoulou-Strack, J.-N. (1986), *Grabbauten des 1. Jahrhunderts n. Chr. im Rheingebiet: Untersuchungen zu Chronologie und Typologie* (Beihefte der Bonner Jahrbücher 43), Bonn: Habelt.

Arce, J. (2005), 'Dress Control in Late Antiquity: *Cod. Theod.* 14.10.1–4', in A. Köb and P. Riedel (eds), *Kleidung und Repräsentation in Antike und Mittelalter*, Munich: Fink, 33–44.

Audley-Miller, L. (2012), 'Dressed to Impress: The Tomb Sculpture of Ghirza in Tripolitana', in M. Carroll and J. P. Wild (eds), *Dressing the Dead in Classical Antiquity*, Stroud: Amberley, 99–114.

Bablitz, L. (2007), *Actors and Audience in the Roman Courtroom*, London and New York: Routledge.

Baldassarre, I. (1991), *Pompei: Pitture e mosaici, vol. III, Regiones II–III–V*, Rome: Istituto della Enciclopedia Italiana.

Baltrusch, E. (1989), *Regimen morum: die Reglementierung des Privatlebens der Senatoren und Ritter in der römischen Republik und frühen Kaiserzeit* (Vestigia 41), Munich: Beck.

Balty, J. C. (1993), *Porträt und Gesellschaft in der römischen Welt*, Mainz: von Zabern.

Banerjee, M. and D. Miller (2003), *The Sari*, Oxford and New York: Berg.

Baratte, F. (2004), 'Le vêtement dans l'antiquité tardive: rupture ou continuité?', *Antiquité Tardive* 12: 121–135.

Barber, C. (1990), 'The Imperial Panels at San Vitale: A Reconsideration', *Byzantine and Modern Greek Studies* 14: 19–42.

Barnes, T. D. (2012), 'The Date of the *Constitutio Antoniniana* Once More', in B. Pferdehirt and M. Scholz (eds), *Bürgerrecht und Krise: Die Constitutio Antoniniana 212 n. Chr. und ihre innenpolitischen Folgen*, Mainz: Schnell & Steiner, 51–52.

Baronowski, D. W. (1984), 'The *formula togatorum*', *Historia* 33: 248–252.

Bartholeyns, G. (2012), 'Le moment chrétien. Fondation antique de la culture vestimentaire médiévale', in F. Gherchanoc and V. Huet (eds), *Vêtements antiques. S'habiller, se déshabiller dans les mondes anciens*, Paris: Errance, 113–134.

Beard, M. (2007), *The Roman Triumph*, Cambridge, MA: Harvard University Press.

Bender, H. (1994), 'De Habitu Vestis: Clothing in the *Aeneid*,' in J. Sebesta and L. Bonfante (eds), *The World of Roman Costume*, Madison: University of Wisconsin Press, 146–152.

Bender Jørgensen, L. (2011), 'Clavi and Non-clavi: Definitions of Various Bands on Roman Textiles', in C. Alfaro, J.-P. Brun, P. Borgard and R. Bierobon Benoit (eds), *Purpureae Vestes III. Textiles y tintes en la ciudad Antigua*, Valencia: Valencia University Press, 75–81.

Bergemann, J. (1990), *Römische Reiterstatuen: Ehrendenkmäler im öffentlichen Bereich*, Mainz: von Zabern.

Bergmann, M. (1977), *Studien zum römischen Portrait des 3. Jahrhunderts n. Chr.*, Bonn: Habelt.

Bertrang, A. (1954), *Le Musée Luxembourgeois*, Arlon: Fasbender.
Bieber, M. (1928), *Griechische Kleidung*, Berlin and Leipzig: De Gruyter.
Bieber, M. (1934), *Entwicklungsgeschichte der griechischen Tracht von der vorgriechischen Zeit bis zur römischen Kaiserzeit*, Berlin: Mann.
Bieber, M. (1959), 'Roman Men in Greek Himation (Romani Palliati): A Contribution to the History of Copying', *Proceedings of the American Philosophical Society* 103 (3): 374–417.
Bieber, M. (1961), *The History of the Greek and Roman Theater*, 2nd edn, Princeton: Princeton University Press.
Bieber, M. (1967), *Entwicklungsgeschichte der griechischen Tracht von der vorgriechischen Zeit bis zur römischen Kaiserzeit*, 2nd edn, Berlin: Mann.
Bieber, M. (1973), 'Charakter und Unterschiede der griechischen und römischen Kleidung', *Arch. Anz.*: 425–447.
Bieber, M. (1977), *Ancient Copies: Contributions to the History of Greek and Roman Art*, New York: New York University Press.
Birk, S. (2013), *Depicting the Dead: Self-representation and Commemoration on Roman Sarcophagi with Portraits*, Aalborg: Aalborg Universitetsforlag.
Blech, M. (1993), 'Die Terrakotten', in M. Blech, T. Hauschild and D. Hertel (eds), *Mulva III* (Madrider Beiträge 21), Mainz: von Zabern, 113–219.
Blümner, H. (1911), *Die römischen Privataltertümer* (I. von Müller, Handbuch der klassischen Altertumswissenschaft 4.2.2), Munich: Beck.
Bodnaruk, M. (2017), 'Administering the Empire: The Unmaking of an Equestrian Elite in the 4th Century CE', in R. Varga and V. Rusu-Bolinde (eds), *Official Power and Local Elites in the Roman Provinces*, London: Routledge, 145–167.
Böhme, A. and W. Schottroff (1979), *Palmyrenische Grabreliefs* (Liebighaus Monografie 4), Frankfurt: Liebighaus.
Bonfante, L. (1975), *Etruscan Dress*, Baltimore and London: Johns Hopkins University Press.
Bonfante, L. (1976), 'Etruscan Influence in Northern Italy', *Archaeological News*: 93–106.
Bonfante, L. (1978), 'The Language of Dress: Etruscan Influences', *Archaeology* 31 (1): 14–26.
Bonfante, L. (2003), *Etruscan Dress*, Updated edn, Baltimore and London: Johns Hopkins University Press.
Bonfante Warren, L. (1966), *Early Etruscan Dress: Studies in Early Italian Art and Culture*, New York: Columbia University Diss.
Bonfante Warren, L. (1970), 'Roman Triumphs and Etruscan Kings: The Changing Face of the Triumph', *JRS* 60: 49–66.
Bonfante Warren, L. (1971), 'Etruscan Dress as Historical Source: Some Problems and Examples', *AJA* 75: 277–284.
Bonfante Warren, L. (1973), 'Roman Costumes: A Glossary and Some Etruscan Derivations', *ANRW* I.4: 584–614.
Borg, B. (1996), *Mumienporträts: Chronologie und kultureller Kontext*, Mainz: von Zabern.

Borg, B. (2013), *Crisis and Ambition: Tombs and Burial Customs in Third-Century AD Rome*, Oxford: Oxford University Press.

Borg, B. and C. Witschel (2001), 'Veränderungen im Repräsentationsverhalten der römischen Eliten während des 3. Jhs. n. Chr.', in G. Alföldy and S. Panciera (eds), *Inschriftliche Denkmäler als Medien der Selbstdarstellung in der römischen Welt*, Stuttgart: Steiner, 47–120.

Boschung, D. (1987), *Antike Grabaltäre aus den Nekropolen Roms*, Bern: Stämpfli.

Bowersock, G. (1976), 'A New Antonine Inscription from the Syrian Desert', *Chiron* 6: 349–355.

Bradley, K. (1994), *Slavery and Society at Rome*, Cambridge: Cambridge University Press.

Brandt, R. and J. Slofstra, eds (1983), *Roman and Native in the Low Countries: Spheres of Interaction*, Oxford: Archaeopress.

Braund, S. (1989), 'City and Country in Roman Satire', in S. Braund (ed.), *Satire and Society in Ancient Rome*, Exeter: University of Exeter Press, 23–47.

Breniquet, C., M. Bèche-Wittmann, C. Bouilloc and C. Gaumat (2017), 'The Gallo-Roman Textile Collection from Les-Martres-de-Veyre in France', *Archaeological Textiles Review* 59: 71–81.

Brennan, C. (2008), 'Tertullian's *de Pallio* and Roman Dress in North Africa', in J. Edmondson and A. Keith (eds), *Roman Dress and the Fabrics of Roman Culture*, Toronto: University of Toronto Press, 257–270.

Breward, C. (2016), *The Suit: Form, Function and Style*, London: Reaktion.

Brown, P. (1971), *The World of Late Antiquity*, London: Thames and Hudson.

Bücheler, F. (1884), 'Altes Latein', *Rh. Mus.* 39: 408–427.

Bulard, M. (1926), *La religion domestique dans la colonie italienne de Délos d'après les peintures murals et les autels historiés*, Paris: de Boccard.

Buraselis, K. (2007), *Theia dōrea: Das göttlich–kaiserliche Geschenk: Studien zur Politik der Severer und zur Constitutio Antoniniana* (trans. W. Schürmann), Vienna: Österreichische Akademie der Wissenschaften.

Burgess, R. (1988), 'Quinquennial Vota and the Imperial Consulship in the Fourth and Fifth Centuries, 337–511', *Num. Chron.* 148: 77–96.

Caldwell, L. (2015), *Roman Girlhood and the Fashioning of Femininity*, Cambridge: Cambridge University Press.

Calza, R. (1964), *Scavi di Ostia V: I Ritratti, Parte I: Ritratti greci e romani fino al 160 circa D.C.*, Rome: Istituto Poligrafico dello Stato.

Cameron, A. (1970), *Claudian: Poetry and Propaganda at the Court of Honorius*, Oxford: Clarendon.

Cameron, A. (1998), 'Consular Diptychs in Their Social Context: New Eastern Evidence', *JRA* 11: 384–403.

Cameron, A. (2013), 'The Origin, Context and Function of Consular Diptychs', *JRS* 103: 174–207.

Camodeca, G. (2000), 'Domiziano e il collegio degli Augustales di Miseno', in G. Paci (ed.), *Epigraphai: miscellanea epigrafica in onore di Lidio Gasperini 1*, Rome: Tipigraf, 171–187.

Caputo, G. (1959), *Il Teatro di Sabratha e l'Architettura Teatrale Africana*, Rome: Bretschneider.
Carandini, A., A. Ricci and M. de Vos (1982), *Filosofiana. La villa di Piazza Armerina. Immagine di un aristocratico romano al tempo di Costantino*, Palermo: Flaccovio.
Cardozo, M. (1996), *Citânia de Briteiros e Castro de Sabroso*, Guimarães: Sociedade Martins Sarmento.
Carpenter, E. (1887), 'Simplification of Life', in E. Carpenter, *England's Ideal and Other Papers on Social Subjects*, London: Swan Sonnenschein, Lowrey and Co., 79–99.
Carroll, M. (2013a), 'Ethnicity and Gender in Roman Funerary Commemoration: Case Studies from the Empire's Frontiers', in L. Nilsson Stutz and S. Tarlow (eds), *The Oxford Handbook of the Archaeology of Death and Burial*, Oxford: Oxford University Press, 559–579.
Carroll, M. (2013b), 'Die Kleidung der Eravisci und Azali an der Donau in römischer Zeit', in A. Wieczorek, R. Schulz and M. Tellenbach (eds), *Die Macht der Toga – Mode im römischen Weltreich*, Exhibition Catalogue, Regensburg: Schnell & Steiner, 194–198.
Carroll, M. (2015), 'Projecting Self-Perception on the Roman Frontiers: The Evidence of Dress and Funerary Portraits', in D. J. Breeze, R. H. Jones and I. A. Oltean (eds), *Understanding Roman Frontiers: A Celebration for Professor Bill Hanson*, Edinburgh: John Donald, 154–166.
Castriota, D. (1995), *The Ara Pacis Augustae and the Imagery of Abundance in Later Greek and Early Roman Imperial Art*, Princeton: Princeton University Press.
Chantraine, P. (1968–1980), *Dictionnaire étymologique de la langue grecque*, Paris: Klincksieck.
Chausson, F. and H. Inglebert, eds (2003), *Costume et société dans l'Antiquité et le haut Moyen Age*, Paris: Picard.
Chauvot, A. (2016), *Les 'barbares' des Romains. Représentations et confrontations*, Metz: CRULH.
Christ, A.T. (1997), 'The Masculine Ideal of "The Race that Wears the Toga"', *Art Journal* 56 (2): 24–30.
Clarke, J. (2003), *Art in the Lives of Ordinary Romans: Visual Representation and Non-Elite Viewers in Italy 100 BC – AD 315*, Berkeley: University of California Press.
Cleland, L., M. Harlow and L. Llewellyn-Jones, eds (2005), *The Clothed Body in the Ancient World*, Oxford: Oxbow.
Coarelli, F. (1968), 'L'"Ara di Domizio Enobarbo" e la cultura artistica in Roma nel II secolo a.C.', *Dialoghi di Archeologia* 3: 302–368.
Coarelli, F. (2011), *Storia dell'arte romana. Vol. 1 – Le origini di Roma. La cultura artistica dalle origini al III sec.*, Milan: Jaca Book.
Colledge, M. A. R. (1976), *The Art of Palmyra*, Boulder: Westview.
Cornwall, A. and N. Lindisfarne (1994), 'Dislocating Masculinity: Gender, Power and Anthropology', in A. Cornwall and N. Lindisfarne (eds), *Dislocating Masculinity: Comparative Ethnographies*, London and New York: Routledge, 11–47.

Courby, F. (1919), s.v. *trabea*, C. Daremberg and E. Saglio, *Dictionnaire des Antiquités Grecques et Romaines* 5.1, Paris: Hachette, 382.
Cunliffe, M. (1959), *George Washington: Man and Monument*, London: Collins.
Curchin, L. (1991), *Roman Spain: Conquest and Assimilation*, London: Routledge.
D'Ambra, E. (1998), *Art and Identity in the Roman World*, London: Weidenfeld & Nicolson.
Dandré Bardon, M. (1784), *Costume des anciens peuples, a l'usage des artistes*, Lyon: Bibliothèque jésuite des Fontaines.
Davies, G. (2005), 'What Made the Roman Toga Virilis?', in L. Cleland, M. Harlow and L. Llewellyn-Jones (eds), *The Clothed Body in the Ancient World*, Oxford: Oxbow, 121–130.
Davies, G. (2010), 'Togate Statues and Petrified Orators', in D. Berry and A. Erskine (eds), *Form and Function in Roman Oratory*, Cambridge: Cambridge University Press, 51–72.
Davies, G. (2018), *Gender and Body Language in Roman Art*, Cambridge and New York: Cambridge University Press.
Davis, F. (1992), *Fashion, Culture and Identity*, Chicago: University of Chicago Press.
Delbrück, R. (1929), *Die Consulardiptychen und verwandte Denkmäler*, Berlin and Leipzig: De Gruyter.
Delbrück, R. (1933), *Spätantike Kaiserporträts von Constantinus Magnus bis zum Ende des Westreichs*, Berlin and Leipzig: De Gruyter.
Delmaire, R. (2003), 'Le vêtement, symbole de richesse et de pouvoir, d'après les textes patristiques et hagiographiques du Bas-Empire', in F. Chausson and H. Inglebert (eds), *Costume et société dans l'Antiquité et le haut Moyen Âge*, Paris: Picard, 85–98.
Delmaire, R. (2004), 'Le vêtement dans les sources juridiques du Bas-Empire', *Antiquité Tardive* 12: 195–202.
Dench, E. (2005), *Romulus' Asylum. Roman Identities from the Age of Alexander to the Age of Hadrian*, Oxford: Oxford University Press.
Deniaux, E. (2003), 'La toga candida et les élections à Rome sous la république', in F. Chausson and H. Inglebert (eds), *Costume et société dans l'Antiquité et le haut Moyen Âge*, Paris: Picard, 49–55.
Deubner, L. (1934), 'Die Tracht des römischen Triumphators', *Hermes*: 316–323.
Dewar, M. J. (2008), 'Spinning the *Trabea*: Consular Robes and Propaganda in the Panegyrics of Claudian', in J. Edmondson and A. Keith (eds), *Roman Dress and the Fabrics of Roman Culture*, Toronto: University of Toronto Press, 217–237.
Dirven, L. (2011), 'The Imperial Cult in the Cities of the Decapolis, Caesarea Maritima and Palmyra: A Note on the Development of Imperial Cults in the Roman Near East', *ARAM* 23: 141–156.
Dirven, L. (forthcoming a), 'Palmyrene Sculpture in Context: Between Hybridity and Heterogeneity', in J. Aruz (ed.), *Palmyra: Mirage in the Desert*, New York: Metropolitan Museum, 120–129.

Dirven, L. (forthcoming b), 'Unity in Diversity? A Note on the Co-existence of Different Styles in Palmyrene Sculpture', in D. Wielgosz-Rondolino (ed.), *Life in Palmyra: Life for Palmyra. Conference, Warsaw, April 2016.*

Dixon, J. (2014), 'Dressing the Adulteress', in M. Harlow and M.-L. Nosch (eds), *Greek and Roman Textiles and Dress*, Oxford: Oxbow, 298–305.

Do Carmo Ribeiro, M. and A. Sousa Melo, eds (2012), *Evolução da paisagem urbana: sociedade e economia*, Braga: CITCEM.

Dohrn, T. (1968), *Der Arringatore*, Berlin: Mann.

Dolansky, F. (2008), '*Togam virilem sumere*: Coming of Age in the Roman World', in J. Edmondson and A. Keith (eds), *Roman Dress and the Fabrics of Roman Culture*, Toronto: University of Toronto Press, 47–70.

Doppelfeld, O., G. Biegel and J. Bracker (1975), 'Das römische Köln, I. Ubier-Oppidum und Colonia Agrippinensium', *ANRW* II.4: 715–782.

Drinkwater, J. (2001), 'The Gallo-Roman Woollen Industry and the Great Debate: The Igel Column Revisited', in D. Mattingly and J. Salmon (eds), *Economies Beyond Agriculture in the Classical World*, London: Routledge, 297–308.

Dross-Krüpe, K. (2011), *Wolle – Weber – Wirtschaft. Die Textilproduction der römischen Kaiserzeit im Spiegelbild der papyrologischen Überlieferung*, Wiesbaden: Harrassowitz.

Dross-Krüpe, K. (2017), 'Production and Distribution', in M. Harlow (ed.), *A Cultural History of Dress and Fashion in Antiquity*, London: Bloomsbury, 37–48.

Dross-Krüpe, K. and A. Paetz gen. Schieck (2014), 'Unravelling the Tangled Threads of Ancient Embroidery', in M. Harlow and M.-L. Nosch (eds), *Greek and Roman Textiles and Dress*, Oxford: Oxbow, 207–235.

Dubourdieu, A. (1986), 'Cinctus Gabinus', *Latomus* 45: 3–20.

Ducati, P. (1929), 'I vetri dorati romani nel Museo Civico di Bologna', *Rivista del Reale Istituto d'Archeologia e Storia dell'Arte* 1: 232–249.

Duncan-Jones, R. (2016), *Power and Privilege in Roman Society*, Cambridge: Cambridge University Press.

Dupont, F. (1992), *Daily Life in Ancient Rome* (Trans. by C. Woodall), Oxford and Cambridge, MA: Blackwell.

Durham, D. (1999), 'Predicaments of Dress: Polyvalency and the Ironies of a Cultural Identity', *American Ethnologist* 26 (2): 389–411.

Dyck, A. R. (2001), 'Dressing to Kill: Attire as a Proof and Means of Characterization in Cicero's Speeches', *Arethusa* 34 (1): 119–130.

Eck, W. (2004), *Köln in römischer Zeit. Geschichte einer Stadt im Rahmen des Imperium Romanum*, Cologne: Greven.

Edmondson, J. (2006), 'Cities and Urban Life in the Western Provinces of the Roman Empire 30 BCE–250 CE', in D. Potter (ed.), *A Companion to the Roman Empire*, Oxford: Wiley-Blackwell, 250–280.

Edmondson, J. (2008), 'Public Dress and Social Control in Late Republican and Early Imperial Rome', in J. Edmondson and A. Keith (eds), *Roman Dress and the Fabrics of Roman Culture*, Toronto: University of Toronto Press, 21–46.

Edmondson, J. (2016), 'Glimpses Inside the *Familia Publica* at Augusta Emerita (Mérida)', in J. Carbonell Manils and H. Gimeno Pascual (eds), *A Baete ad fluvium Anam: Cultura epigráfica en la Bética Occidental y territorios fronterizos. Homenaje al prof. J. L. Moralejo Álvarez*, Alcalá de Henares: Universidad de Alcalá, Servicio de Publicaciones, 67–83.

Edmondson, J. and A. Keith, eds (2008), *Roman Dress and the Fabrics of Roman Culture*, Toronto: University of Toronto Press.

Edmondson, J., T. Nogales Basarrate and W. Trillmich, eds (2001), *Imagen y Memoria – monumentos funerarios con retratos en la Colonia Augusta Emerita* (Monografías Emeritenses 6), Madrid: Publicaciones del Gabinete de Antigüedades de la Real Academia de la Historia/Bibliotheca Archaeologica Hispana.

Edwards, C. (1993), *The Politics of Immorality in Ancient Rome*, Cambridge: Cambridge University Press.

Entwhistle, J. (2000), *The Fashioned Body: Fashion, Dress and Modern Social Theory*, Cambridge: Polity, 40–55.

Ewald, B. C. (2003), 'Sarcophagi and Senators: The Social History of Roman Funerary Art and Its Limits: Rev. Wrede, *Senatorische Sarkophage*', *JRA* 16: 561–571.

Facsády, A. (2007), 'Aquincumi fülbevalók / Earrings from Aquincum', *Budapest Régiségei* 40: 51–70.

Fantham, E. (2008), 'Covering the Head at Rome: Ritual and Gender', in J. Edmondson and A. Keith (eds), *Roman Dress and the Fabrics of Roman Culture*, Toronto: University of Toronto Press, 158–171.

Fear, T. (2005), 'Propertian Closure: The Elegiac Inscription of the Liminal Male and Ideological Contestation in Augustan Rome', in R. Ancona and E. Greene (eds), *Gendered Dynamics in Latin Love Poetry*, Baltimore: Johns Hopkins University Press, 13–40.

Fejfer, J. (2008), *Roman Portraits in Context*, Berlin: De Gruyter.

Ferris, I. M. (2000), *Enemies of Rome: Barbarians through Roman Eyes*, Stroud: Sutton.

Filges, A. (2000), 'Himationträger, Palliaten und Togaten', in T. Mattern and D. Korol (eds), *Munus. Festschrift Hans Wiegartz*, Münster: Scriptorium, 95–109.

Fischer, T. and M. Trier (2013), *Das römische Köln*, Cologne: Bachem.

Fittschen, K. (1970), 'Der Arringatore: ein römischer Bürger?', *MDAI(R)* 77: 177–184.

Fittschen, K. (1992), 'Mädchen nicht Knaben', *MDAI(R)* 99: 301–305.

Fittschen, K. (2008), 'Der Arringatore: kein römischer Bürger?', in E. La Rocca, P. Leon and C. Parisi Presicce (eds), *Le due patrie acquisite: studi di archeologia dedicati a Walter Trillmich*, Rome: Bretschneider.

Fittschen, K. and P. Zanker (1983), *Katalog der römischen Porträts in den Capitolinischen Museen und den anderen kommunalen Sammlungen der Stadt Rom vol. III: Kaiserinnen- und Prinzessinnenbildnisse. Frauenporträts*, Mainz: von Zabern.

Fittschen, K. and P. Zanker (2011), *Katalog der römischen Porträts in den Capitolinischen Museen und den anderen kommunalen Sammlungen der Stadt Rom vol. II: Die männlichen Privatporträts*, Berlin: De Gruyter.

Flohr, M. (2013), 'The Textile Economy of Pompeii', *JRA* 6: 447–450.
Flory, M. B. (1978), 'Family in Familia: Kinship and Community in Slavery', *AJAH* 3: 78–95.
Flower, H. (2017), *The Dancing Lares and the Serpent in the Garden: Religion at the Roman Street Corner*, Princeton: Princeton University Press.
Fraschetti, A. (1999), 'Roman Youth', in G. Levi and J.-C. Schmitt (eds), *A History of Young People in the West 1: Ancient and Medieval Rites of Passage*, Cambridge, MA: Harvard University Press, 51–82.
Frazer, J. G. (1890), *The Golden Bough*, London and New York: Macmillan.
Freeman, P. W. M. (1993), '"Romanization" and Roman Material Culture. Rev. of Millett 1992', *JRA* 6: 438–445.
Freigang, Y. (1997), 'Die Grabmäler der gallo-römischen Kultur im Moselland. Studien zur Selbstdarstellung einer Gesellschaft', *JRGZM* 44 (1): 277–440.
Frenz, H. G. (1977), *Untersuchungen zu den frühen römischen Grabreliefs*, Frankfurt: Goethe-Universität diss.
Fröhlich, T. (1991), *Lararien- und Fassendenbilder in den Vesuvstädten*, Mainz: von Zabern.
Gabelmann, H. (1977), 'Die ritterliche Trabea', in *JDAI*, 92: 322–374.
Gabelmann, H. (1984), *Antike Audienz- und Tribunalszenen*, Darmstadt: Wissenschaftliche Buchgesellschaft.
Gabelmann, H. (1985), 'Römische Kinder in Toga Praetexta', *JDAI* 100: 497–541.
Galinier, M. (2012), 'Domi forisque: les vêtements romains de Vertu', in F. Gherchanoc and V. Huet (eds), *Vêtements antiques. S'habiller, se déshabiller dans les mondes anciens*, Paris: Errance, 189–208.
Galsterer, B. and H. Galsterer (1975), *Die römischen Steininschriften aus Köln*, Cologne: Greven & Bechtold.
Garbsch, J. (1965), *Die norisch-pannonische Frauentracht im 1. und 2. Jahrhundert*, Munich: Beck.
Gardner, J. (1986), 'Proofs of Status in the Roman World', *BICS* 33: 1–14.
Gardner, J. (1993), *Being a Roman Citizen*, London: Routledge.
Garnsey, P. (1974), 'Aspects of the Decline of the Urban Aristocracy in the Empire', *ANRW* II.1: 229–252.
Gawlikowski, M. (1970), *Monuments funéraires de Palmyre*, Warsaw: Państwowe Wydawnictwo Naukowe.
Gehn, U. (2012), *Ehrenstatuen in der Spätantike. Chlamydati und Togati*, Wiesbaden: Reichert.
George, M. (2001), 'A Roman Funerary Monument with a Mother and Daughter', in S. Dixon (ed.), *Childhood, Class and Kin in the Roman World*, London and New York: Routledge, 178–189.
George, M. (2006), 'Social Identity and the Dignity of Work in Freedmen's Reliefs', in E. D'Ambra and G. Métraux (eds), *The Art of Citizens, Soldiers and Freedmen in the Roman World*, Oxford: Archaeopress, 19–29.

George, M. (2008), 'The "Dark" Side of the Toga', in J. Edmondson and A. Keith (eds), *Roman Dress and the Fabrics of Roman Culture*, Toronto: University of Toronto Press, 94–112.

Gercke, W. (1968), *Untersuchungen zum römischen Kinderporträt von den Anfängen bis in hadrianische Zeit*, University of Hamburg diss.

Giard, J. B. (1976), *Catalogue des monnaies de l'Empire Romaine 1*, Paris: Bibliothèque Nationale.

Giroire, C. and D. Roger (2007), *Roman Art from the Louvre*, Manchester VT: Hudson Hills Press.

Giuliani, L. (1986), *Bildnis und Botschaft: Hermeneutische Untersuchungen zur Bildniskunst der Römischen Republik*, Frankfurt: Suhrkamp.

Giuliano, A. (1981), *Museo Nazionale Romano. Le sculture 1.2*, Rome: de Luca.

Gleason, M. (1990), 'The Semiotics of Gender: Physiognomy and Self-fashioning in the Second Century CE', in D. M. Halperin, J. Winkler and F. Zeitlin (eds), *Before Sexuality: The Construction of Erotic Experience in the Ancient Greek World*, Princeton: Princeton University Press, 389–416.

Gleason, M. (1999), 'Elite Male Identity in the Roman Empire', in D. Potter and D. Mattingly (eds), *Life, Death and Entertainment in the Roman Empire*, Ann Arbor: Michigan University Press, 67–84.

Gleba, M. and J. Pásztókai-Szeőke, eds (2013), *Making Textiles in Pre-Roman and Roman Times. Peoples, Places, Identities*, Oxford and Oakville, CT: Oxbow.

Goethert, F. W. (1931), *Zur Kunst der römischen Republik*, Berlin: Bark & Schröter.

Goethert, F. W. (1937), s.v. toga, *PW* VI A.2: 1651–1660.

Goethert, F. W. (1939), 'Studien zur Kopienforschung 1: Die stil- und trachtgeschichtliche Entwicklung der Togastatue in den beiden ersten Jahrhunderte der römischen Kaiserzeit', *MDAI(R)* 54: 176–219.

Goette, H. R. (1990), *Studien zu römischen Togadarstellungen* (Beiträge zur Erschliessung hellenistischer und frühkaiserzeitlicher Skulptur und Architektur 10), Mainz: von Zabern.

Goette, H. R. (2012), 'Zur Darstellung von religiöser Tracht in Griechenland und Rom', in S. Schrenk, K. Vössing and M. Tellenbach (eds), *Kleidung und Identität in religiösen Kontexten der römischen Kaiserzeit: altertumswissenschaftliches Kolloquium, Universität Bonn, 30. und 31. Oktober 2009* (Mannheimer Geschichtsblätter Sonderveröffentlichung 4), Regensburg: Schnell und Steiner, 20–34.

Goette, H. R. (2013), 'Die römische "Staatstracht" – *toga, tunica* und *calcei*', in A. Wieczorek, R. Schulz and M. Tellenbach (eds), *Die Macht der Toga – Mode im römischen Weltreich*, Exhibition Catalogue, Regensburg: Schnell & Steiner, 39–52.

Goldhill, S. (2001), *Being Greek under Rome: Cultural Identity, the Second Sophistic, and the Development of Empire*, Cambridge and New York: Cambridge University Press.

Goldman, B. (1994), 'Graeco-Roman Dress in Syro-Mesopotamia', in J. Sebesta and L. Bonfante (eds), *The World of Roman Costume*, Madison: University of Wisconsin Press, 163–181.

Goldman, N. (1994), 'Reconstructing Roman Clothing', in J. Sebesta and L. Bonfante (eds), *The World of Roman Costume*, Madison: University of Wisconsin Press, 213–237.

González, J. and M. Crawford (1986), 'The Lex Irnitana: A New Copy of the Flavian Municipal Law', *JRS* 76: 147–243.

Granger-Taylor, H. (1982), 'Weaving Clothes to Shape in the Ancient World: The Tunic and Toga of the Arringatore', *Textile History* 13: 3–25.

Granger-Taylor, H. (1987), 'The Emperor's Clothes: The Fold Lines', *Bulletin of the Cleveland Museum of Art* 74 (3): 114–123.

Granger-Taylor, H. (2007), 'Weaving Clothes to Shape in the Ancient World 25 Years On: Corrections and Further Details with Particular Reference to the Cloaks from Lahun', *Archaeological Textiles Newsletter* 45: 26–35.

Granger-Taylor, H. (2008), 'A Fragmentary Roman Cloak Probably of the 1st Century CE and Off-cuts from Other Semi-circular Cloaks', *Archaeological Textiles Newsletter* 46: 6–16.

Graver, M. (1998), 'The Manhandling of Maecenas: Senecan Abstractions of Masculinity', *AJP* 119 (4): 607–632.

Grilli, A. (1997), 'Cicerone nell'età della toga virile', *La parola del passato* 52: 161–176.

Grömer, K. (2010), *Prähistorische Textilkunst in Mitteleuropa*, Vienna: Naturhistorisches Museum.

Gunderson, E. (2003), *Declamation, Paternity and Roman Identity. Authority and the Rhetorical Self*, Cambridge: Cambridge University Press.

Hackworth Petersen, L. (2003), 'The Baker, His Tomb, His Wife, and Her Breadbasket: The Monument of Eurysaces in Rome', *The Art Bulletin* 85 (2): 230–257.

Hackworth Petersen, L. (2006), *The Freedman in Roman Art and Art History*, Cambridge: Cambridge University Press.

Hackworth Petersen, L. (2009), '"Clothes Make the Man": Dressing the Roman Freedman Body', in T. Fögen and M. M. Lee (eds), *Bodies and Boundaries in Graeco-Roman Antiquity*, Berlin and New York: De Gruyter, 181–212.

Hafner, G. (1969), 'Etruskische togati', *Antike Plastik* 9: 25–44.

Hanson, W. S. (1994), 'Dealing with the Barbarians. The Romanization of Britain', in B. Vyner (ed.), *Building on the Past. Papers Celebrating 150 Years of the Royal Archaeological Institute*, London: Royal Archaeological Institute, 149–163.

Harlow, M. (2005), 'Dress in the *Historia Augusta*: The Role of Dress in Historical Narrative', in L. Cleland, M. Harlow and L. Llewellyn-Jones (eds), *The Clothed Body in the Ancient World*, Oxford: Oxbow, 143–153.

Harlow, M. (2018), 'Textile Crafts and History', in C. Ebert, S. Frisch, M. Harlow, E. Andersson Strand and L. Bjerregaard (eds), *Traditional Textile Craft: An Intangible Cultural Heritage?*, Copenhagen: CTR, 133–139.

Harlow, M. and R. Laurence (2002), *Growing Up and Growing Old in Ancient Rome: A Life Course Approach*, London: Routledge.

Harrill, J. A. (2002), 'Coming of Age and Putting on Christ: The *Toga Virilis* Ceremony, Its Paraenesis and Paul's Interpretation of Baptism in Galatians', *Novum Testamentum* 43 (3): 252–277.

Hartnett, J. (2017), *The Roman Street: Urban Life and Society in Pompeii, Herculaneum, and Rome*, Cambridge and New York: Cambridge University Press.

Havé-Nikolaus, F. (1998), *Untersuchungen zu den kaiserzeitlichen Togastatuen griechischer Provenienz: Kaiserliche und private Togati der Provinzen Achaia, Creta (et Cyrene) und Teilen der Provinz Macedonia*, Mainz: von Zabern.

Heinen, H. (1985), *Trier und das Trevererland in römischer Zeit*, Trier: Spee.

Helbig, W. (1904), 'Toga und Trabea', *Hermes* 39 (2), 161–181.

Hertel, D. (1993), 'Die Skulpturen', in M. Blech, T. Hauschild and D. Hertel (eds), *Mulva III* (Madrider Beiträge 21), Mainz: von Zabern, 35–112.

Herzog-Hauser, G. (1937), s.v. Trauerkleidung, *PW* VII: 942–951.

Hesberg, H. von and P. Zanker, eds (1987), *Römische Gräberstrassen. Selbstdarstellung – Status – Standard. Kolloquium in München vom 28. bis 30. Oktober 1985*, Munich: Beck.

Heskel, J. (1994), 'Cicero as Evidence for Attitudes to Dress in the Late Republic', in J. Sebesta and L. Bonfante (eds), *The World of Roman Costume*, Madison: University of Wisconsin Press, 133–145.

Heurgon, J. (1961), *La vie quotidienne chez les Étrusques*, Paris: Hachette.

Heuzey, L. (1922), *Histoire du costume antique d'après des études sur le modèle vivant*, Paris: Bibliothèque Nationale.

Heyn, M. (2017), 'Western Men, Eastern Women? Dress and Cultural Identity in Roman Palmyra', in M. Cifarelli and L. Gawlinski (eds), *What Shall I Say of Clothes? Theoretical and Methodological Approaches to the Study of Dress in Antiquity*, Boston: AIA, 210–217.

Hillers, D. R. and E. Cussini (1996), *Palmyrene Aramaic Texts*, Baltimore: Johns Hopkins University Press.

Hingley, R. (2005), *Globalizing Roman Culture. Unity, Diversity and Empire*, Oxford and New York: Routledge.

Holder, P. (2006), *Roman Military Diplomas V*, London: University of London, ICS.

Hollander, A. (1978), *Seeing Through Clothes*, New York: Viking.

Hollander, A. (1994), *Sex and Suits*, Brinkworth: Claridge.

Holleran, C. (2012), *Shopping in Ancient Rome: The Retail Trade in the Late Republic and the Principate*, Oxford: Oxford University Press.

Hope, T. (1809), *Costumes of the Greeks and Romans*, London: Bulmer.

Hope, V. M. (2001), *Constructing Identity: The Roman Funerary Monuments of Aquileia, Mainz and Nîmes*, Oxford: Archaeopress.

Howells, D. T. (2015), *A Catalogue of the Late Antique Gold Glass in the British Museum*, London: British Museum.

Howgego, C. (2005), 'Coinage and Identity in the Roman Provinces', in C. Howgego, V. Heuchert and A. Burnett (eds), *Coinage and Identity in the Roman Provinces*, Oxford: Oxford University Press, 1–17.

Huet, V. (1999), 'Napoleon I: A New Augustus?', in C. Edwards (ed.), *Roman Presences: Receptions of Rome in European Culture, 1789–1945*, Cambridge: Cambridge University Press, 53–69.

Huet, V. (2012), 'Le voile du sacrifiant a Rome sur les reliefs romains: une norme?', in F. Gherchanoc and V. Huet (eds), *Vêtements antiques. S'habiller, se déshabiller dans les mondes anciens*, Paris: Errance, 47–62.

Hula, E. (1895), *Die Toga der späteren Kaiserzeit*, Brno: Kindl.

Huskinson, J. (1996), *Roman Children's Sarcophagi*, Oxford: Clarendon.

Inan, J. and E. Alföldi-Rosenbaum (1966), *Roman and Early Byzantine Portrait Sculpture in Asia Minor*, Oxford: Oxford University Press.

James, D. (1996), '"I Dress in This Fashion": Transformations in Sotho Dress and Women's Lives in a Sekhukhuneland Village, South Africa', in H. Hendrickson (ed.), *Clothing and Difference: Embodied Identities in Colonial and Post-Colonial Africa*, Durham, SC and London: Duke University Press, 34–65.

Jantsch, F. (1934), 'Norische Trachtendarstellungen in Kärnten', *Carinthia* 124: 65–73.

Jenkyns, R. (1991), *Dignity and Decadence: Victorian Art and the Classical Inheritance*, London: HarperCollins.

Johnstone, H. W. (1903), *The Private Life of the Romans*, Chicago: Scott Foresman.

Jones, A. H. M. (1960), 'The Cloth Industry under the Roman Empire', *The Economic History Review* NS 13 (2): 183–192.

Jones, A. H. M. (1973), *The Later Roman Empire*, Oxford: Basil Blackwell.

Joshel, S. (1992), *Work, Identity and Legal Status at Rome*, Norman and London: Oklahoma University Press.

Kaizer, T. (2002), *The Religious Life of Palmyra: A Study of the Social Patterns of Worship in the Roman Period*, Stuttgart: Steiner.

Kaizer, T. (2016), 'Divine Constellations at Palmyra: Reconsidering the Palmyrene "Pantheon"', in A. Kropp and R. Raja (eds), *The World of Palmyra*, Copenhagen: Kongelige Danske Videnskabernes Selskab, 17–30.

Kampen, N. (1981), *Image and Status: Roman Working Women in Ostia*, Berlin: Mann.

Karali, L. and C. Alfaro (2008), *Purpureae vestes II. Vestidos, textiles y tintes: estudios sobre la producción de bienes de consumo en la Antigüedad*, Valencia: Valencia University Press.

Karanastasi, P. (2013), 'Die statuarische Repräsentation der römischen Kaiser im östlichen Imperium', in A. Wieczorek, R. Schulz and M. Tellenbach (eds), *Die Macht der Toga – Mode im römischen Weltreich*, Exhibition Catalogue, Regensburg: Schnell & Steiner, 94–97.

Keay, S. (1988), *Roman Spain*, London: British Museum.

Keay, S. and N. Terrenato, eds (2001), *Italy and the West: Comparative Issues in Romanization*, Oxford: Oxbow.

Kleiner, D. E. E. (1976), *Roman Group Portraiture: The Funerary Reliefs of the Late Republic and Early Empire*, New York: Columbia University diss.

Kleiner, D. (1978), 'The Great Friezes of the Ara Pacis Augustae. Greek Sources, Roman Derivatives, and Augustan Social Policy', *MÉFRA* 90: 753–785.

Kleiner, D. E. E. (1987), *Roman Imperial Funerary Altars with Portraits* (Archaeologica 62), Rome: Bretschneider.

Kleiner, D. E. E and F. S. Kleiner (1980–1981), 'Early Roman Togate Statuary', *Bull. Com. Arch.* 87: 125–133.

Kneissl, P. (1983), 'Mercator – negotiator. Römische Geschäftsleute und die Terminologie ihrer Berufe', *Münstersche Beiträge zur antiken Handelsgeschichte* 2: 73–90.

Köb, A. and P. Riedel (2005), *Kleidung und Repräsentation in Antike und Mittelalter*, Munich: Fink.

Koch, G. and H. Sichtermann (1982), *Römische Sarkophage* (I. von Müller, Handbuch der klassischen Altertumswissenschaft 6. Handbuch der Archäologie), Munich: Beck.

Kockel, V. (1993), *Porträtreliefs stadtrömischer Grabbauten: ein Beitrag zur Geschichte und zum Verständnis des spätrepublikanisch-frühkaiserzeitlichen Privatporträts* (Beiträge zur Erschliessung hellenistischer und kaiserzeitlicher Skulptur und Architektur 12), Mainz: von Zabern.

Kohl, J. (2018), '*Martiali verna dulcissimo*: Children's Busts, Family, and Memoria in Roman Antiquity and the Renaissance', in T. Greub and M. Roussel (eds), *Figurationen des Porträts*, Paderborn: Fink/Brill, 241–276.

Kolb, F. (1973), 'Römische Mäntel: paenula, lacerna, μανδύη', *MDAI(R)* and 80: 69–162.

Kolb, F. (1974), 'Die paenula in der Historia Augusta', *Historia-Augusta-Kolloquium, Bonn 1971*: 81–101.

König, R. (1973), *The Restless Image*, London: George Allen and Unwin.

Krier, J. (1981), *Die Treverer ausserhalb ihrer civitas. Mobilität und Aufstieg* (Trierer Zeitschrift Beiheft 5), Trier: Rheinisches Landesmuseum Trier.

Kühnert, B. (1991), 'Die plebs urbana bei Horaz', *Klio* 73: 130–142.

Kuttner, A. (2004), 'Roman Art during the Republic', in H. Flower (ed.), *The Cambridge Companion to the Roman Republic*, Cambridge: Cambridge University Press, 294–321.

La Follette, L. (1994), 'The Costume of the Roman Bride', in J. Sebesta and L. Bonfante (eds), *The World of Roman Costume*, Madison: University of Wisconsin Press, 54–64.

Lahusen, G. (1983), *Untersuchungen zur Ehrenstatue in Rom: literarische und epigraphische Zeugnisse*, Rome: Bretschneider.

Laird, M. L. (2015), *Civic Monuments and the Augustales in Roman Italy*, Cambridge: Cambridge University Press.

Larsson Lovén, L. (2007), 'Wool-work as a Gender Symbol in Ancient Rome', in C. Gilles and M.-L. Nosch (eds), *Ancient Textiles: Production, Craft and Society*, Oxford: Oxbow, 229–236.

Larsson Lovén, L. (2013), 'Römische Frauen, Kleidung und öffentliche Identitäten', in A. Wieczorek, R. Schulz and M. Tellenbach (eds), *Die Macht der Toga – Mode im römischen Weltreich*, Exhibition Catalogue, Regensburg: Schnell & Steiner, 98–103.

Latham, J. (2016), *Performance, Power and Processions in Ancient Rome: The* pompa circensis *from the Late Republic to Late Antiquity*, Cambridge: Cambridge University Press.

Launitz, V. D. (1865), *Über die Toga der Römer und die Palla der Römerinnen*, Heidelberg: Heidelberg University Press.

Laurence, R. (2012), 'Investigating the Emperor's Toga: Privileging Images on Coins', in M. Harlow (ed.), *Dress and Identity*, Oxford: Archaeopress, 69–81.

Lavan, M. (2016a), 'The Spread of Roman Citizenship, 14–212 CE: Quantification in the Face of High Uncertainty', *P&P* 230 (1): 3–46.

Lavan, M. (2016b), 'Father of the Whole Human Race': Ecumenical Language and the Limits of Elite Integration in the Early Roman Empire', in M. Lavan, R. Payne and J. Weisweiler (eds), *Cosmopolitanism and Empire: Universal Rulers, Local Elites and Cultural Integration in the Ancient Near East and Mediterranean*, Oxford: Oxford University Press, 153–168.

Lenaghan, J. (2016), 'Fourth-century Portrait Sculpture and Re-use', in R. R. R. Smith and B. Ward-Perkins (eds), *The Last Statues of Antiquity*, Oxford: Oxford University Press, 267–279.

Lesky, M. (1998), 'Zum Gewand des Vel Saties in der Tomba François', in L. Aigner-Foresti (ed.), *Die Integration der Etrusker und das Weiterwirken etruskischen Kulturgutes im republikanischen und kaiserzeitlichen Rom*, Vienna: Österreichischen Akademie der Wissenschaften, 177–185.

Linderski, J. (2002), 'The Pontiff and the Tribune: The Death of Tiberius Gracchus', *Athenaeum* 90 (2): 339–366.

Long, J. (1996), *Claudian's In Eutropium: Or, How, When, and Why to Slander a Eunuch*, Chapel Hill and London: University of North Carolina Press.

Lurie, A. (1992), *The Language of Clothes*, London: Bloomsbury.

MacCormack, S. (1981), *Art and Ceremony in Late Antiquity*, London, Berkeley and Los Angeles: University of California Press.

MacLean, R. (2018), *Freed Slaves and Roman Imperial Culture: Social Integration and the Transformation of Values*, Cambridge and New York: Cambridge University Press.

MacMahon, A. (2005), 'The *Taberna* Counters of Pompeii and Herculaneum', in A. MacMahon and J. Price (eds), *Roman Working Lives and Urban Living*, Oxford: Oxbow, 70–87.

Maiuri, A. (1953), *Roman Painting*, Geneva: Skira.

Malnati, T. P. (1988), 'Juvenal and Martial on Social Mobility', *CJ* 83: 133–141.

Mander, J. (2013), *Portraits of Children on Roman Funerary Monuments*, Cambridge: Cambridge University Press.

Mannering, U. (2000), 'Roman Garments from Mons Claudianus', in D. Cardon and M. Feugère (eds), *Archéologie des textiles des origine au Ve siècle*, Montagnac: Monique Mergoil, 283–290.

Marlowe, E. (2013), *Shaky Ground: Context, Connoisseurship and the History of Roman Art*, London and New York: Bloomsbury.

Marquardt, J. (1886), *Das Privatleben der Römer*, Leipzig: Hirzel.
Marrou, H. I. (1964), *Mousikos aner: Étude sur les scènes de la vie intellectuelle figurant sur les monuments funéraires romains*, reprint from 1938, Rome: Bretschneider.
Marrou, H. I. (1977), *Décadence romaine ou Antiquité tardive?* Paris: Seuil.
Martelli, M. (2014), 'Alchemical Textiles: Colourful Garments, Recipes and Dyeing Techniques in Graeco-Roman Egypt', in M. Harlow and M.-L. Nosch (eds), *Greek and Roman Textiles and Dress*, Oxford: Oxbow, 111–129.
Mathieu, J.-M. (1992), 'Peut-on parler d'une "révolution du costume" de l'Antiquité tardive?', *Kentron: revue du monde antique et de psychologie historique* 8: 73–86.
Matthews, J. (1975), *Western Aristocracies and Imperial Court AD 364–425*, Oxford: Clarendon.
Matthews, J. (1984), 'The Tax Law of Palmyra: Evidence for Economic History in a City of the Roman East', *JRS* 74: 157–180.
Mattingly, D. J. (1997), 'Dialogues of Power and Experience in the Roman Empire', in D. J. Mattingly (ed.), *Dialogues in Roman Imperialism: Power, Discourse, and Discrepant Experience in the Roman Empire* (JRA Supp. Series 23), Portsmouth (USA): Journal of Roman Studies, 7–26.
Mattingly, H. (1923), *Coins of the Roman Empire in the British Museum. Vol. I, Augustus to Vitellius*, London: British Museum.
Mattingly, H. (1930), *Coins of the Roman Empire in the British Museum. Vol. II, Vespasian to Domitian*, London: British Museum.
Maynard, M. (2004), *Dress and Globalisation*, Manchester: Manchester University Press.
Mazrui, A. A. (1970), 'The Robes of Rebellion', *Encounter* 34: 19–32.
McDonnell, M. (2006), *Roman Manliness: Virtus and the Roman Republic*, Cambridge: Cambridge University Press.
McGinn, T. A. J. (1998), *Prostitution, Sexuality, and the Law in Ancient Rome*, Oxford: Oxford University Press.
McKechnie, P. (1992), 'Tertullian's *De pallio* and Life in Roman Carthage', *Prudentia* 24 (2): 44–66.
McKie, S. (forthcoming), *Living and Cursing in the Roman West: Curse Tablets and Society*, London: Bloomsbury.
Mehl, A. (1997), 'Wirtschaft, Gesellschaft, Totenglauben: Die "Igeler Säule" bei Trier und ihre Grabherren', *Laverna* 8: 59–92.
Meyer, E. A. (1990), 'Explaining the Epigraphic Habit in the Roman Empire: The Evidence of Epitaphs', *JRS* 80: 74–96.
Meyer, W. (1879), *Zwei antike Elfenbeintafeln der K. Staats-Bibliothek in München: Festgabe zum fünfzigjährigen Jubiläum des Deutschen Archaeologischen Instituts in Rom*, Munich: Verlag der K. Akademie.
Meyer-Zwiffelhoffer, E. (2003), 'Bürger sein in den griechischen Städten der römischen Kaiserzeit', in K.-J. Hölkeskamp, J. Rüsen, E. Stein-Hölkeskamp and H. T. Grütter (eds), *Sinn (in) der Antike. Wertkonzepte, Leitbilder und Orientierungssysteme im Altertum*, Mainz: von Zabern, 375–402.

Micali, G. (1835), *Storia degli antichi popoli Italiani*, Florence: Tipografia all' insegna di Dante.
Michalowski, K. (1960), *Palmyre I. Fouilles polonaises 1959*, Warszaw: Państwowe Wydawnictwo Naukowe.
Millar, F. (1993), *The Roman Near East, 31 B.C.-A.D. 337*, Cambridge, MA: Harvard University Press.
Millar, F. (2006), *Rome, the Greek World, and the East: Volume 3: The Greek World, the Jews and the East*, Chapel Hill, NC: University of North Carolina Press.
Millett, M. (1992), *The Romanization of Britain: An Essay in Archaeological Interpretation*, 2nd edn, Cambridge: Cambridge University Press.
Millett, M. (2001), 'Roman Interaction in North-western Iberia', *OJA* 20 (2): 157-170.
Mitchell, S. (1993), *Anatolia. Land, Men, and Gods in Asia Minor. Vol. 1: The Celts in Anatolia and the Impact of Roman Rule*, Oxford: Clarendon.
Mittag, P. F. (2009), '"Processus consularis", "adventus" und Herrschaftsjubiläum: zur Verwendung von Triumphsymbolik in der mittleren Kaiserzeit', *Hermes* 137 (4): 447-462.
Mócsy, A. (1959), *Die Bevölkerung von Pannonien bis zu den Markomannenkriegen*, Budapest: Ungarische Akademie der Wissenschaften.
Mócsy, A. (1974), *Pannonia and Upper Moesia. A History of the Middle Danube Provinces of the Roman Empire*, London: Routledge.
Molinier-Arbo, A. (2003), '*Imperium in virtute esse non in decore*: le discours sur le costume dans l'*Histoire Auguste*', in F. Chausson and H. Inglebert (eds), *Costume et société dans l'Antiquité et le haut Moyen Âge*, Paris: Picard, 67-84.
Mommsen, T. (1887), *Römisches Staatsrecht III.1*, Leipzig: Hirzel.
Mommsen, T. (1888), *Römisches Staatsrecht III.3*, Leipzig: Hirzel.
Mommsen, T. (1969), *Römisches Staatsrecht* (Handbuch der römischen Alterthümer 1-3), 2nd edn, Graz: Akademische Druck- und Verlagsanstalt.
Müller, A. (1869), 'Die Toga bis trium ulnarum bei Horat. Epod. IV, 8', *Philologus* 28: 116-122.
Müller, A. (1888), 'Toga', in A. Baumeister (ed.), *Denkmäler des klassischen Altertums zur Erläuterung des Lebens der Griechen und Römer in Religion, Kunst und Sitte* III, Munich and Leipzig: Oldenburg, 1822-1846.
Mustakallio, K. (2010), 'Creating Roman Identity: Exemplary Marriages. Roman Model Marriages in the Sacral and Historical Sphere', in L. Larsson Lovén and A. Strömberg (eds), *Ancient Marriage in Myth and Reality*, Cambridge: Cambridge Scholars, 12-24.
Nadig, M. (1986), *Die verborgene Kultur der Frau: Ethnopsychoanalytische Gespräche mit Bäuerinnen in Mexiko. Subjektivität und Gesellschaft im Alltag von Otomi-Frauen*, Frankfurt: Fischer.
Neri, V. (2004), 'Vestito e corpo nel pensiero dei padre tardoantichi', *Antiquité Tardive* 12: 223-230.
Nicolet, C. (1960), 'Consul togatus: remarques sur la vocabulaire politique de Cicéron et de Tite-Live', *Rev. Ét. Lat.* 38: 236-263.

Nicolet, C. (1966), *L'ordre équestre à l'époque républicaine (312–43 av. J.–C.): définitions juridiques et structures sociales*, Paris: De Boccard.

Nicolet, C. (1989), 'Il cittadino, il politico', in A. Giardina (ed.), *L'uomo romano*, Bari and Rome: Laterza, 3–44.

Niemeyer, H. G. (1968), *Studien zur statuarischen Darstellung der römischen Kaiser*, Berlin: Mann.

Noelke, P. (1998), 'Grabreliefs mit Mahldarstellungen in den germanisch-gallischen Provinzen – soziale und religiöse Aspekte', in P. Fasold, T. Fischer, H. von Hesberg and M. Witteyer (eds), *Bestattungssitte und kulturelle Identität: Grabanlagen und Grabbeigaben der frühen römischen Kaiserzeit in Italien und den Nordwest-Provinzen: Kolloquium in Xanten vom 16. bis 18. Februar 1995*, Bonn: Habelt, 399–418.

Noelke, P. (2000), 'Zur Chronologie der Grabreliefs mit Mahldarstellung im römischen Germanien', in H. Walter (ed.), *La sculpture d'époque romaine dans le nord et à l'est des Gaules et dans les régions avoisinantes: acquis et problématiques actuelles*, Besançon: Presses Universitaire Franche-Comté, 59–70.

Noll, R. (1963), *Das römerzeitliche Gräberfeld von Salurn* (Archäologische Forschungen in Tirol 2), Innsbruck: Archäologisches Institut der Universität.

Nordholt, H. ed., (1997), *Outward Appearances: Dressing State and Society in Indonesia*, Leiden: KITVL Press.

Olson, K. (2006), 'Matrona and Whore: Clothing and Definition in Roman Antiquity', in C. A. Faraone and L. McClure (eds), *Prostitutes and Courtesans in the Ancient World*, Madison: University of Wisconsin Press, 186–206.

Olson, K. (2008a), 'The Appearance of the Young Roman Girl', in J. Edmondson and A. Keith (eds), *Roman Dress and the Fabrics of Roman Culture*, Toronto: University of Toronto Press, 139–157.

Olson, K. (2008b), *Dress and the Roman Woman*, London: Routledge.

Olson, K. (2014a), 'Toga and *Pallium*: Status, Sexuality, Identity', in M. Masterson and N. Rabinowitz (eds), *Sex in Antiquity: New Essays on Gender and Sexuality in the Ancient World*, London: Routledge, 422–448.

Olson, K. (2014b), 'Masculinity, Appearance, and Sexuality: Dandies in Roman Antiquity', *Journal of the History of Sexuality* 23 (2): 182–205.

Olson, K. (2017a), 'Status', in M. Harlow (ed.), *A Cultural History of Dress and Fashion. Vol. I: Antiquity*, London: Bloomsbury, 105–118.

Olson, K. (2017b), *Masculinity and Dress in Roman Antiquity*, London: Routledge.

Opper, T. (2008), *Hadrian: Empire and Conflict*, Cambridge, MA: Harvard University Press.

Ortiz, J., C. Alfaro, L. Turell and M. J. Martínez, eds (2016), *Purpureae Vestes V: Textiles, Basketry and Dyes in the Ancient Mediterranean World*, Valencia: Valencia University Press.

Packer, J. E. (1997), *The Forum of Trajan in Rome: A Study of the Monuments*, Berkeley: University of California Press.

Pallottino, M. (1952), *Etruscan Painting*, Geneva: Skira.

Palmer, R. E. A. (1998), 'Bullae insignia ingenuitatis', *AJAH* 14: 1-69.
Parlasca, K. and H. Seemann (1999), *Augenblicke. Mumienporträts und ägyptische Grabkunst aus römischer Zeit*, Frankfurt and Munich: Klinkhardt & Biermann.
Pausch, M. (2003), *Die römische Tunika. Ein Beitrag zur Peregrinisierung der römischen Kleidung*, Augsburg: Wißner.
Pfuhl, E. and H. Möbius (1977), *Die ostgriechischen Grabreliefs*, Mainz: von Zabern.
Pitts, M. (2007), 'The Emperor's New Clothes: The Utility of Identity in Roman Archaeology', *AJA* 111 (4): 693-713.
Pitts, M. and M. J. Versluys, eds (2015), *Globalisation and the Roman World: Archaeological and Theoretical Perspectives*, Cambridge: Cambridge University Press.
Pochmarski, E. (2004), 'Das sagum. Urtrachtlicher keltischer Umhang und/oder römischer Uniformmantel', in H. Heftner and K. Tomaschitz (eds), *Ad fontes! Festschrift Gerhard Dobesch*, Vienna: Wiener Humanistischen Gesellschaft, 571-578.
Pochmarski, E. (2006), 'Zu Fragen der Typologie und der Chronologie der römischen Porträtstelen in Noricum', *Römisches Österreich* 29: 89-114.
Potthoff, A. (1992), *Lateinische Kleidungsbezeichnungen in synchroner und diachroner Sicht* (Innsbrucker Beiträge zur Sprachwissenschaft 70), Innsbruck: Institut für Sprachwissenschaft.
Poulsen, F. (1940), *Katalog over antike Skulpturer der Ny Carlsberg Glyptotek*, Copenhagen: Ny Carlsberg Glyptotek.
Prayon, F. (1999), 'Individualporträt in der etruskischen Kunst?', in H. v. Steuben (ed.), *Antike Porträts. Zum Gedächtnis von Helga von Heintze*, Möhnesee: Bibliopolis, 85-90.
Precht, G. (1975), *Das Grabmal des Lucius Poblicius, Rekonstruktion und Aufbau*, Cologne: RGM.
Price, S. (1984), *Rituals and Power: The Roman Imperial Cult in Asia Minor*, Cambridge: Cambridge University Press.
Quiroga, P. L. B. de (1995), 'Freedmen Social Mobility in Roman Italy', *Historia* 44 (3): 326-348.
Raepsaet-Charlier, M.-T. (2001), 'Caractéristiques et particularités de l'onomastique trévire', in M. Dondin-Payre and M.-T. Raepsaet-Charlier (eds), *Noms, identités culturelles et romanisation sous le Haut-Empire*, Brussels: Timperman, 343-398.
Raja, R. (2016), 'Representations of Priests in Palmyra: Methodological Considerations on the Meaning of the Representation of Priesthood in the Funerary Sculpture from Roman Period Palmyra', *Religion in the Roman Empire* 2 (1): 125-146.
Raja, R. (2017a), 'You Can Leave Your Hat On. Priestly Representations from Palmyra: Between Visual Genre, Religious Importance and Social Status', in R. Gordon, G. Petridou and J. Rüpke (eds), *Beyond Priesthood. Religious Entrepreneurs and Innovators in the Roman Empire*, Berlin: de Gruyter, 417-442.
Raja, R. (2017b), 'Between Fashion Phenomena and Status Symbols: Contextualising the Wardrobe of the So-called "Former Priests" of Palmyra', in C. Brøns and M.-L. Nosch (eds), *Textiles and Cult in the Ancient Mediterranean*, Oxford: Oxbow, 209-229.

Raja, R. (2017c), 'To Be or Not to Be Depicted as a Priest in Palmyra: A Matter of Representational Spheres and Societal Values', in T. Long and A. H. Sørensen (eds), *Positions and Professions in Palmyra*, Copenhagen: Royal Danish Academy of Sciences and Letters, 115–130.

Raja, R. (2018), 'The Matter of the Palmyrene "Modius". Remarks on the History of Research into the Terminology of the Palmyrene Priestly Hat', *Religion in the Roman Empire* 2 (4): 237–259.

Rawson, B. (2003), *Children and Childhood in Roman Italy*, Oxford: Oxford University Press.

Rebenich, S. (1991), 'Zum Theodosiusobelisken in Konstantinopel', *MDAI(I)* 41: 447–476.

Reinach, S. (1897), *Répertoire de la statuaire grecque et romaine*, Paris: Leroux.

Reinach, S. (1912), *Répertoire de reliefs grecs et romains*, Paris: Leroux.

Reinhold, M. (1970), *History of Purple as a Status Symbol in Antiquity* (Collection Latomus 116), Brussels: Latomus.

Reinhold, M. (1971), 'Usurpation of Status and Status Symbols', *Historia* 20: 275–302.

Reinsberg, C. (2006), *Vita-Romana Sarkophage. Die Sarkophage mit Darstellungen aus dem Menschenleben. 3. Die antiken Sarkophagreliefs*, Berlin: Mann.

Revell, L. (2009), *Roman Imperialism and Local Identities*, Cambridge: Cambridge University Press.

Revell, L. (2013), 'Code-switching and Identity in the Western Provinces', *Herom* 2 (1): 121–139.

Richard, C. J. (1994), *The Founders and the Classics: Greece, Rome, and the American Enlightenment*, Cambridge, MA: Harvard University Press.

Richardson, E. H. (1953), 'The Etruscan Origins of Early Roman Sculpture', *Amer. Acad. Rome* 21: 75–124.

Richardson, E. H. and L. Richardson (1966), 'Ad cohibendum brachium toga', *YClS* 19: 251–268.

Richardson, J. (1986), *Hispaniae: Spain and the Development of Roman Imperialism 218-82 BC*, Cambridge: Cambridge University Press.

Richardson, J. (2008), *The Language of Empire: Rome and the Idea of Empire from the Third Century BC to the Second Century AD*, Cambridge: Cambridge University Press.

Richlin, A. (1997), 'Gender and Rhetoric: Producing Manhood in the Schools', in W. J. Dominik (ed.), *Roman Eloquence: Rhetoric in Society and Literature*, London and New York: Routledge, 90–110.

Roche, D. (1994), *The Culture of Clothing: Dress and Fashion in the 'Ancien Régime'*, trans. J. Birrell, Cambridge: Cambridge University Press.

Roche-Bernard, G. (1993), *Costumes et textiles en Gaule romaine*, Paris: Errance.

Rogers, P. W., L. B. Jørgensen and A. Rast-Eicher, eds (2001), *The Roman Textile Industry and its Influence: A Birthday Tribute to John Peter Wild*, Oxford: Oxbow.

Ross, C. F. (1911), 'The Reconstruction of the Later Toga', *AJA* 15: 24–31.

Ross Taylor, L. (1931), *The Divinity of the Roman Emperor*, Middletown: American Philological Association.

Rothe, U. (2009), *Dress and Cultural Identity in the Rhine-Moselle Region of the Roman Empire*, Oxford: Archaeopress.

Rothe, U. (2012), 'Dress in the Middle Danube Provinces: The Garments, Their Origins and Their Distribution', *JÖAI* 81: 137–231.

Rothe, U. (2013), 'Whose Fashion? Men, Women and Roman Culture as Reflected in Dress in the Cities of the Roman North-west', in E. Hemelrijk and G. Woolf (eds), *Women and the Roman City in the Latin West*, Leiden: Brill, 243–268.

Rothe, U. (2014), 'Ethnicity in the Roman North-west', in J. McInerney (ed.), *A Companion to Ethnicity in the Ancient Mediterranean*, Oxford: Wiley-Blackwell, 497–513.

Rothe, U. (2017), 'Ethnicity', in M. Harlow (ed.), *A Cultural History of Dress and Fashion, Vol. 1: Antiquity*, London: Bloomsbury, 119–134.

Rothe, U. (in prep.), 'Who Wore the Trousers? Myth and Reality in Northern European Dress in the Roman Period'.

Rothfus, M. A. (2010), 'The *Gens Togata*: Changing Styles and Changing Identities', *AJP* 131: 425–452.

Roxan, M. (1978), *Roman Military Diplomas 1954–77* (Institute of Archaeology Occasional Publication 2), London: Institute of Archaeology.

Roxan, M. (1985), *Roman Military Diplomas 1978–1984*, with contributions by H. Ganiaris and J. C. Mann (Institute of Archaeology Occasional Publication 9), London: Institute of Archaeology.

Roxan, M. (1994), *Roman Military Diplomas 1985–93* (Institute of Archaeology Occasional Publication 14), London: Institute of Archaeology.

Roxan, M. and P. A. Holder (2003), *Roman Military Diplomas IV* (BICS Supplement 82), London: ICS.

Rubens, A. (1665), *De re vestiaria veterum praecipue de lato clavo, libri duo*, Antwerp: Balthasar Moreti.

Ryberg, I. S. (1967), *Panel Reliefs of Marcus Aurelius* (AIA Monographs 14), New York: AIA.

Salanitro, M. (1992), 'Un'espressione della lingua dell'uso e la vanità della toga in Marziale', *Invigilata lucernis* 13/14: 281–288.

Salles, C. (2003), 'Le costume satirique dans la poésie satirique latine', in F. Chausson and H. Inglebert (eds), *Costume et société dans l'Antiquité et le haut Moyen Âge*, Paris: Picard, 57–66.

Schäfer, T. (1989), *Imperii insignia: Sella Curulis und Fasces. Zur Repräsentation römischer Magistrate*, Mainz: von Zabern.

Scheid, J. (1986), 'Le flamine de Jupiter, les Vestales et le général triomphant: Variations romaines sur le thème de la figuration des dieux', in C. Malamoud and J. P. Vernant (eds), *Corps des dieux*, Paris: Gallimard, 213–230.

Scheid, J. (1995), '*Graeco Ritu*: A Typically Roman Way of Honouring the Gods', *Harv. Stud.* 97: 15–31.

Schlippschuh, O. (1974), *Die Händler im römischen Kaiserreich in Gallien, Germanien und den Donauprovinzen*, Amsterdam: Hakkert.

Schlüter, E. (1998), *Hispanische Grabstelen der Kaiserzeit. Eine Studie zur Typologie, Ikonographie und Chronologie*, Lüneburg: Camelion.

Schmidt-Colinet, A. (2004), 'Palmyrenische Grabkunst als Ausdruck lokaler Identität(en): Fallbeispiele', in A. Schmidt-Colinet (ed.), *Lokale Identitäten in Randgebieten des Römischen Reiches. Akten des Internationalen Symposiums in Wiener Neustadt, 24.–26. April 2003*, Vienna: Phoibos, 189–198.

Schmidt-Colinet, A. (2009), 'Nochmal zur Ikonographie zweier palmyrenischer Sarkophage', in M. Blömer, M. Facella and E. Winter (eds), *Lokale Identität im römischen Nahen Osten. Kontexte und Perspektiven. Tagung Münster 2007*, Stuttgart: Steiner, 223–234.

Schmidt-Colinet, A. and K. al-As'ad (2007), 'Zwei Neufunde palmyrenischer Sarkophage', in G. Koch (ed.), *Akten des Symposiums des Sarkophag-Corpus. Marburg 2.–7. Juli 2001*, Mainz: von Zabern, 271–278.

Scholz, B. I. (1992), *Untersuchungen zur Tracht der römischen Matrona*, Cologne: Böhlau.

Schramm, P. (1954), 'Von der Trabea triumphalis des römischen Kaisers über das byzantinische Lorum zur Stola des abendländischen Herrschers', in P. Schramm, *Herrschaftzeichen und Staatssymbolik 1*, Stuttgart: Hiersemann, 25–50.

Sebesta, J. L. (2005), 'The *Toga Praetexta* of Roman Children and Praetextate Garments', in L. Cleland, M. Harlow and L. Llewellyn-Jones (eds), *The Clothed Body in the Ancient World*, Oxford: Oxbow, 113–120.

Sebesta, J. and L. Bonfante, eds (1994), *The World of Roman Costume*, Madison: University of Wisconsin Press.

Sehlmeyer, M. (1999), *Stadtrömische Ehrenstatuen der republikanischen Zeit. Historizität und Kontext von Symbolen nobilitären Standesbewußtseins*, Stuttgart: Steiner.

Seipel, W. (1998), *Bilder aus dem Wüstensand: Mumienportraits aus dem Ägyptischen Museum Kairo*, Exhibition Catalogue, Milan: Skira.

Sherwin-White, A. N. (1973), *The Roman Citizenship*, 2nd edn, Oxford: Clarendon.

Sinn, F. (1987), *Stadtrömische Marmorurnen* (Beiträge zur Erschließung hellenistischer und kaiserzeitlicher Skulptur und Architektur 8), Mainz: von Zabern.

Smith, R. R. R. (1993), *The Monument of C. Julius Zoilos*, Mainz: von Zabern.

Smith, R. R. R. (1998), 'Cultural Choice and Political Identity in Honorific Portrait Statues in the Greek East in the Second Century AD', *JRS* 88: 56–93.

Smith, R. R. R. (1999), 'Late Antique Portraits in a Public Context: Honorific Statuary at Aphrodisias in Caria, AD 300–600', *JRS* 89: 155–189.

Smith, R. R. R. (2007), 'Statue Life in the Hadrianic Baths at Aphrodisias, AD 100–600: Local Context and Historical Meaning', in F. A. Bauer and C. Witschel (eds), *Statuen in der Spätantike*, Wiesbaden: Reichert, 203–235.

Smith, R. R. R. and B. Ward-Perkins, eds (2016), *The Last Statues of Antiquity*, Oxford: Oxford University Press.

Solin, H. (1983), 'Juden und Syrer im westlichen Teil der römischen Welt. Eine ethnisch-demographische Studie mit besonderer Berücksichtigung der sprachlichen Zustände', *ANRW* II 29.2: 587–789; 1222–1249.
Spagnuolo Vigorita, T. (1993), 'Cittadini e sudditi tra II e III secolo', in A. Carandini, L. Cracco Ruggini and A. Giardina (eds), *Storia di Roma* III: *L'età tardoantica, 1 Crisi e trasformazioni*, Turin: Einaudi.
Starbatty, A. (2010), *Aussehen ist Ansichtssache: Kleidung in der Kommunikation der römischen Antike*, Munich: Utz.
Stauffer, A. (2013), 'Kleidung als Botschaft: die Mäntel aus den vorrömischen Fürstengräbern von Verucchio', in A. Wieczorek, R. Schulz and M. Tellenbach (eds), *Die Macht der Toga – Mode im römischen Weltreich*, Exhibition Catalogue, Regensburg: Schnell & Steiner, 69–71.
Stein, E. (1968), *Opera minora selecta*, Amsterdam: Hakkert.
Stek, T. (2013), 'Material Culture, Italic Identities and the Romanization of Italy', in J. DeRose Evans (ed.), *A Companion to the Archaeology of the Roman Republic*, Malden, MA, Oxford and Chichester: Wiley-Blackwell, 337–353.
Stewart, P. (2003), *Statues in Roman Society: Representation and Response*, Oxford: Oxford University Press.
Stewart, P. (2008), *The Social History of Roman Art*, Cambridge: Cambridge University Press.
Stewart, P. (2009), 'Totenmahl Reliefs in the Northern Provinces: A Case-study in Imperial Sculpture', *JRA* 22: 253–274.
Stone, S. (1994), 'The Toga: From National Costume to Ceremonial Costume', in J. Sebesta and L. Bonfante (eds), *The World of Roman Costume*, Madison: University of Wisconsin Press, 13–45.
Tarlo, E. (1996), *Clothing Matters: Dress and Identity in India*, Chicago: University of Chicago Press.
Terrenato, N. (1998), 'The Romanization of Italy: Global Acculturation or Cultural Bricolage?', in C. Forcey, J. Hawthorne and R. Witcher (eds), *TRAC 97: Proceedings of the Seventh Annual Theoretical Roman Archaeology Conference, Nottingham April 1997*, Oxford: Oxbow, 20–27.
Toynbee, J. (1956), 'Picture-language in Roman Art and Coinage', in R. A. G. Carson and C. H. V. Sutherland (eds), *Essays in Roman Coinage Presented to Harold Mattingly*, Oxford: Oxford University Press, 205–226.
Treggiari, S. (1969), *Roman Freedmen during the Late Republic*, Oxford: Clarendon.
Tuchelt, K. (1979), *Frühe Denkmäler Roms in Kleinasien: Beiträge zur archäologischen Überlieferung aus der Zeit der Republik und des Augustus. Teil I. Roma und Promagistrate*, Tübingen: Wasmuth.
Upson-Saia, K. (2011), *Early Christian Dress: Gender, Virtue, and Authority*, London: Routledge.
Urbano, A. P. (2014), 'Sizing up the Philosopher's Cloak: Christian Verbal and Visual Representations of the *tribon*', in K. Upson-Saia, C. Daniel-Hughes and A. J. Batten

(eds), *Dressing Judaeans and Christians in Antiquity*, Farnham and Burlington: Ashgate, 175–194.

Uzzi, J. D. (2005), *Children in the Visual Arts in Imperial Rome*, Cambridge: Cambridge University Press.

Verdone, M. (2003), *Il Cinema a Roma*, Rome: Edilazio.

Vermaseren, M. J. (1957), 'The *suovetaurilia* in Roman Art', *BaBesch*. 32: 1–12.

Versluys, M. J. (2014), 'Understanding Objects in Motion: An Archaeological Dialogue on Romanization', *Archaeological Dialogues* 21 (1): 1–20.

Versnel, H. S. (1970), *Triumphus*, Leiden: Brill.

Veyne, P. (1960), 'Iconographie de la "Transvectio equitum" et des Lupercales', *Rev. Ét. Anc.* 62: 100–112.

Veyne, P. (1961), 'Vie de Trimalcion', *Annales. Économies, Sociétés, Civilisations* 16: 213–247.

Veyne, P. (1999), 'L'identité grecque devant Rome et l'Empereur', *Rev. Ét. Grec.* 112: 510–567.

Veyne, P. (2001), 'Préface', in G. Degeorge, *Palmyre, Métropole Caravanière*, Paris: Imprimerie Nationale, 8–57.

Vicari, F. (2001), *Produzione e commercio dei tessuti nell'Occidente romano*, Oxford: Archaeopress.

von Haase, F.-W. (2013), 'Zur Kleidung im frühen Etrurien', in A. Wieczorek, R. Schulz and M. Tellenbach (eds), *Die Macht der Toga – Mode im römischen Weltreich*, Exhibition Catalogue, Regensburg: Schnell & Steiner, 72–79.

von Moock, D. W. (1998), *Die figürlichen Grabstelen Attikas in der Kaiserzeit*, Mainz: von Zabern.

von Rummel, P. (2007), *Habitus barbarus. Kleidung und Repräsentation spätantiker Eliten im 4. und 5. Jahrhundert* (RGA Ergänzungsbände 55), Berlin: De Gruyter.

Vössing, K. (2012), 'Das "philosophische" Pallium in der paganen Welt und im Christentum der ersten drei Jahrhunderte', in S. Schrenk, K. Vössing and M. Tellenbach (eds), *Kleidung und Identität in religiösen Kontexten der römischen Kaiserzeit: altertumswissenschaftliches Kolloquium, Universität Bonn, 30. und 31. Oktober 2009* (Mannheimer Geschichtsblätter Sonderveröffentlichung 4), Regensburg: Schnell und Steiner, 174–195.

Vout, C. (1996), 'The Myth of the Toga: Understanding the History of Roman Dress', *G & R* 43: 204–220.

Vout, C. (2010), 'Hadrian, Hellenism and the Social History of Art', *Arion: A Journal of Humanities and the Classics* 18 (1): 55–78.

Wallace-Hadrill, A. (1982), '*Civilis Princeps*: Between Citizen and King', *JRS* 72: 32–48.

Wallace-Hadrill, A. (2008), *Rome's Cultural Revolution*, Cambridge: Cambridge University Press.

Warde-Fowler, W. (1896), 'On the Toga Praetexta of Roman Children', *CR* 10: 317–319.

Warde-Fowler, W. (1920), 'The Religious Meaning of the Toga Praetexta of Roman Children', in W. Warde-Fowler, *Roman Essays and Interpretations*, Oxford: Clarendon, 42–52.

Webster, J. (2001), 'Creolizing the Roman Provinces', *AJA* 105: 209–225.
Wegner, M. (1939), *Die Herrscherbildnisse in antoninischer Zeit* (Das römische Herrscherbild II.4), Berlin: Mann.
Wegner, M. (1956), *Hadrian* (Das römische Herrscherbild II.3), Berlin: Mann.
Wegner, M., J. Bracker and W. Real (1979), *Gordian III bis Carinus* (Das römische Herrscherbild III.3), Berlin: Mann.
Wegner, M., G. Daltrop and U. Hausmann (1966), *Die Flavier* (Das römische Herrscherbild II.1), Berlin: Mann.
Wierschowski, L. (1991), 'Handels- und Wirtschaftsbeziehungen der Städte in den nordwestlichen Provinzen des römischen Reiches', in W. Eck and H. Galsterer (eds), *Die Stadt in Oberitalien und in den nordwestlichen Provinzen des römischen Reiches*, Mainz: von Zabern, 121–139.
Wierschowski, L. (1995), *Die regionale Mobilität in Gallien nach den Inschriften des 1. bis 3. Jahrhunderts n. Chr. Quantitative Studien zur Sozial- und Wirtschaftsgeschichte der westlichen Provinzen des römischen Reiches* (Historia Einzelschrift 91), Stuttgart: Steiner.
Wiggers, H. B. and M. Wegner (1971), *Caracalla. Geta. Plautilla. Macrinus bis Balbinus* (Das römische Herrscherbild III.1), Berlin: Mann.
Wightman, E. M. (1970), *Roman Trier and the Treveri*, London: Hart-Davis.
Wild, J. P. (1970), *Textile Manufacture in the Northern Roman Provinces*, Cambridge: Cambridge University Press.
Wild, J. P. (1985), 'The Clothing of Britannia, Gallia Belgica and Germania Inferior', *ANRW* II.12.3: 362–423.
Williams, C. A. (2010), *Roman Homosexuality*, 2nd edn, Oxford: Oxford University Press.
Wilpert, G. (1898), *Un capitolo di storia del vestiario* (L'Arte 1.3–5), Rome: Tipografia dell'Unione Cooperativa Editrice.
Wilson, A. and M. Flohr (2016), *Urban Craftsmen and Traders in the Roman World*, Oxford: Oxford University Press.
Wilson, L. M. (1924), *The Roman Toga*, Baltimore: Johns Hopkins University Press.
Wiseman, T. P. (1970), 'The Definition of "Eques Romanus" in the Late Republic and Early Empire', *Historia* 19 (1): 67–83.
Wissowa, G. (1912), *Religion und Kultus der Römer*, 2nd edn, Munich: Beck.
Wolff, H. (1976), *Die Constitutio Antoniniana und Papyrus Gissensis 40.I*, University of Cologne diss.
Wolff, H. (1995), 'Die römische Erschliessung der Rhein- und Donauprovinzen im Blickwinkel ihrer Zielsetzung', in R. Frei-Stolba and M. A. Speidel (eds), *Römische Inschriften. Neufunde, Neulesungen und Neuinterpretationen. Festschrift für Hans Lieb. Zum 65. Geburtstag dargebracht von seinen Freunden und Kollegen*, Basel: Reinhardt, 309–340.
Woolf, G. (1998), *Becoming Roman: The Origins of Provincial Civilization in Gaul*, Cambridge: Cambridge University Press.

Wrede, H. (1988), 'Zur Trabea', *JDAI* 103: 381–400.
Wrede, H. (1995), 'Rev. Goette: *Studien zu römischen Togadarstellungen*', *Gnomon* 67: 541–550.
Wrede, H. (2000), *Cunctorum splendor ab uno. Archäologie, Antikensammlung und antikisierende Ausstattungen in Nepotismus und Absolutismus*, Stendal: Winckelmann-Gesellschaft.
Wrede, H. (2001), *Senatorische Sarkophage Roms*, Mainz: von Zabern.
Wueste, E. (2017), 'The Costumes of Late Antique Honorific Monuments: Conformity and Divergence within the Public and Political Sphere', in M. Cifarelli and L. Gawlinski (eds), *What Shall I Say of Clothes? Theoretical and Methodological Approaches to the Study of Dress in Antiquity*, Boston: AIA, 179–201.
Wyke, M. (1997), *Projecting the Past: Ancient Rome, Cinema and History*, London and New York: Routledge.
Yon, J.-B. (2002), *Les notables de Palmyre*, Beirut: Ifpo.
Zadoks-Jitta, A. N. (1932), *Ancestral Portraiture in Rome and the Art of the Last Century of the Republic* 1, Amsterdam: N. V. Noord-Hollandische Uitgevers-Mij.
Zadoks-Jitta, A. N. (1939–1940), 'De romeinsche toga', *Hermeneus* 12: 126–130.
Zanker, P. (1983a), *Provinzielle Kaiserportraits: zur Rezeption der Selbstdarstellung des Princeps* (Abhandlungen Bayrische Akademie der Wissenschaften 90), Munich: Beck.
Zanker, P. (1983b), 'Zur Bildrepräsentation führender Männer in mittelitalischen und campanischen Städten', in *Les 'Bourgeoisies' municipales italiennes aux 2e et 1er siècles av. J.-C.*, Paris: Editions du CNRS, 254–266.
Zanker, P. (1989), 'Statuenrepräsentation und Mode', in S. Walker and A. Cameron (eds), *The Greek Renaissance in the Roman Empire*, London: University of London, ICS, 102–107.
Zanker, P. (1992), 'Bürgerliche Selbstdarstellung am Grab im römischen Kaiserreich,' in H. Schalles, H. von Hesberg and P. Zanker (eds), *Die römische Stadt im 2. Jh. n. Chr., Kolloquium Xanten 1990* (Xantener Berichte 2), Cologne and Bonn: Rheinland/Habelt, 339–358.
Zanker, P. (2010), *Power of Images in the Age of Augustus*, 19th edn, Ann Arbor: University of Michigan Press.
Ziegler, R. (1995), 'Die Polis in der römischen Kaiserzeit: Selbstdarstellung und Rangstreitigkeiten', in G. Hödl and J. Grabmayer (eds), *Leben in der Stadt. Gestern – heute – morgen*, Vienna, Cologne and Weimar: Böhlau, 83–105.
Zimmer, G. (1982), *Römische Berufsdarstellungen*, Berlin: Mann.
Zimmer, G. (1992), 'Statuenaufstellung auf Forumsanlagen des 2. Jahrhunderts n. Chr.', in H. Schalles, H. von Hesberg and P. Zanker (eds), *Die römische Stadt im 2. Jh. n. Chr., Kolloquium Xanten 1990* (Xantener Berichte 2), Cologne and Bonn: Rheinland/Habelt, 301–313.

Index

Locators in **bold** denote figures

Achaia 141
adlocutio 113–16, **115**, 118, **119**
adolescence, *see togam virilem sumere and*
    marriage
adventus 32, 61, **61**, 73, 120, 150–1
Aeneas 6, 10, **10**, 21–2, 47–8, 77, 111
Agricola 125
Agrippa 38, 52
Agrippina the Younger 115
Ajaccio (Corsica) **160**, 161
Alexander Severus, *see* Severus
    Alexander
Alexandria 107
alimenta 117, **117**
amphitheatre 84
Antoninus Pius 118
    Column of 80, **80**
Antony, Mark, *see* Mark Antony
Apana, gravestone of 127, 131–2, **131**,
    136, 146
Aphrodisias 150, 201 n.105
Appian 77, 83, 186 n.88
Apuleius 66, 76, 187 n.102
Ara Pacis 10, **10**, 21–2, 31, 38, 47–8, 62, 74,
    75, 94, 111–12, 128
'armsling' toga 20, 28, 30, **30**, **39**, 35, 54,
    67–8, 89, 111, 127, 131, *see also*
    draping styles of the toga *and*
    fashion
army, *see* soldiers and togas
'Arringatore' statue 28, **29**, 51–2, 60
artisans 96–9, **98**
Asia Minor 18, 23, 139
Asiaticus, M. Valerius Anteros
    (freedman on a gravestone from
    Brescia) 90
Athens 50, 141, 201 n.105
Attica 139
augurs 22, 60, 79, 104, 182, 184
Augurs, Tomb of the 18–19, **18**

Augustine 11, 149
Augustus 9, 25, 31, 34, 43, 48, 52, 68, 83–4,
    103–4, 107, 110–15, 118, 122, 131,
    153, 160
    Forum of 52, 64
Aulus Gellius, *see* Gellius
Aulus Metellus, *see* 'Arringatore' statue
Aurelian 142, 150
Ausonius 149, 152–3

Baker, Tomb of the, *see* Eurysaces,
    Tomb of
balteus 27–8, **27**, 30–2, 56, 128, 142, 163,
    172 n.111
banishment, *see* exile
birrus 149, 163
boys and togas 37–8, 41, 59–66, 80–1, 90,
    90, 94–5, 111, 115–16, 120, 133,
    203 n.2, 204 n.16
Britannicus 115–16
Britain/Britons 82, 114, 125–6
'Brothers' Sarcophagus 32, **32**, 36, 154
bulla 20, 60, 64, 77, 90, **90**, 97
Byzantine Empire 150, 158, **158**, *see also*
    loros

Caecina Alienus, A. (first-century CE
    general) 44
Caesar, Julius 3, 4, 45–6, 58, 75, 78, 84, 99,
    101–2, 107, 122, 124, 131, 191 n.15
calcei 5, 20–1, 44, 51–2, 79, 114, 163
caligae 4, 163
Caligula 52, 58, 64, 115
Campus Martius 52, 67, 87
capite aperto 48
capite velato 10, **10**, 20, 46–8, **47**, 111, 113,
    118, 163, 166 n.36, 187 n.103,
    202 n.124
Capua 84
Caracalla 127, 147, 194 n.84

Carthage 87, 147, 166 n.39
Cassius Dio, *see* Dio Cassius
Castricius, Titus (second-century CE rhetorician) 67
Catiline 103, 108
Cato the Elder 26, 63
Cato the Younger 7, 21, 35, 107
Catullus 61
Celerinus, M. Valerius (veteran on a gravestone from Cologne) 128–9, **129**
Celje (Celeia) 136–9, **137**, 146
censors 72, 75
children and togas 37–41, **39**, 60–3, 73, 89–90, **90**, 100, 111, 115–17, **117**, 127–8, 165 n.10, 195 n.93, 197 n.44, *see also* boys *and* girls
chlaina 17, 74, 163
chlamys 20, **33**, 76, 148–50, 155–6, **155**, 158, 163, 165 n.10, 195 n.89
Christianity 148–9, 157, 203 n.2
Cicero 3–5, 7, 12, 28, 35, 38–9, 42–6, 51, 58, 61–2, 66–7, 74, 84, 95, 100, 103–5, 108–9, 174 n.29
Cimber, L. Tillius 101
Cincinnatus 43, 85
cinctus Gabinus 22, **47**, 74
citizenship, Roman 6–9, 12, 21, 33, 42, 44–5, 51–2, 60, 81–2, 88–9, 97, 99, 109, 123–32, 136–8, 140–1, 143, 145–8, *see also ius Latii*
non-citizens wearing togas 5, 75, 81, 107, 131–2, **131**, 136–8, **137**
civil/civilian sphere (as opposed to military) 42, 45–6, 51, 84, 108–10, 114, 116–18, 120–1, 147–8, 152–3, 156–8
civil unrest, the toga and 102, 108, 116
Claudian 152–3, 156
Claudius (first-century emperor) 7, 58, 81–2, 114–15, 124–5, 137
Claudius Gothicus 43, 150
clavi **11**, **29**, **47**, 51, 60, 79, 114, 124, 151, 163, 196 n.9, 205 n.35
client kings 106–7
clients, *see* patronage
Cloelia (early Roman figure) 21, 40–1
collegia, professional 99
colobium 151

Cologne (oppidum Ubiorum/Colonia Claudia Ara Agrippinensium) 127–32, **129**, 146
Colonia Claudia Ara Agrippinensium, *see* Cologne
coloniae 73, 126–8
Columella 23
coming of age, *see togam virilem sumere and* marriage
Commodus 87, 119, 166 n.39
Constantine the Great **33**, 150, 154
Arch of 32–3, **33**, 36, 95, 148, 150
Constantinople 148, 154–6, **155**
Constantius III 158
constitutio Antoniniana 33, 127, 130, 143, 147
consular diptychs 33, 151–2, **152**, 158
consuls 33, 72, 74–5, 78–9, 101, 104–8, 118, 120–1, 141, 150–8, **152**, **155**
contabulated toga
fully 32, **32**, 33, **33**, 154
partly **11**, 32, 36, 38, 133, **135**, 194 n.84
see also draping styles of the toga *and* fashion
Corinth 141
Cornelia (stepdaughter of Augustus) 38
Cornificius, Quintus (late Republican general) 109
Cotta, C. Aurelius (late Republican consul) 107
court hearings/personnel, the toga and 43, 59, 62, 64, 67, 81, 86, 88, 91, 102, 104–5, 108, 147–9
Crassus, M. Licinius 45, 105, 110
Crete 141
Çukurbağ, *see* Nicomedia

dalmatica 119, 163, 205 n.35
'dandies' 58–9
Danube region, *see* Noricum
Decennalia Base 36
Digesta 62, 81
Dio Cassius 78, 109, 115, 119, 122
Diocletian's Price Edict 26, 149
Diodorus of Sicily 17
Dionysius of Halicarnassus 17–18, 20, 79, 167 n.6
diplomacy, toga and 106–7

Doctus, C. Fundilius (actor in a statue from Nemi) 89
Domitia (daughter of Antonia the Elder and L. Domitius Ahenobarbus) 38
Domitian 116
Domitius Ahenobarbus, Altar of 28, 47
draped vs tailored clothing 55–6, 148, 159
draping styles of the toga 26–36, **27**, *see also* fashion, 'armsling toga', 'imperial toga', contabulated toga, 'magistrate-type' toga

eastern provinces, *see* Greek East
Egypt 25, 33, 73, 126, 139
Elagabalus 73, 120
emperors and the toga 36, 43, 46, 48, 51, 58, 73–5, 78, 104, 107, 110–22, **115**, **117**, **119**, 149–51, 155, 157–8, *see also* names of individual emperors
Ennius 6, 21
equestrians 79–80, **80**, 87, 95, 118, 147, 151, 154, 157, 163, *see also transvectio equitum*
Esquiline Tomb Frescoes 21, 28
Etruscan art **18**, 49–51
Etruscan dress 14, 17–22, **18**, 28, 59–60, 75–7, 79, 83
Eurysaces, Tomb of 84
Eutropius 153
Eutyches (*verna* on a gravestone from Rome) 81, *see also* Nico
exemplum (concept) **31**, 53–4, **53**, 72, 112, 149
exercitus, see adlocutio
exile/exiled persons 11, 81, 105
exomis 163, 190 n.159

fasces 5, 72–3, 77
fashion 33–6, 87, 89, 117–18, 121, 127, 131, 154, 197 n.31, *see also* draping styles of the toga
Festus 62, 77
fibulatorium 149
flamines 20, 74, **75 Fig. 4.1**, 111, *see also* priests
Florus 5, 17, 45
formula togatorum 21, 82–3, 168 n.29
Forum Augustum, *see* Augustus, Forum of

Forum Romanum 50, 64, 68, 83–4, 87, 105, 110
freeborn status 37, 60, 62–3, 73, 81, 88–90, **90**, 97, 128, 164, *see also toga praetexta* of children
freedpeople 6, 9, 14, 30, 35, 40, 54, 62, 72, 74, 82, 88–91, **90**, 95–8, 100, 124, 126, 128, 147
Fronto 25, 43
funerals 48–9, 72–3, 75, 86, 99, 103

Gaius Gracchus, *see* Gracchus, Gaius
Galba 116
Galicia 131–3, **131**, 136, 146
Gallic dress 44, 124, 132–6, **135**, 146
games 58, 73, 76, 110, 115–16, 119, 151, 155, **155**, 157, *see also* amphitheatre, theatre, master of games
Gandhi 55
Gaul 12, 23, 129–30, 132–6, **134**, **135**, 146
Gauls 1, 7, 9, 124–5, 132–6, **135**, 146, 149, 166 n.32
Gellius, Aulus 59, 66–8
genii 21, 36, 61, 73, **47**, 87, 118
Germanic culture 65
Geta 194 n.84
girls and toga 9, 21, 37–41, **39**, 63–4, 111, 127
globalization 5, 57, 126, 136, 146
Gordian I 78, 121
Gortyn 141
governors, provincial 44–5, 55, 88, 108, 122, 125, 141, 156
Gracchus, Gaius 101
Gracchus, Tiberius 101, 105
Graecus ritus, see capite aperto
Grania Faustina, grave ara of 81
Gratian 152
Greek dress 17, 20, 22, 28, 30, 33, 35, 37, 41, 44–5, 48, 76–7, 87, 89, 107–8, 118, 121, 139–46, 156, *see also chlamys, chlaina, exomis, palla, pallium*
Greek East 121–2, 139–46
Greek influence on Roman culture 7–9, 17, 20, 22, 28, 30, 33, 37, 41–2, 49, 76–7, 87, 89, 118, 156

Hadrian 32, 87, 118–19, **119**, 121, 195 n.89
Hadrumetum 11, **11**

himation, see pallium
Historia Augusta 73, 78, 114, 118–21, 150
Homer 76
honestiores 147
Honor (deity) 48
Horace 28, 39–40, 45, 53, 58, 84, 94–6, 110
Hortensius Hortalus, Q. (late Republican orator) 4, 59
humiliores 147

ideology, political, toga and, *see* political ideology
Igel Pillar 133–6, **134**, **135**
imperial cult 143–6, **144**, *see also seviri Augustales*
imperial imagery, *see* emperors and the toga
'imperial toga' 24, **27**, 30–2, **31**, **32**, 36, **47**, 54, 60, 89, 110–12, **115**, **117**, 118, 127, 132, 137, **137**, 142, **144**, 154, **160**, 161, *see also umbo*, draping styles of the toga, fashion
India 55, 57, 59, 63, 94, *see also* Gandhi, sari
Isidore of Seville 102
ius Latii 82, 130–1, 137, 196 n.20

judges, *see* court hearings
Julia (daughter of Agrippa) 38
Julia Felix, House of (Pompeii) 53, **53**, 85, 95, 170 n.73
Julian 204 n.22
Julius Caesar, *see* Caesar, Julius
Jupiter Optimus Maximus, Temple of (Capitol) 45, 64, 76–8, 120, 184 n.49
Juvenal 4, 26, 38, 44, 77, 85, 91–3, 96

Laberius, Decimus (author) 11–12
lacerna 44, 67, 83–4, 93
lacinia 27, **27**, 86, 163
Laelius, M. (mid-Republican augur) 60
laena 17, 74–5, **75**, 99, 111, 163
Lares/lararia 22, **47**, 60–1, 64, 73–4, 87
Latin citizenship, *see ius Latii*
law courts, *see* court hearings
Lentulus, P. Cornelius 73, 104
Lepidus, Aemilius (mid-Republican consul) 60
Lex Irnitana 196 n.20

Lex Ursonensis 125, 141
Liberalia 64
liberti, see freedpeople
Livy 1, 12, 17, 19, 21, 38, 43, 46, 64, 83, 85, 108, 130
loros 158, **158**
Lucan 45, 83
Lucullus, L. Licinius (late Republican general) 12
Lugo (Spain) **131**, 132
Lyon Tablet 124

Macrobius 4, 58, 60
'magistrate type' toga 33, **34**, 151, 155, **155**, *see also* draping styles of the toga, fashion
magistrates **32**, 33, **34**, 38, 52, 59–62, 72–8, 85–7, 102–3, 105, 113–14, 116, 140, 147, 151, 154–5, 187 n.103, 193 n.47
manufacture of togas, *see* material, production, acquisition of togas
Marcus Aurelius 117–20, 143
  Arch of 36, 95, 117
  Column of 48
Mark Antony 5, 9, 39–40, 44–5, 78, 102, 109–10
marriage **32**, 38, 49, 62, 64, 90, 127–8, 137–8, 154, 191 n.4
Martial 4, 23–4, 26, 38–9, 43–4, 59, 84–6, 91–6, 100
Martianus Capella 148
Masinissa 106
master of games 151, 157, 205 n.35
material, production, acquisition of togas 23–6
memoria (concept) 53–4
Metellus, Aulus, *see* 'Arringatore' statue
Metellus, Q. Caecilius (late Republican tribune) 45
military, *see* soldiers and togas
'*modius*' hat 143, **144**
mos maiorum 8, 107, 111, 118
mourning 61, 103–7, 119, *see also toga pulla*
Mulva (Munigua) 130–1
Munigua, *see* Mulva

Napoleon Bonaparte 160–1, **160**
Nemi 89

Nero 115–16, **115**, 195 n.89
Nicephorus III 158, **158**
Nico (boy on a gravestone from Rome) 81, *see also* Eutyches
Nicomedia 60, **61**, 73, 150
Nîmes, Musée de la Romanité 161, **161**
non-elite, toga and the 82–8, 92–5, 96–9
Noricum 32, 136–9, **137**, 146
North Africa 145, 149

'*oblitus togae*' 5, 45, 110
oppidum Ubiorum, *see* Cologne
orators/oratory 6, 16, 23–4, 28–9, 34–5, 43, 51–2, 54, 56, 58–9, 63, 67, 103, 147, 169 n.51
origins of the toga 17–22
Ostia 36
Ovid 26, 58, 64, 94

paenula **33**, 113, 148–9, 156–7, 163, 175 n.34, 205 n.35
palla 37–8, **39**, 41, 127, 163
pallium/himation 4, 6, 11, 17, 20, 28, 30, **32**, 35, 44, 57, 63, 76, 81, 86–7, 89, 107, 111, 115, 118, 120–1, 128, 140–2, 148, 154, 156, 163, 166 n.36, 175 n.45, 188 n.117, 191 n.15
Palmyra 142–6, **144**
Pannonia Inferior/Superior 136
Parentalia 103
Parthian-style dress 142–5
parties, toga 159
patricians vs plebs 108
patronage (patron–client system) 15, 26, 44, 50, 67, 71, 84, 91–2, 96, 147, *see also salutatio*
Paulus (late Roman jurist) 61
Persius 61, 66–7, 103
Perugia 28, 51
Petronius 88, 90
Philopappos 141
Piazza Armerina 205 n.35
Plautus 17, 25
Pliny the Elder 3, 17, 19, 21–3, 34, 41, 50, 73, 76, 86, 103, 113
Pliny the Younger 11, 35, 44, 85
Plutarch 17, 48–9, 63, 65–6, 73, 76, 101–3
Poblicius, L. (veteran on a grave monument in Cologne) 127–8, 130, 146

political ideology, toga and 107–22, **115**, **117**, **119**, 149–57
political protest, toga and 105–6
Polybius 3, 72, 83, 99
polychromy 73, 199 n.84, 206 n.60
Pompeii 47, 53, **53**, 60–1, 73, 85–6, 95
Pompey 4, 45, 102, 105, 187 n.103
potters 97, **98**
praetorian guard 46
praetors 72–4, 78, 154
priests 20, 33, 38, 46, 61, 72, 74, **75**, 90, 111, 133, 143–6, **144**, 204 n.22
Primus, Sex. Titius (freedman on a gravestone from Ancona) 90
Probus 73, 157
processus consularis, *see adventus*
production, *see* material, production, acquisition of togas
Propertius 4, 10, 38
protest, *see* political protest
provinces, dress of emperor in 121–2
Prudentius 78, 102, 149
Prusias (king of Bithynia) 3, 106
Ptolemy (king of Numidia/Mauretania) 106
public life, toga as a symbol of 42–9
purchase of togas, *see* material, production, acquisition of togas
purple (dye) 59–61, 75, *see also toga purpurea* and *toga praetexta*
Puteoli 107

Quartus Sirae (man on a gravestone in Celje) 127, 137–9, **137**
Quintilian 23–4, 28, 34–5, 43, 54, 56, 58–9, 63, 102, 104

republicanism, the toga and modern 159–60
rhetoric/rhetoricians, *see* orators/oratory
Romanus ritus, *see capite velato*
Romulus 7, 21, 123, 185 n.58, 191 n.16
Rostra **33**, 50, 72, 118–19, 148, 150, 191 n.16

sagum 4, 22, 26, 46, 104, 130, 133, 138, 148–9, 163, 175 n.34, 191 n.15
Sallust 12, 107
salutatio 44, 84, 91–2, 119, 147, *see also* patronage

Santa Sabina, Church of 148
sari 55–9, 63, 94, *see also* India
Saturn 48
Saturnalia 43, 81
Scaevola, Q. Mucius 67
Scipio Africanus 77
Scipio Nasica 101, 103, 109
Secundinii (Treveran family) 133–6, **134**, **135**
sella curulis 1–2, 17, 19–20, 60, 72, 77, 106, 113–14, 116, 184 n.56
Sempronius Tuditanus (son of the consul of 129 BCE) 58
senate/senators (and dress) 5, 43, 46, 50–2, 67, 73, 75–6, 78–9, 85, 87, 103–7, 109, 114–20, 124, 147, 151, 156–7, 196 n.9, 204 n.28
Seneca the Elder 6, 68
Seneca the Younger 5, 63, 68, 81, 125
Septimius Severus 36, 120, 150, 194 n.84
Servile Wars 22, 75, 107, *see also* Tryphon
Servius (late Roman commentator) 18, 79, 149
Servius Tullius (early Roman king) 22, 168 n.28
Severus Alexander 78, 120
seviri Augustales 72, 74, 90, *see also* priests
SHA, *see Historia Augusta*
Sidonius 148
sinus **27**, 30–3, 35, 56, 60, 110–11, 151, 163
slaves (and dress) 3, 5, 57, 81, 93, 96, 112, 165 n.10, 182 n.1
soldiers (and dress) 4, 22, 45, 73, 80, 83, 108–10, 114, 116, 119, 126, 130, 150, 155, 168 n.30, 169 n.39, 191 n.15, *see also* praetorian guard
Spanish provinces 22–3, 81, 125, 130–2, **131**, 146
statues, toga 21, 28, **29, 31, 34**, 49–54, 56, 60, 68, 73, 85, 113, 116, 118, 125, 141–3, 150, 154, 156–7, *see also* 'Arringatore' *and* 'Togatus Barberini'
Stilicho 152–3
stola 4, 37, 40–1, 164, 165 n.10
Strabo 81, 125
stuprum 62
Suetonius 4–5, 25, 42, 52, 58, 68, 74, 77, 79, 81, 83–4, 101, 107, 110, 114, 116
suit, *see* western suit

Sulla 4, 185 n.59, 187 n.103
sumptuary laws 108
Supertamarici 132
symmetry 74, 204 n.33
synthesis 43, 115, 164, 175 n.34
Syphax (king of Numidia) 106
Syria 126, 142–6, **144**

Tacitus (author) 44, 46, 65, 67–8, 98, 106, 115, 125
Tarquinia, tombs at 18, **18**, 168 n.25
Tarquinius Priscus 60
tebenna 18–21, **18, 19**, 24, 28, 49, 59, 76, 149, 164
Tertullian 57, 78, 87, 93, 147–8
Tetrarchy 150
theatre 43, 58, 84, 96, 110
Theoderic 149
Theodosius I/II 150
  Obelisk of Theodosius I 155–6, **155**
Thrace 139
Tiberius 46, 74, 104, 106, 114, 121, 175 n.45
Tiberius Gracchus, *see* Gracchus, Tiberius
Tibullus 38
tirocinium fori 67–8
Titus, Arch of 32
toga candida 24, 102–3, 108, 122, 164
toga contabulata, see contabulated toga
'*toga exigua*' 28
'*toga libera*' 65, *see also toga virilis* and *togam virilem sumere*
toga muliebris, see women and toga
toga perversa 104–5
toga picta 1, 72, 76–8, 106, 115, 118, 120–1, 150, 153, 164, *see also* triumph *and tunica palmata*
toga praetexta 24, **47**, 59–64, **61**, 106, 163
  of children 21, 37–9, **39**, 41, 61–4, 89–90, **90**, 115, 127–8, 165 n.10, 204 n.16
  of magistrates 2, 17, 22, 52, 73–5, 99, 103–4, 109, 114, 120–1, 150–1, 204 n.22
toga pulla 103–5, 122, 164, *see also* mourning
toga pura, see toga virilis
toga purpurea 24, 72, 75–7, 85, 99, 106–8, 116, 119, 164

'*toga sordida*' 104
toga virilis/*toga pura* 38–9, 62, 64–6, 68–9, 102, 104, 115, 119–20, 149, 164, *see also togam virilem sumere*
togam virilem sumere, 38–9, 62, 64–8, 115, 120, 149, 200 n.90, *see also toga virilis*
'Togatus Barberini' statue **31**, 53
'*togula*' 92, 95
'*Totenmahl*' scenes 128, **129**
trabea 33, 79–80, **80**, 95, 149–53, **152**, 156–8, 164
tradespeople, *see* artisans
Trajan 117, **117**, 141, 150
　Arch of (Benevento) 36
　Column of 48
transvectio equitum 50, 80, **80**, 95, *see also* equestrians *and trabea*
Trebonianus Gallus 157
tribunes (of the plebs) 45, 103, 105, 108
Trimalchio 88, 90, 182 n.14, 189 n.152
triumph 1, 51, 60, 72–3, 76–8, 104, 108–9, 114–16, 118, 120, 150–1, 153, *see also toga picta* and *tunica palmata*
Tryphon (leader of Slave Revolt) 75, 99, 107
Tullus Hostilius 60
tunic, Roman female 37, 127, 165 n.10
tunic, Roman male 4, 11, 21–3, 26, 33, 35, 44, 51, 56–8, 61, 67, 79, 84–6, 96–9, **98**, 103, 106–8, 111, 115, 120, 137, 141, 151, 165 n.10
tunica palmata 76–8, 153, 164, *see also toga picta and* triumph

Ubii 128
umbo 8, **27**, 31–3, 36, 57–8, 80, 89, 110–12, 118, 127–8, 132, 137, 142, 154, 161, 164, 172 n.111, *see also* 'imperial toga'

Valerius Maximus 12, 22, 43, 58, 60, 101, 109
Varro (author) 6, 23, 74
Vatinius, P. (late Republican politician) 103
Vergil 10–11, **11**, 37, 47, 77, 79, 110
Verres, C. (governor of Sicily) 38, 44, 61–2, 108
Vertumnus 4
Verucchio 19–20, **19**, 24, 60–1
Vespasian 116, 130
vestem mutare, see vestis mutatio
vestiplicus 93–4
vestis mutatio/*vestem mutare* 103–6, *see also* mourning, *sagum* and *toga pulla*
veterans, military 127–9, **129**
Virgil, *see* Vergil
viri consulares, see consuls
Vitellius 116
Vulci 6, 21, 76

Washington, George 159–60
wearing a toga (learning the skill) 54–6, 63
weaving, *see* material, production, acquisition of togas
weddings, *see* marriage
western suit 36, 54–5, 57, 86, 94, 112, 125–6, 135–6
women and toga 9, 20–1, 37–41
work scenes 97–9

www.ingramcontent.com/pod-product-compliance
Lightning Source LLC
Chambersburg PA
CBHW050325020526
44117CB00031B/1804